"I love these dead celebrities! They're the stars I grew up wat' 'ing, and they deserve to be remembered even i̇ screen than they were in the kitchen. Frank cle is I do, and after reading *The Dead Celebrity Co*

—Rosie O'Donnell

"I adore this book so much I find myself on the horns of a dilemma—make the recipes or kill myself so I can be in the sequel."

—**Brini Maxwell**, author of *Brini Maxwell's Guide to Gracious Living* and creator of felixpopuli.com

"Celebrities die—eventually—but their recipes live on, thanks to Frank DeCaro's thorough and thoroughly delicious book. DeCaro's dry wit is tasty, and judging from these yummy concoctions, most of these celebs died really happy!"

—**Michael Musto**, *Village Voice*

"Finally, Frank DeCaro has put his sick obsession with dead celebs to some good use! Hilarious and bursting with usable recipes. Even if you do not know how to turn on the toaster oven, you will adore this gossip-filled cackle-fest."

—**Simon Doonan**, author of *Gay Men Don't Get Fat*

"Hankering for star-powered recipes? With this laugh-out-loud encyclopedia of Hollywood culinaria, Frank DeCaro brings out the real 'celebrity chefs' in spades. Or with a spade."

—**Bruce Weinstein** and **Mark Scarbrough**, bestselling authors of more than twenty cookbooks including *Lobsters Scream When You Boil Them and 100 Other Myths About Food and Cooking*

"Frank DeCaro has the most delectable treats I've ever tasted—and the recipes aren't bad, either! My dying wish is to have one of my recipes in *The Dead Celebrity Cookbook II.* Anyone for the Queen of Mean's 'So-Good-You'll-Slap-Yo-Mama Chicken 'n Waffles'?"

—**Lisa Lampanelli**, comedienne

"Frank DeCaro's two obsessions—food and the famous—have been hilariously united in *The Dead Celebrity Cookbook.* Reading Frank is like breaking your diet with your funniest best friend."

—**Bob Smith**, author of
Remembrance of Things I Forgot

"With *The Dead Celebrity Cookbook,* you can spend endless hours attempting to duplicate puddings, pies, and polenta from the recipes of famous dead people, some of whom may have died from their own cooking. It's like microwave roulette—fun even if you don't last until the last chapter."

—**Bruce Vilanch,** writer/performer

THE DEAD CELEBRITY COOKBOOK

A Resurrection of Recipes from More
Than 145 Stars of Stage and Screen

Frank DeCaro

Health Communications, Inc.
Deerfield Beach, Florida

www.hcibooks.com

Library of Congress Cataloging-in-Publication Data

DeCaro, Frank, 1962–
   The dead celebrity cookbook / Frank DeCaro.
      p. cm.
   Includes bibliographical references and index.
   ISBN-13: 978-0-7573-1596-1 (pbk.)
   ISBN-10: 0-7573-1596-8 (pbk.)
   ISBN-13: 978-0-7573-9164-4 (e-book)
   ISBN-10: 0-7573-9164-8 (e-book)
   1. Cooking.   2. Cookbooks.   3. Celebrities—Miscellanea.   I. Title.
TX714.D435 2011
641'.5—dc23

                                            2011025281

Publisher: Health Communications, Inc.
          3201 S.W. 15th Street
          Deerfield Beach, FL 33442–8190

Cover design by Justin Rotkowitz
Interior design and formatting by Lawna Patterson Oldfield
Interior illustrations by Larissa Hise Henoch

THIS BOOK IS DEDICATED TO
THE MEMORY OF MY TWO FAVORITE
DEAD CELEBRITIES—
MARIAN AND FRANK DECARO SR.—
WHOSE GREATEST OBSERVATIONS ABOUT FOOD
ARE TOO SALTY TO MENTION HERE.

How can I make an apple pie with a difference?

Use peaches.

Hermione Gingold 1897–1987

contents

INTRODUCTION

E XCEPT FOR A 2008 record release party at Charo's place in Beverly Hills, our Dead Celebrity Party was the best house party I've ever attended. At Northwestern University in the early 1980s, our little tribe of misfits decided we should give a costume shindig where everyone had to dress as a star who'd gone to the Great Studio Commissary in the Sky. That night, in a dancer-friend's apartment, we gathered in our guises and partied ourselves silly.

In that room were a bunch of kids who'd go on to be filmmakers, novelists, voice actors, at least one Tony Award winner, and an adorably chubby radio show host—each dressed as someone famous but dead. The guests ran the gamut from Sid Vicious to Ernest Hemingway, Bill "Bojangles" Robinson to Jack Soo, who played Yemana on *Barney Miller*. Me? I went as Euell Gibbons, the noted outdoorsman who claimed in a Grape-Nuts commercial that many parts of a pine tree are edible. The dancer whose apartment we borrowed dressed as Judy Garland. The pill bottle he carried all night read: TAKE UNTIL DEAD.

The one thing missing from our Dead Celebrity Party way back when was the food of the dead celebrities we were celebrating. Since that night, I've been collecting recipes of the stars. Having scoured flea markets and yard sales and eBay for decades, I have stacks of out-of-print celebrity cookbooks—

Candy Hits by ZaSu Pitts is my favorite title—musty biographies, vintage magazines and dusty giveaway pamphlets from supermarkets, banks, realty offices, and corporations. They're filled with a pantry full of recipes—some best forgotten—from a galaxy of stars, all of whom deserve to be remembered. From them, I've learned that there was a time when if you bought a microwave, you received a free cookbook from the guy who played Mel Cooley on *The Dick Van Dyke Show*.

I miss those days when celebrities still had mystery about them, and a glimpse inside their radar ranges seemed, for any fan, like a window into a world of glamour and excitement, which is why I put together this book. For decades, I've wanted others to share my fantasy of feasting on Frank Sinatra's Barbecued Lamb, lunching on Lucille Ball's Chinese-y Thing, diving ever-so-neatly into Joan Crawford's Poached Salmon, and wrapping my lips around Rock Hudson's Cannoli. Really, who hasn't fantasized about that?

I'm incredibly lucky because I've made a living my entire adult life indulging such fantasies. As the flamboyant movie critic on *The Daily Show with Jon Stewart* for six-and-a-half years, I let loose my passion for movies. As a contributor to *TV Guide*, the *New York Times*, and most recently CBS's *Watch!* magazine, I've sat in front of the television and called it work. On Sirius XM Satellite Radio, where I've spent my mornings for the past seven-plus years, I've welcomed celebrities from all points on the showbiz map—many of whom are icons from the TV shows upon which I was raised. Honestly, how many people can say they got to chit-chat with three of the four *Golden Girls* as the nation listened in? Among my radio guests have been some of the brightest lights in the world of gourmet food, too. I've been able to talk—and often taste—the deliciousness that people like Martha Stewart, Mario Batali, and any number of Deens bring to the world. With *The Dead Celebrity Cookbook*, I've combined all of these interests. My goal is to share my enthusiasm for food and pop culture with you.

If you're willing to share my dream—and if you're reading this book, I assume you are—then hold on to your oven mitts! *The Dead Celebrity Cookbook* is here to remind you that before there were celebrity chefs, there were celebrities who fancied themselves chefs. These stars championed a style of home entertaining that's ripe for reexamination, if not revival. They were whipping up culinary delights for their fans decades before the Food Network ushered chefs out of the kitchen and under the hot lights.

Hollywood, you'll soon discover, doesn't make celebrities (or cooks) like it used to. Looking at some of these recipes, intrepid gourmands, you may think that might be a good thing. I disagree. I'm sure the food was better at Julia Child's house, but really, wouldn't you rather have been invited to Liberace's?

These stars, mega and minor, may be gone, but their culinary prowess lives on. With *The Dead Celebrity Cookbook*, I invite you to put the kitsch back into the kitchen, while fondly and respectfully remembering the stars of classic television, beloved films, Broadway, and more. Along with the food, I've suggested ways to enjoy these artists' greatest works after you've put the dishes in the Maytag.

I like to say that the book you're holding contains recipes that the stars are dying for you to make. Please don't bury it in your cupboard.

1

TALK
CHOW

WHEN MIKE DOUGLAS, who'd had a big band hit with "Ole Buttermilk Sky" in 1946, and Merv Griffin, who scored a million seller with the 1950 novelty song "I've Got a Lovely Bunch of Coconuts," became talk show hosts, they made sure their programs had cooking segments. They—or at least their producers—knew who their audience was: housewives. These women weren't singing about buttermilk and coconuts, they were cooking with them in kitchens across America, and every day their eyes were glued to their sets. In fact, the marquee outside the Douglas studio for a while read YOUR WIFE SPENT THE AFTERNOON WITH MIKE DOUGLAS.

The man born Michael Delaney Dowd Jr. but rechristened Mike Douglas by bandleader Kay Kyser often said that no matter how much excitement or controversy guests on his syndicated talk show might stir up, the celebrity cooking segments generated the most mail (and this was a man who spent a week chatting and singing with John Lennon and Yoko Ono during the Vietnam War, mind you!). He estimated, in 1969's *The Mike Douglas Cookbook,* that as many as 70,000 fans wrote in for recipes each week.

Cooking shows today make stars of chefs. Talk shows made chefs of stars. Watching a celebrity don an apron did something that no other part of a talk show could do: it humanized celebrities. Many of these singers, comedians, and actors were extraordinarily talented performers. But in the kitchen, they were just like us.

A New Jersey housewife would never be able to sing "Splish Splash" as engagingly as Bobby Darin did on a 1970 installment of *Mike Douglas,* but at home on her range she could recreate the stir-fry noodles with mushrooms, onions, and tamari sauce that he made that day; and the noodles would turn out just as yummy as his, and maybe even better. At dinner, she'd be the one making the splash.

Cooking segments also made for good comedy. Frequent talk show guest Hermione Gingold, an actress and raconteuse extraordinaire who appeared in such films as *Gigi*, *Bell, Book and Candle*, and *A Little Night Music*, recounts, in her hilarious 1988 memoir *How to Grow Old Disgracefully*, her experience making her signature chicken dish on *The Merv Griffin Show*. Before curtain time, she put the recipe down the front of her dress for safekeeping. When the moment came to cook, she couldn't find the paper and she began rooting around in her cleavage on national television. Ever the helpful host, Merv asked if she needed help. "No," the bawdy Brit barked, "I know my way 'round."

Dinah Shore, a singer, actress, and avid golfer who most famously dated a much younger Burt Reynolds in the 1970s, knew her way 'round, too. A kitchen, that is. Shore's stints hosting the talk shows *Dinah!*, *Dinah's Place*, and *Dinah and Friends* led to a second career as a cookbook author. Her book *Someone's in the Kitchen with Dinah* is worth checking out. During a show, one cooking segment went particularly awry, though. Shore's guest was the legendarily confrontational comedian Andy Kaufman, appearing in the guise of his lounge-lizard character Tony Clifton. He sang "On the Street Where You Live," then was belligerent with Dinah and Charles Nelson Reilly. Tony was slated to cook, but insisted on singing instead. As the story goes, he dumped a pan of raw eggs over Shore's head, and she was so offended she demanded the footage be destroyed. The spot never aired.

All of these years later, you can decide if the recipes of the legendary talk show hosts that follow deserve air time.

Jack Paar 1918–2004

KNOWN AS AN EMOTIONAL AND URBANE TV presence, Jack Paar is considered one of the greatest talk show hosts of all time. A former actor (he played Marilyn Monroe's boyfriend in one film) and comic, Paar filled the very large shoes of Steve Allen as the host of *The Tonight Show* and was as comfortable talking with Richard Nixon as he was gossiping with Elsa Maxwell. He saw magic in the strange pairings of guests on his show. Thus, on one installment, Muhammad Ali recited poetry while Liberace played piano accompaniment. As for his special recognition, Paar was as famous for quitting *The Tonight Show* as he was for hosting it. When the network censors nixed a joke about a "water closet" in 1960, he walked off the show and didn't come back for three weeks. During that time, no doubt, he had plenty of time to make his favorite soup.

Jack Paar's
CLUPP SOUP

1 quart water

1 teaspoon allspice

3 bay leaves

1 onion, diced

Salt and pepper, to taste

1 pound ground beef

½ cup cracker crumbs

1 egg, slightly beaten

2 tablespoons milk

1 small onion, minced

½ teaspoon salt

4 tablespoons flour

4 tablespoons vinegar

½ cup cream

Combine water, allspice, bay leaves, onion, and salt and pepper and bring to a boil. Simmer until the flavor of the spices releases. In a large bowl, combine ground beef, cracker crumbs, egg, milk, minced onion, and salt. Mix well and form into meatballs about the size of walnuts. Drop into boiling spiced water. Cover pan and boil for 30 minutes. Combine flour and vinegar to form a paste. Add a little water to thin if necessary. Drizzle into soup slowly, stirring until mixture is thick. Add cream. Remove meatballs. Strain liquid. Serve over rice or riced potatoes; that is, potatoes put through a potato ricer.

Mike Douglas 1925–2006

AN AFFABLY SQUARE FAMILY MAN who was married to the same woman for more than sixty years, Mike Douglas launched his talk show in Cleveland in 1961, moved it to Philadelphia four years later, and finally to Los Angeles where it ran from 1978 to 1982. *The Mike Douglas Show* was the first syndicated program to win an Emmy Award. At the height of the show's popularity, *TV Guide* wrote, "Dishes go unwashed and shirts remain un-ironed when Mike Douglas comes on." His was the kind of show that would seat Gene Simmons of Kiss next to comedienne Totie Fields, whose Mish Mosh recipe appears in Chapter 20. The show set the tone for friendly modern chat shows like those hosted by Rosie O'Donnell and Ellen DeGeneres. In his home kitchen, Douglas was best known for his version of the classic Caesar salad.

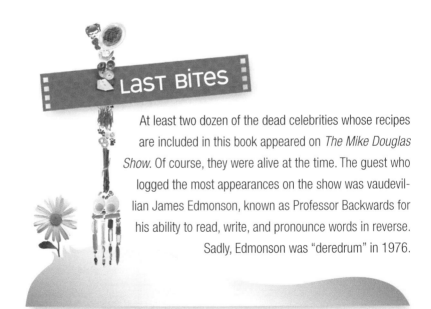

Last Bites

At least two dozen of the dead celebrities whose recipes are included in this book appeared on *The Mike Douglas Show.* Of course, they were alive at the time. The guest who logged the most appearances on the show was vaudevillian James Edmonson, known as Professor Backwards for his ability to read, write, and pronounce words in reverse. Sadly, Edmonson was "deredrum" in 1976.

Mike Douglas's Caesar Douglas Salad

1 clove garlic, quartered

1 teaspoon salt

½ teaspoon freshly ground
   pepper

⅔ cup olive oil

2 eggs, coddled

2 heads romaine lettuce

1 head iceberg lettuce

1 large ripe avocado

2 tablespoons anchovy paste

Juice of two lemons

2 tablespoons red wine
   vinegar

⅔ cup croutons

½ cup Parmesan cheese

Put garlic, salt, and pepper in the olive oil and let it marinate several hours or overnight. Remove garlic. Coddle eggs by placing two room temperature eggs into boiling water for one minute and then removing and setting aside until needed. Wash and dry lettuce, tear into bite-size pieces, and refrigerate until needed. Cut avocado in half, remove pit, spoon out pulp and mash in a large wooden salad bowl. Add anchovy paste, lemon juice, vinegar, and oil mixture. Mix well. Add greens and toss. Garnish with croutons, cheese, and coddled eggs; toss lightly again and serve.

JOHNNY CARSON 1925–2005

CONSIDERED THE KING OF LATE NIGHT television, Johnny Carson hosted *The Tonight Show* for thirty years, first out of New York, then from Burbank, California. His mannerisms—most notably, his golf swing—made him easy to imitate but, as a talk show host, he was impossible to duplicate. Everyone who was anyone in entertainment sat on his couch, and if he invited a comic over to chat after a set, the guy or gal had it made. Carson played his own characters—Carnac the Magnificent was the best—which further endeared him to audiences. When he hosted animal guests, the results were often screamingly funny. Along with sidekick Ed McMahon and bandleader Doc Severinsen, Carson tucked America in at night. When he bid his final audience "a very heartfelt good night," an era was over. His way with whitefish, however, lives on.

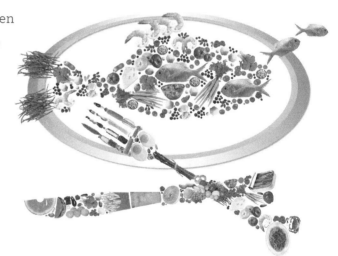

JOHNNY CARSON'S WHITEFISH WITH ANGEL HAIR PASTA

1 medium zucchini,
cut into ½-inch cubes

1 carrot, cut into
½-inch dice

¼ pound green beans,
trimmed and cut into
1-inch pieces

2 pounds whitefish fillets

¼ teaspoon salt

⅛ teaspoon freshly
ground pepper

¼–½ teaspoon filé
powder

Pinch cayenne pepper

1 pound angel hair pasta

1 ripe tomato, peeled,
seeded and diced

2 tablespoons extra-
virgin olive oil

½ cup fresh basil,
chopped

In a large pot of boiling salted water, cook the zucchini until tender, about 1 minute. Remove with a slotted spoon and set aside. Add the carrots and cook in the still-boiling water until tender, 2–3 minutes. Remove with a slotted spoon and set aside. Finally add the green beans and cook until tender, 2–3 minutes and remove. Keep the water at a full boil until ready to cook the pasta.

Preheat the broiler and broiling pan. Season the fish with salt, black pepper, filé powder, and cayenne pepper to taste. Broil 4–5 inches away from heat until the fish is lightly browned, firm to the touch, and opaque, 7–10 minutes. Transfer to a platter, remove the skin and keep warm.

Add the pasta to the pot of boiling water and cook until al dente. Drain well. Return the drained pasta to the pot, set over moderately high heat. Add the cooked vegetables, chopped tomato, olive oil, and basil. Toss until blended and heated through. Transfer to a large serving platter. Place fish on top and serve at once.

DINAH SHORE 1916–1994

BEFORE SHE WAS SYNONYMOUS with an all-girl weekend held each year in Palm Springs, singer/actress Dinah Shore made three of the greatest guest-star turns in TV history. She played the Olivia de Havilland role in the venerated *The Carol Burnett Show* spoof "Went with the Wind." She played herself in a hilarious episode of *Mary Hartman, Mary Hartman.* And she sang the world's longest version of "The 12 Days of Christmas" on the *Pee-wee's Playhouse Christmas Special.* These unforgettable moments barely ice the cake of a very long and delicious career. She had a string of hits during the Big Band era, her own TV variety shows in the '50s and '60s, and various talk shows in the '70s, '80s, and '90s. Most recently, the cast of *Glee* recreated one of Shore's vintage commercials for Chevy, singing "See the U.S.A. in Your Chevrolet" in a spot that aired during the 2011 Super Bowl. Millions of people, whether they knew it or not, were witnessing a giant "mwah"—as Dinah's signature kisses were called—to a very special lady and a helluva good cook.

LAST BITES

Dinah was born Frances Rose Shore in Tennessee. In her teens, as the story goes, she so often sang the popular song "Dinah" at auditions that a prominent disc jockey who couldn't remember her name called her "that Dinah girl" on the air and the name stuck. Thank heaven! Would you really have run home from school to watch a TV show called *Frances's Place*?

Dinah Shore's Red Snapper

4 red snapper filets

½ stick butter, melted

Salt and pepper, to taste

Juice of 2 limes

½ bunch fresh parsley, chopped

Brush red snapper filets with melted butter and sprinkle with salt and pepper. Broil quickly on each side under a very hot broiler. Sprinkle generously with lime juice. Before serving, pour on a bit more melted butter. Garnish with lime halves and sprinkle with chopped parsley.

STeve aLLen 1921–2000

A UTHOR, COMPOSER, COMEDIAN, AND ACTOR Steve Allen all but created the late night talk show in 1953 as the original host of *The Tonight Show*. A versatile entertainer from a family of vaudevillians, he pioneered such late-night staples as "man on the street" interviews and prankish gags. He also played the title character in the 1955 film *The Benny Goodman Story*, wrote more than 5,000 songs including the hit "This Could Be the Start of Something Big," and went on to host *The Steve Allen Show* where he gave a generation of second bananas—Louis Nye, Tom Poston, Don Knotts among them—their big break. A minor accomplishment, but an accomplishment nonetheless, Allen is said to have coined the phrase "Is it bigger than a breadbox?" as a regular on *What's My Line?* A better kitchen question might be, is your recipe tastier than his rack of lamb?

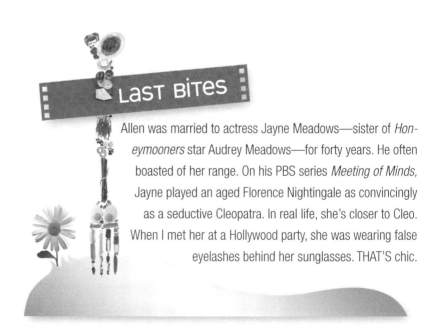

LasT BiTes

Allen was married to actress Jayne Meadows—sister of *Honeymooners* star Audrey Meadows—for forty years. He often boasted of her range. On his PBS series *Meeting of Minds*, Jayne played an aged Florence Nightingale as convincingly as a seductive Cleopatra. In real life, she's closer to Cleo. When I met her at a Hollywood party, she was wearing false eyelashes behind her sunglasses. THAT'S chic.

steve allen's
rack of lamb

1 rack of lamb

1 bottle honey-mint sauce

Lemon-pepper seasoning

Salt, to taste

Marinate lamb in honey-mint sauce for 12 hours, turning twice. Season rack with lemon-pepper seasoning and salt. Stand lamb on a metal roasting rack in a flat pan. Bake, uncovered and unbasted, for 45–50 minutes at 325° for pink, medium doneness. Cover ends with foil to avoid burning. To serve, cut lamb rack into chops of 2 at thickest part, and 3 at the narrow end. Dress ends of chops with "lamb pants" in various colors.

Merv Griffin 1925–2007

BETWEEN HIS START AS A BIG-BAND SINGER and becoming a stinking-rich businessman, Merv Griffin created the two greatest game shows ever, *Jeopardy!* and *Wheel of Fortune*, and he hosted a must-watch TV talk show. Gabbing with all manner of celebrities, the "eternally jovial Irishman," as the *New York Times* called him in his obituary, created a cocktail party atmosphere on his show and thus managed to get the biggest stars to let it all hang out. Although rumor has it he was gay, Griffin was often seen on the arm of Eva Gabor, whose goulash recipe appears in Chapter 13. When asked at age 80 about his sexuality, he told interviewers to "get a life." An astute businessman who bought casinos and hotels—and relished his rivalry with Donald Trump—Griffin made what was possibly his smartest move when he wrote the theme song to *Jeopardy!* and then maintained the rights to it, even after selling the show. He bragged that his royalties from the song earned him upwards of $80 million. That's a lot of stuffed squash.

Merv Griffin's Stuffed Squash

In a large bowl, toss together stuffing, lemon juice with zest, pineapple with water, dried apricots, onions, nuts, coconut, and butter. Stuff squash with mixture. Bake squash halves for one hour in a preheated 325° oven. Garnish with the 2 tablespoons of toasted coconut.

12 ounces cornbread stuffing mix

Juice and zest of 1 lemon

1 can (20 ounces) pineapple chunks in water

1½ cups dried apricots, slivered

1 cup chopped onion

1 cup walnuts, pecans, or macadamia nuts, coarsely chopped

½ cup flaked coconut (reserve 2 tablespoons for toasting)

½ cup melted butter

4 small acorn, golden nugget, or sweet dumpling squash, halved and seeded

POST MORTEM

This recipe makes way more stuffing than you need to fill eight squash halves, but who ever complained about having leftover stuffing? With or without the squash, the fruity flavors of the stuffing make a great accompaniment to pork chops, ham, or even chicken. Yum!

A PIONEERING WOMAN IN THE TALK SHOW GAME, Virginia Graham had one of the fastest, funniest tongues (and the best bouffant hairdo) ever on television. As the host of *Girl Talk* and *The Virginia Graham Show* in the 1960s and '70s, she interviewed the most fascinating women of the time. Everyone from Gloria Swanson (whose Potassium Broth recipe appears in Chapter 18) to Joan Rivers matched wits with her, and millions tuned in every time. Her often self-deprecating humor infused everything she did. Her books include *There Goes What's Her Name* and *Don't Blame the Mirror*. When I interviewed Graham in 1989 for a style story on Barbara Bush, I asked her if she thought the new First Lady would be a fashion role model. Graham said, "Well, she might be a *roll* model." Her recipe for Coffee Toffee Pie can help you be one, too.

virginia graHam's coffee Toffee pie

For the pastry, combine pastry ingredients and mix well with a fork. Turn into a well-greased 11-inch pie plate. Press firmly against bottom and sides of plate. Bake 15 minutes in a 375° oven. Cool on rack.

For filling, using electric mixer on medium speed, beat butter until creamy. Gradually add sugar. Beat until light. Blend in chocolate and instant coffee. Add eggs one at a time, beating after each one. Then beat for five more minutes. Pour into the cool pie shell. Put in refrigerator, covered. Chill overnight. For topping, combine heavy cream, instant coffee, and confectioners' sugar. Chill in refrigerator for two hours. Then beat until stiff. Spread topping on pie. Chill for three hours before serving.

Pastry Shell:

1 package pie crust mix

½ cup firmly packed brown sugar

1½ cups walnuts, finely chopped

2 squares unsweetened chocolate, grated

2 teaspoons vanilla

2 tablespoons water

Filling:

1 cup soft butter

1½ cups sugar

2 squares unsweetened chocolate (melted and cooled)

4 teaspoons instant coffee

4 eggs

Topping:

3 cups heavy cream

3 tablespoons instant coffee

¾ cup confectioners' sugar

after-dinner viewing

enjoy a talk-show marathon

Take the opportunity to enjoy the talk shows of yore on DVD. There's a treasure trove of vintage *The Tonight Show* with Johnny Carson episodes, like the 12-disc collection called *Heeere's Johnny: The Definitive Collection.* Merv Griffin has a 3-disc best-of box set, *The Merv Griffin Show—40 of the Most Interesting People of Our Time,* which includes an interview with Orson Welles hours before he died. There's *The Jack Paar Collection*, three discs, two with clips, another with three complete episodes. But the disc that brings back the most nostalgia for me is *Mike Douglas: Moments & Memories,* a documentary on his life and work, with bonus excerpts of interviews with such varied personalities as Ingrid Bergman, John Lennon and Yoko Ono, Paul Newman, Alfred Hitchcock, Alex Haley, Mother Teresa—MOTHER TERESA—and Ron Howard discussing the birth of his daughter, star-to-be Bryce Dallas Howard.

2

Batman's Kitchen Capers

THE DELICIOUSLY DERANGED writers of the classic TV show *Batman* clearly had food issues. Beginning with its 1966 premiere, a two-part episode that launched all-out "Bat-mania" in America, the series was a candy-colored feast of exploding cakes, flung fish, doped orange juice, man-eating giant clams, and puns so rancid you couldn't wait to spit them out the next day at school. When Batman (Adam West) faced his feline foe Catwoman (Julie Newmar), and she tried to scald him with coffee in an outsized cup, the announcer asked, "Are Batman and Robin still good to the last drip?"

In three mostly high-rated seasons on ABC, the wacky wordsmiths in the writers' room nearly disposed of the caped crusader and his sidekick Robin (Burt Ward) in more food-related ways than you could shake a wooden spoon at. The icy Mr. Freeze (Otto Preminger) tried to turn the Dynamic Duo into giant Frosty Freezies. (Each would be big enough to slushy the entire cast of *Glee* today.) The malevolent Minstrel (Van Johnson), another special guest villain, made every effort to barbecue the bat and the bird on a large rotisserie. The Penguin (Burgess Meredith) attempted to dunk Batman and Robin to death by turning them into human teabags hung over a boiling vat.

Olga, an evil Cossack queen played by Anne Baxter, and Egghead, an ovum-obsessed one played by Vincent Price, tried to drown Batgirl (Yvonne Craig) in caviar and then make Bessarovian Wedding Borscht out of Robin and Commissioner Gordon (Neil Hamilton). Bookworm (Roddy McDowall, whose red cabbage recipe appears in Chapter 22) trapped the Dynamic Duo in an oversized cookbook. Then there was the time when the Joker (Cesar Romero) turned the entire Gotham City water supply into strawberry jelly. As Robin said when he opened the taps in the Batcave to find only a font of red goo, "Holy jelly molds!" That was only one of the Boy Wonder's many food-related interjections on the show.

Robin's other cuisine-related rejoinders included:

"Holy oleo!"

"Holy guacamole!"

"Holy ravioli!"

"Holy hamburger!"

"Holy popcorn!"

"Holy mashed potatoes!"

"Holy fruit salad!"

"Holy egg shells!"

"Holy hole in a doughnut!"

"Holy birthday cake!"

"Holy wedding cake!"

"Holy red snapper!"

"Holy red herring!"

"Holy sardines!"

And my favorite: "Holy astringent plum-like fruit!"

They don't write them like that anymore.

The following recipes represent the culinary contributions of Batman's greatest foes—Mr. Freeze, Catwoman, the Penguin, the Riddler, and the Joker— or at least the actors who so memorably played them on television decades ago. In the cafeteria of the Gotham State Penitentiary of the Great Beyond, I like to think they're cooking up something other than their next crimes.

OTTO Preminger 1905–1986

PRODUCER, DIRECTOR AND ACTOR Otto Preminger was one of three men to play Mr. Freeze on *Batman*, and certainly the most memorable. Arnold Schwarzenegger's take on the character in the 1997 kitsch-fest *Batman & Robin* owes him everything. Despite Preminger's reputation as an awful man to work for—Laurence Olivier called him a bully; others called him worse—he made some wonderful films, among them, *Laura*, *Anatomy of a Murder*, and *The Man with the Golden Arm*. He was twice nominated for the Best Director Academy Award, which is pretty cool. Sadly, though, his deviled eggs don't freeze well.

POST Mortem

Otto, Otto, Otto. The cheeses, the vinegar . . . you've overwhelmed the yolks. All the egginess is gone from your deviled eggs. What would Egghead say? With this recipe, you've thrown a cheese dip party and then invited an egg at the last minute. I'll never be the super villain you were, but my recipe—yolks flavored with a little mayo, a little Indian relish, a little Sriracha sauce and some prepared mustard—beats yours cold. As you used to say, they're "wild, simply wild!"

OTTO PREMINGER'S DEVILED EGGS

Put eggs in pan and fill with enough cold water to cover the eggs with an inch to spare. Bring to a full boil. Cover, remove from heat, and let sit for 15–18 minutes. Then drain and submerge eggs in cold water. When they're cool, peel eggs and set aside. Whip cheeses, mustard, red pepper, sugar, and salt. Split the eggs in half lengthwise, carefully removing the yolks from the whites. Mash egg yolks very finely, add the vinegar, then the mayonnaise. Add to cheese mixture, along with Parmesan cheese, and whip until smooth. Generously fill egg white halves with yolk mixture, rounding off the top. Sprinkle with paprika or parsley.

Serves 6

6 eggs

4 ounces cream cheese, softened

1 cup cottage cheese

¼ teaspoon English dry mustard

⅛ teaspoon red pepper

Dash sugar

Dash salt

1 tablespoon tarragon vinegar

2 tablespoons mayonnaise

1 teaspoon Parmesan cheese

Paprika or parsley

earTHa KiTT 1927–2008

ACTRESS, CHANTEUSE, AND INTERNATIONAL sex kitten Eartha Kitt slipped into Catwoman's catsuit in the final season of *Batman*. (Julie Newmar was off making a movie.) In the mid-seventies, she played a funky-fierce fashion designer named Madame Rena in the very fun blax-ploitation film *Friday Foster*, opposite Pam Grier. Her voice-acting was much lauded in her later years. No one could purr any sexier than she could. Kitt is best remembered, though, as the singer of the Christmas favorite "Santa Baby." Others from Madonna to Miss Piggy have recorded the song. But Kitt's original remains the definitive version. In comparison, the others are just kitty litter. Oh, meow.

eartha kitt's chicken wings

Put wings in a pot with water and tomatoes and simmer for 20 minutes covered. Meanwhile, chop the vegetables. Add them with the seasoning to the chicken wings and simmer uncovered for 10–15 minutes until tender, but not overcooked, and most of the liquid has been absorbed.

3 pounds chicken wings

1 cup water

1 (19-ounce) can tomatoes

2–3 carrots, cut lengthwise

1 green pepper, chopped

2 medium onions, chopped

1 clove garlic

1 red pepper pod

1 bay leaf

1 teaspoon chili powder

½ teaspoon celery salt

Salt and freshly ground pepper, to taste

B ETWEEN PLAYING THE MEEK little man who breaks his glasses just when he finds the time to get some reading done in the classic post-apocalyptic *Twilight Zone* episode "Time Enough at Last" in 1959, and playing perverted old Grandpa Gustafson in the Grumpy Old Men movies of the 1990s, Emmy Award–winning character actor Burgess Meredith became synonymous with a cagey bird known as the Penguin. His waddle, his quack—do penguins really quack?—and his way with a cigarette holder endeared him to Bat fans. *Rocky* fans loved him as Rocky Balboa's trainer Mickey Goldmill. Meredith was great in *The Day of the Locust* and *Magic*, too. But there's something about him wearing a tuxedo and top hat and riding a giant umbrella that I'll always love best.

Burgess Meredith's Nacho Salad

Mix the beans, corn, rice, onion, cilantro, and tomatoes in a large bowl. In a small bowl, stir together the lime juice, olive oil, salt, and pepper. Pour over the vegetable mixture and let it sit for a bit. Then toss and serve on a bed of lettuce and tortilla chips. Top with grated cheese, sour cream, and salsa.

Serves
4

1 (15-ounce) can black beans

1 cup canned yellow corn kernels

1 cup cooked rice

1 onion, chopped

1 bunch of fresh cilantro (leaves only), chopped

3 medium tomatoes, seeded and diced

Juice of 1 lime

3 tablespoons olive oil

Salt and pepper, to taste

1 head lettuce

1 large bag of tortilla chips

Shredded cheese, for garnish

Sour cream, for garnish

Fresh salsa, for garnish

Frank Gorshin 1933–2005

IMPRESSIONIST FRANK GORSHIN was nominated for an Emmy Award for his portrayal of the Riddler, a characterization said to have been based on Richard Widmark's character Tommy Udo in the 1947 noir classic *Kiss of Death*. At the very least, the two evildoers shared the same manic laugh. Gorshin also had a very memorable turn on another time-honored series, the original *Star Trek*. He guest-starred as the black-on-one-side, white-on-the-other alien Bele in the 1969 episode "Let That Be Your Last Battlefield." Gorshin played plenty of other roles in his career—in his final years, he even impersonated George Burns on Broadway—but Batman was his ticket to immortality. Although a little less lithe in his leotard, he played the Riddler again in 1979 in *Legend of the Superheroes*, an off-the-wall TV special that must be seen to be believed. In 2005, shortly before his death, he voiced another Bat charac- ter, Hugo Strange, in three episodes of the animated series *The Batman*.

Frank Gorshin's Pepper Steak

1½ pounds top sirloin

1 tablespoon flour

½ teaspoon salt

2 tablespoons bacon fat

1 medium onion, minced

1 small clove garlic,
finely minced

2 teaspoons sweet
Hungarian paprika

Pinch cayenne

1 cup beef stock

¼ cup tomato puree

2 Italian frying peppers,
cut in ¼-inch strips

Freshly ground black
pepper, to taste

Cut the beef on the diagonal into ½-inch-thick slices. Place the beef between sheets of waxed paper and pound with a kitchen mallet until ¼-inch thick. Sprinkle lightly with flour and salt. Heat the bacon fat in a large heavy skillet over medium heat. Add beef and brown well on all sides. Remove and keep warm. Add the onion to the skillet and sauté over medium heat until translucent. Add the garlic, stir, and cook for less than a minute. Add the paprika and pinch of cayenne pepper; cook for a few seconds. Stir in the beef stock and the tomato puree, scraping up the bottom of the pan. As the mixture begins to simmer, return the beef to the pan. Partially cover and cook until the beef is tender, about 45 minutes. Add the Italian frying peppers, re-cover partially and simmer until the peppers are softened, about 15–20 minutes. Serve with sour cream on a bed of caraway-seeded wide egg noodles.

A RECIPE FROM CESAR ROMERO would fit in at least four different chapters in this book. He always played Latin lovers, he was Sophia's suitor on *The Golden Girls*, and let's just say that he wasn't cast in *The Gay Caballero* for nothing. But Romero's *ne plus ultra* portrayal of the Joker—sorry Jack, sorry Heath—is the role for which he is best remembered. So here with his cohorts in crime he shall be. Although the New York–born Cuban-American actor refused to shave off his signature mustache and the makeup men had to cover it with white greasepaint, his Joker remains Batman's greatest archenemy. Other memorable parts include his 1957 appearance on *The Lucy-Desi Comedy Hour*, his recurring roles on such fondly remembered TV series as *Zorro*, *Julia*, and *Alias Smith and Jones*, and his stint as Peter Stavros, Jane Wyman's love interest on *Falcon Crest*. She must have adored his rice.

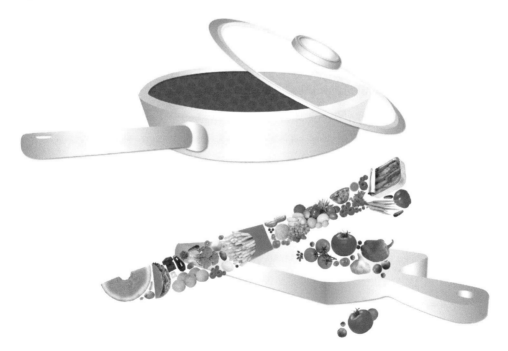

cesar Romero's spanish Rice

Heat the olive oil in a skillet. Add the rice and cook, stirring, until golden brown. Add the onions, peppers, and tomatoes and mix well. Then add the boiling water, cover, and let simmer for about a half hour without stirring. Sprinkle with Parmesan cheese before serving.

1 cup uncooked rice, washed

½ cup olive oil

¾ cup boiling water

2 onions, chopped

2 green peppers, chopped

2 cups tomatoes, chopped

Salt and pepper to taste

Parmesan cheese, for garnish

POST Mortem

For a more traditional take on Spanish rice, season the dish with a couple of teaspoons of chili powder, a teaspoon of cumin, and a pinch of oregano before adding vegetables. Use chicken broth instead of water and omit the Parmesan cheese.

after-dinner viewing

Batman: the Movie

There are many theories why the *Batman* TV series has never come to home video: rights issues, squabbling studios, embarrassment about the show's camp aspects. Whatever the reason, the exclusion stinks more than Egghead's onion-scented teargas eggs. The 1966 big-screen spinoff of *Batman*, however, is not only out on DVD, it's out on Blu-ray and it's an excellent way to get your Joker jollies after you've been fed. In the film, Batman and Robin battle not only the original Clown Prince of Crime, but also the Riddler, the Penguin, and a lite-version of Catwoman, played by Lee Meriwether. A former Miss America, she looks great in leopard but she has no menace. Still, two hours of high-definition *Batman* is better than none. A dessert suggestion while you're watching: serve an ice cream cake. If everyone's too full to eat it, paraphrase the movie's most famous line. Tell your guests, in your most exasperated tone, "Some days, you just can't get rid of a bombe!"

3

MUSICAL MUNCHIES

LIBERACE PUT THE CONNECTION BETWEEN FOOD AND MUSIC in perspective in his 1970 book *Liberace Cooks!* when he called them "the two best things in life." Take that with a grain of salt. He was a man so obsessed with food and music that at one point he lived in a home with seven dining rooms; he also had a home with a piano-shaped swimming pool out back. But the diamond-encrusted megastar was on to something. Food and music share the power to fuel a man's fantasy life, and as he points out in the book, they also share the power to build bridges to other cultures. Put it this way: you might be too squeamish to travel to India—poor people! Blech!—but a little Chicken Tikka Masala from the take-out place isn't daunting, it's Tuesday's dinner. Put a little sitar music on the hi-fi and you're practically in New Delhi.

Certainly Liberace wasn't the only legendary musical performer to find his inspiration in the kitchen. A love of food has begotten plenty of music. From "Shortnin' Bread" to "Clambake," musicians from Fats Waller to Elvis Presley love to sing about what they love to eat. Yes, sometimes it only sounds like they're going on about food. When Memphis Minnie sang about selling her "pork chops" and giving her "gravy" away, I'm quite sure that a box of Shake 'N Bake and a bottle of Kitchen Bouquet were the furthest things from her mind. (Kids, Kelis and her "Milkshake" had nothing on that old broad!) But "Hamburger Hop" really was about burgers and "The Candy Man" genuinely was so sweet you could get cavities from just one listen. Please, you could even eat the dishes!!!

Let's not forget, too, that there has always a superfluity of bands named after food. Hot Chocolate, the Electric Prunes, and the Black Eyed Peas are but a few. Peaches & Herb becomes twice as culinary if you don't pronounce the "H"! And one of my favorite albums since I was but a wee thing, *Whipped Cream and Other Delights* by Herb Alpert & the Tijuana Brass, is totally food themed. On the cover, there's a bare-naked lady covered in Chantilly (cream not lace). None of those musicians' recipes are included here (either I couldn't find a good one or they're not dead), and this chapter's only meat loaf belongs to Lawrence Welk. But there's plenty here to sing about. Put on a platter and then whip up a platter of any or all of these tasty dishes. With all apologies to Shakespeare, if music be food, eat on . . .

H OW A SULTRY SOPHISTICATED URBAN PRESENCE like singer/ songwriter Peggy Lee sprang from the little town of Jamestown, North Dakota, is beyond me. But thank heaven she found her way from that so-called Buffalo City to success on stage and screen. The brilliant chanteuse is best known to baby boomers for such songs as "Fever," "Is That All There Is?" and "I'm a Woman," the w-o-m-a-n song that Miss Piggy sang with Raquel Welch that time on *The Muppet Show*. Lee's title song to *Johnny Guitar* is faboo, too. A Grammy winner, Lee also acted and was nominated for an Oscar for her supporting role in the 1955 film *Pete Kelly's Blues*. To so many of us, though, she's the voice of the dog Peg in the Disney animated classic *Lady and the Tramp*. In 2005, Bette Midler (both a lady and a tramp) released her tribute album, *Bette Midler Sings the Peggy Lee Songbook*. It's fun, but Lee's originals— like the recipe that follows—will give you fever, baby.

MiSS PeGGY Lee's JaDe SaLaD

Serves
6

Wash and thoroughly dry lettuce, cut into julienne strips and place in a large bowl. Chop green onions into ¼-inch pieces and mix with oil, vinegar, mustard, garlic powder, pepper, sugar, sesame seeds, and Parmesan. Pour dressing over lettuce and toss thoroughly to coat. Sprinkle with almonds.

2 heads romaine lettuce

2 bunches green onions

1⅓ cups olive oil

⅔ cup red wine vinegar

2 teaspoons Dijon mustard

½ teaspoon garlic powder

½ teaspoon black pepper

2 tablespoons sugar

¼ cup toasted sesame seeds

¼ cup grated Parmesan cheese

½ cup sliced almonds

POST MorTem

Two bunches of green onions is overpowering. But Miss Peggy Lee's vaguely Asian dressing is delicious. Make enough salad or your guests will be saying, "Is That All There Is?"

Tammy Wynette 1942–1998

BROTHER BOY, THE INSTITUTIONALIZED DRAG QUEEN played by Emmy-winner Leslie Jordan in Del Shores' hilarious TV series *Sordid Lives*, worshipped Tammy Wynette, and if you've ever heard her music you probably do, too. The woman knew pain and how to emote it, and she still looked glamorous all the while. Wynette is famous for such songs as "D-I-V-O-R-C-E" and "Stand By Your Man," for which she won a Grammy in 1969. Her biggest hit on the pop charts, though, came in 1991 performing with the British dance band The KLF on a curiosity called "Justified and Ancient (Stand by the JAMs)." It's guaranteed to keep your feet moving as you wait for her favorite starter to be ready to serve. When your salad takes a whole day to prepare, you need something to listen to.

Sonny Bono 1935–1998

EVERYBODY LOVED SONNY BONO almost as much as Cher did. We just didn't know it until he died in a tragic skiing accident. Bono was a terrible singer, an even worse actor (YOU try sitting through his film *Good Times*), and (gasp!) he was a Republican, but he was so damn likeable. And behind the scenes, as a writer and music producer, he was brilliant. He wrote (or cowrote) such timeless pop classics as "Needles and Pins" and "Bang Bang (My Baby Shot Me Down)," and Sonny and Cher's two biggest hits, "I Got You Babe" and "The Beat Goes On." For those of us who grew up in the 1970s, Sonny and Cher were our Liz and Dick, and when they split up, we were heartbroken, too. Their 1987 reunion on David Letterman's late-night talk show had us weeping in our midnight snacks. You'll weep with joy when you discover just how handy the former U.S. congressman and mayor of Palm Springs, California, was in the kitchen, too. Here's Bono's favorite pasta dish.

Tammy Wynette's 24-Hour Salad

Layer lettuce in bottom of large salad bowl. Add layer of spinach. Layer onions on spinach. Top with cauliflower. Sprinkle with bacon bits. Add sugar. Spread salad dressing spread over top and cover with shredded cheese. Cover with plastic wrap. Chill in refrigerator 24 hours. Toss and serve.

1 head lettuce, washed and torn into pieces

1 package cleaned fresh spinach, torn into pieces

3 onions, diced

1 head cauliflower, chopped

½ cup bacon bits

¼ cup sugar

⅓ cup Parmesan cheese

1 cup salad dressing spread (Miracle Whip)

1 cup shredded cheddar cheese

Sonny Bono's Spaghetti with Fresh Tomato Sauce

Cook pasta according to package directions. While cooking, prepare sauce. Blanch tomatoes in boiling water for 1 minute, then peel and dice. Sauté garlic in oil over medium heat until tender. Add tomatoes and sauté one minute. Add basil, stir, and remove from heat. Toss pasta with tomato sauce. Season to taste. Sprinkle with red pepper and Parmesan.

1 pound spaghetti

5 large ripe tomatoes

1 clove garlic, minced

¼ cup olive oil

1 bunch basil, chopped

Salt and pepper, to taste

Crushed red pepper, to taste

Parmesan cheese, to taste

Isaac Hayes 1942–2008

BEFORE HE LENT HIS INCREDIBLY DEEP VOICE to the outrageous cartoon *South Park*, Isaac Hayes was a Grammy- and Academy Award–winning singer/songwriter. He took home the Oscar for the "Theme from Shaft" in 1972, putting him, at the time, in the very rarefied company of Sidney Poitier and Hattie McDaniel as one of the few African Americans to win the award. He cowrote some great pop songs, among them "Soul Man" and "Hold On, I'm Comin'," recorded some amazing albums, and acted in fun movies like *I'm Gonna Git You Sucka*. He'll probably be remembered most as the voice of Chef on *South Park* though. Hayes was a bad mother, "Shut yo' mouth!" but his Cornish hens were as sweet as can be. You'll have to decide for yourself if they're as mouthwatering as his "Chocolate Salty Balls."

BOBBY Darin 1936–1973

HE SPLISHED. HE SPLASHED. He married Sandra Dee. He died. But the legacy of singer and actor Bobby Darin is a lot more than just a novelty hit about taking a bath and a tabloid-ready marriage. Darin's jazzy version of "Mack the Knife" is killer—the man name-checks "ole Lotte Lenya" so smoothly in the song that it sounds like Brecht expected it to be sung that way!!! And his version of "Beyond the Sea" is transporting. I love his rendition of "Artificial Flowers" from the Broadway musical *Tenderloin*. Darin had a film career, too. He won a Golden Globe for his work in *Pressure Point* and was nominated for an Oscar for *Captain Newman, M.D.* Kevin Spacey, a terrific actor, played Darin in *Beyond the Sea,* a terrible biopic. Darin's Special Spinach will make you a lot happier than the movie.

Isaac Hayes's Cornish Hens

Place hens breast side up on a rack in a roasting pan. Rub them with salt and butter. Roast at 350° for 30 minutes per pound, basting frequently with ¼ cup butter melted in ⅔ cup boiling water. Turn hens often. While they're cooking, make sauce. Mix the rind, fruit juices, sugar, salt, and beaten egg yolks in a saucepan. Cook over low heat, stirring constantly, until thickened. Add egg whites. Beat the sauce until stiff. Cool and add vanilla. Serve hens with sauce.

2 Cornish hens

¼ cup butter, plus butter to rub on hens

⅔ cup boiling water

Grated rind of ½ lemon

Juice of ½ lemon

½ cup orange juice

⅓ cup sugar

Pinch of salt

2 eggs, separated

1 teaspoon vanilla

Bobby Darin's Special Spinach

Cook spinach according to package directions, and then drain thoroughly. Melt the butter over very low heat. Add onion and cook until soft, stirring occasionally. Add flour, stirring to remove any lumps. Add milk slowly and cook until it thickens. Add salt and nutmeg, and then combine spinach and sauce, mixing well. Heat a bit more over low heat and serve.

2 packages frozen, chopped spinach

3 tablespoons butter

2 tablespoons onion, finely chopped

2 tablespoons flour

1 cup whole milk

½ teaspoon salt

⅛ teaspoon ground nutmeg

Lawrence Welk 1903–1992

THE CHAMPAGNE MUSIC MAKER, Lawrence Welk was a bandleader with a hell of an accent, "Ah-one! Ah-two!" and an accordionist who could polka with the best of them. His evergreen TV series, *The Lawrence Welk Show*, still shown on public television, was a soothing antidote to the turbulent 1960s. Parents adored it and, secretly, so did the rest of us. It was so ridiculously corny, but it had bubbles, and Welk was so square he was mesmerizing. He toyed with his own image in 1970 with a memorable appearance on *Here's Lucy* in which Lucy tried to pass off a wax dummy of Welk as the real thing. It wasn't hard to do. In recent years, Fred Armisen has impersonated Welk on *Saturday Night Live*, bringing the maestro to a new generation. Welk's meat loaf is "wunnerful, wunnerful."

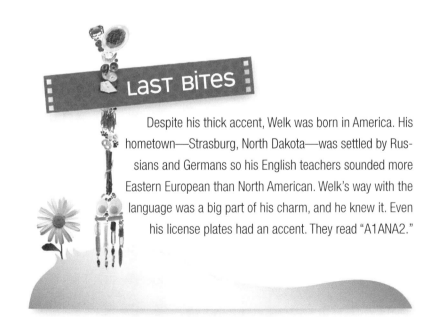

Last Bites

Despite his thick accent, Welk was born in America. His hometown—Strasburg, North Dakota—was settled by Russians and Germans so his English teachers sounded more Eastern European than North American. Welk's way with the language was a big part of his charm, and he knew it. Even his license plates had an accent. They read "A1ANA2."

Lawrence Welk's Lake Tahoe Meat Loaf

Mix meat loaf ingredients well. Shape into a loaf and place in a 13 x 9-inch pan and add ¾ cup water to pan. Bake at 400° for 30 minutes. While the meat loaf bakes make sauce. Cook down tomatoes with the salt, pepper, and sugar for 10–15 minutes. Spread over the top of meat loaf. Bake 40 minutes more.

Serves 4
with leftovers

For meat loaf:

2¼ pounds ground beef

4 or 5 slices bread, soaked in milk (squeeze out some milk)

1 bunch fresh parsley, chopped

2 onions, minced

4 hard-boiled eggs, chopped

3 fresh eggs

¼ cup Parmesan cheese

Salt and pepper, to taste

1 clove minced garlic

For sauce:

1 (15-ounce) can chopped tomatoes

Salt and pepper, to taste

1 teaspoon sugar

H E WAS THE MAN IN BLACK, a troubled but spiritually inclined genius who was one of the most original voices ever to spring from the world of country music. Johnny Cash wrote so many songs—more than 1,000, it is said—and had so many signature hits, including: "I Walk the Line," "Folsom Prison Blues," "Ring of Fire," and "A Boy Named Sue" that he is immortal in the realm of American pop culture. He fought drug addiction, but he was never really the outlaw that he made himself out to be—as he did when he sang about shooting a man just to watch him die. His wife, June Carter Cash, was brilliant in her own right, and two of his kids, Roseanne and John, are very talented musicians. Johnny was talented in the kitchen, too.

JOHNNY CASH'S PAN-FRIED OKRA

2 pounds okra

1 large yellow onion

½ cup cornmeal

¼ cup flour

1 teaspoon salt

Freshly ground black
  pepper, to taste

Bacon drippings or
  vegetable oil, for frying

Wash and dry okra. Cut off stems. If pods are small, leave them whole; otherwise, cut into 1-inch pieces. Peel and chop onion. Place cornmeal, flour, salt, and pepper in brown paper bag. Shake to blend ingredients. Heat bacon drippings or vegetable oil in heavy skillet. Put okra and onion in the paper bag with the seasoned cornmeal mixture; shake vigorously until vegetables are well coated. Fry vegetables in hot fat for several minutes until slightly brown, stirring to brown evenly. Do not overcook.

JOHN Denver 1943–1997

NAMED THE POET LAUREATE of Colorado in 1977, John Denver parlayed his boyish good looks, down-home charm, and gorgeous voice into stardom in many areas of show business. He had numerous chart hits with such songs as "Take Me Home, Country Roads," "Thank God I'm a Country Boy," and "Rocky Mountain High." He was pretty darn good in the 1977 film *Oh, God!* opposite George Burns, scored on TV with the Muppets—he looked like one, actually—and won an Emmy for the televised concert *An Evening with John Denver*. An activist and avid pilot, Denver died doing something he loved, flying, when his plane crashed into the Pacific. His music lives on, though, and Denver's Flemish Apple Cake? Well, as he liked to say, it's "far out!"

JOHN DENVER'S FLEMISH APPLE CAKE

Sauté apples in butter. Season with nutmeg, cinnamon, and salt. Stir for a few minutes, then add maple syrup and set aside. Sift flour, baking powder, baking soda, and ginger. Cream butter and honey. Add eggs and sour cream or yogurt to butter and honey and mix well. Mix dry ingredients into creamed mixture. Fold in apples and bake in a greased loaf pan at 400° for 35–40 minutes.

2 pounds golden delicious apples, peeled, cored, and cut into eighths

¼ cup butter

½ teaspoon nutmeg

1 teaspoon cinnamon

Pinch of salt

¼ cup maple syrup

3½ cups whole wheat flour

2 teaspoons baking powder

1 teaspoon baking soda

1 teaspoon ground ginger

1 cup unsalted butter
   (at room temperature)

1 cup honey

3 eggs, beaten

½ cup sour cream or yogurt

karen carpenter 1950–1983

I F MAMA CASS HAD GIVEN Karen Carpenter that ham sandwich, they'd both be alive today. I've always loved that joke. But Carpenter's immense talent was no laughing matter. Her angelic voice, showcased best on the 1971 track "Superstar," was unlike any other and one of the greatest hits of all time. Her hits, performed along with her brother, Richard, included such soft-rock classics as "(They Long to Be) Close to You," "Rainy Days and Mondays," and "For All We Know." Karen's tragic, untimely death, brought on by anorexia, shocked the world. How could someone squeaky clean enough to sing the saccharine children's song "Sing" and get away with it, be so troubled? The comforting thing is her cautionary tale helped others battling the disease, and her music lives on. Here's how I look at it: if you meet someone who doesn't like The Carpenters, don't be friends with them. And certainly don't give them a taste of your pie.

Last Bites

Director Todd Haynes, best known for his Oscar-nominated 2002 film *Far From Heaven* and the Emmy-adored 2011 HBO miniseries *Mildred Pierce*, cast Barbie to play the title character in his controversial 1988 biopic *Superstar: The Karen Carpenter Story*. Some say the plastic doll did a better job portraying her than Cynthia Gibb did a year later in the TV movie *The Karen Carpenter Story*.

karen carpenter's chewy pie

Crush saltines. Mix sugar and baking powder together and add to saltines. Beat egg whites until stiff, and then fold in saltine mixture. Fold in nuts. Add vanilla and pour into well-buttered pie dish. Bake 35 minutes. Open oven door and let sit with the door open about 10 minutes. After it is completely cool, beat whipping cream and cover, sprinkle with chocolate shavings and refrigerate. Chill until ready to serve.

Serves 8

16 saltine crackers, crushed

1 cup sugar

½ teaspoon baking powder

3 egg whites

¾ teaspoon vanilla

½ pint whipping cream

¾ cup nuts, chopped

Chocolate shavings

DUSTY SPRINGFIELD 1939–1999

I N THE REALM OF POP CULTURE, singer Dusty Springfield is not an elective, she's a requirement. Like Karen Carpenter, she had one of the most distinctive voices ever preserved on vinyl. She started out as a folk singer, but on a walk through New York's Greenwich Village she heard the sound of the Exciters singing "Tell Him" pouring out of a music shop and had an epiphany. She switched to pop and the rest, as lesbians (like Springfield) like to say, is "herstory." The British singer's versions of such Burt Bacharach and Hal David songs as "Wishin' and Hopin'" and "I Just Don't Know What to Do with Myself" are among the best interpretations of those songwriters' oeuvre. Only Dionne Warwick comes close. Springfield's album *Dusty in Memphis*, which contained her signature hit "Son of a Preacher Man," is a classic. Her biggest chart hit, though, was her duet with Pet Shop Boys on "What Have I Done to Deserve This?" To get a good overview of Springfield's music, seek out her compilation CD *The Silver Collection*. Then do what I did: buy every Springfield recording you can get your hands on. She's that good. Then you can decide if her banana pudding lives up to those high standards.

DUSTY SPRINGFIELD'S BANANA PUDDING

½ cup flour

1 cup sugar

3⅛ cups whole milk

2 egg yolks

1 tablespoon vanilla extract

1 box vanilla wafer cookies

6 or 7 bananas

2½ cups heavy cream

Mix the flour, sugar, and milk in a medium-size saucepan. Stir over low heat until the mixture thickens, then add the egg yolks. Cook for a minute more and then remove from heat. Add the vanilla extract and place a cover over the saucepan. Line a 2-quart dish with the cookies, add a layer of bananas and pour enough of the mixture from the saucepan to completely cover the bottom of the dish. Start again with the cookies, bananas, and mixture until all are used. Beat the heavy cream until thick. Pour over the top of the pudding. Refrigerate until ready to serve.

RENOWNED AS MR. SHOWMANSHIP, Liberace was a rhinestone's best friend, a highly paid (and highly worth it) Las Vegas entertainer, and television personality whose luxurious lifestyle and extravagant wardrobe defined showbiz excess. "Too much of a good thing can be wonderful," the Paderewski-worshipping pianist liked to say, quoting his friend Mae West. When critics were cruel—usually lambasting his flamboyance, not his talent—Liberace coined the phrase, "I cried all the way to the bank." In his four books and in the media, Liberace was very much in control of his image, being coy about his effeminacy so that the women who adored him—and they were legion—wouldn't be disappointed that he was a confirmed bachelor, ahem. Lee (his nickname to friends, his full real name was Wladziu Valentino Liberace) broke box office records, gave command performances for Queen Elizabeth, had an audience with Pope Pius XII, played twin villains on *Batman* in the 1960s, and delighted millions during his long career. And while the Las Vegas museum dedicated to his legacy, once described by the *New York Times* as "a tourist attraction on par with Hoover Dam," closed in 2010, no less than Lady Gaga acknowledges his undying influence, dropping his name into her hit "Dance in the Dark." The following recipe, one of many Liberace left behind, is my favorite in this book, and not just because of the name.

POST Mortem

If Liberace didn't have a way with sticky buns, no one did. These are like Cinnabon for grown-ups, and yummier than a recipe that starts with store-bought crescent rolls should ever be. One bite and you'll be able to play "Boogie-Woogie" just like Lee! Okay, maybe not, but heavens, you'll love eating them.

Liberace's Sticky Buns

1 cup white raisins

¼ cup light rum

1½ cups brown sugar

2 sticks unsalted butter

½ teaspoon cinnamon

¼ teaspoon nutmeg

¼ teaspoon allspice

¼ teaspoon cloves

¼ teaspoon ginger

3 packages refrigerated
   unbaked crescent rolls

1 cup chopped pecans

1 cup whole pecans

Non-stick baking spray with
   flour for greasing pan

Preheat oven to 325°. Spray two muffin pans with non-stick baking spray. Combine raisins and rum in a small bowl and warm in microwave on high for 45 seconds. Set aside. In a saucepan, melt butter and then stir in spices and brown sugar. Cook, stirring frequently, until it becomes a bubbling syrup. Put a teaspoon of syrup and a few whole pecans in each muffin cup. Unroll one package of crescent rolls on a piece of parchment paper. Pinch seams together to form one flat piece. Drizzle a quarter of the syrup over the dough. Sprinkle a third of the raisins and a third of the chopped pecans on it. Roll it jelly roll style. Cut into 1-inch thick pieces. Place one slice of dough, cut side up, in each muffin tin. Repeat with each package of crescent rolls. Bake 13–15 minutes or until golden brown. Remove from oven and immediately flip the buns onto a cookie sheet covered with parchment paper. Replace any nuts that may have stuck to the pan and serve warm.

MiCHaeL JaCKSon 1958–2009

B EFORE HE WAS WEIRD, HE WAS ADORABLE. But even at his strang-est—dangling his baby off a balcony, sleeping in a hyperbaric chamber, befriending a chimp—Michael Jackson was one of the most talented perform-ers who ever graced a stage. He had thirteen Grammys and twenty-six Ameri-can Music Awards to prove he was a "Thriller" and then some. One just had to watch him glide through his signature "moonwalk" or hear him sing anything from "Ben" to "Billie Jean" to know Jackson was a one-of-a-kind cultural pres-ence, the likes of which we'll never see again. Heck, we even loved him as the scarecrow in the awful movie version of *The Wiz,* and that took some serious charm. He deservedly was called the King of Pop, but was he the King of Pie? You decide.

Michael Jackson's sweet potato pie

3 eggs

½ cup sugar

¼ cup butter, melted

½ teaspoon salt

⅓ cup milk

1 teaspoon vanilla extract

1 teaspoon ground cinnamon

2 tablespoons fresh lemon or orange juice

2½ cups mashed sweet potatoes (canned or freshly cooked)

1 teaspoon nutmeg

½ cup pecan halves

1 unbaked pie shell

Beat eggs and sugar. Add melted butter, salt, milk, vanilla, and spices. Blend egg mixture with mashed sweet potatoes and lemon or orange juice. Pour into an unbaked pie shell. Garnish with pecan halves. Bake 10 minutes in a preheated 400° oven. Reduce oven temperature to 375° and bake 40 minutes longer or until golden.

POST MORTEM

As it turns out, Michael Jackson WAS the King of Pie. Even using canned sweet potatoes and omitting the pecans, his Sweet Potato Pie is a "Thriller." Cover the crust with aluminum foil if it gets too brown before the filling is set. Although it's not that "Bad" even if it does. Warm from the oven, you can't "Beat it." Okay, I'm done now. Oh, one more: "Don't Stop 'Til You Get Enough."

Dinner Music

A Dead Celebrity Baker's Dozen

1. "Everybody Eats When They Come to My House"
   by Cab Calloway

2. "Clambake" by Elvis Presley

3. "Jambalaya (On the Bayou)" by Jo Stafford

4. "(Do the) Mashed Potatoes" by James Brown

5. "The Frim Fram Sauce" by the Nat King Cole Trio

6. "Coconut" by Harry Nilsson

7. "Hey Pete! Let's Eat More Meat" by Dizzy Gillespie

8. "Let's Turkey Trot" by Little Eva

9. "Shortnin' Bread" by Fats Waller

10. "Hamburger Hop" by Johnny Hicks

11. "The Candy Man" by Sammy Davis Jr.

12. "Selling My Pork Chops" by Memphis Minnie

13. "Black Coffee" by Peggy Lee

an.
ALL-NiGHT
oscar
BUFFeT

THERE WAS A TIME WHEN the Academy Awards telecast was called the "Gay Super Bowl." Movie queens went nuts every March. Everyone else either watched or didn't. It was no biggie. But now that the greatest nights in football and Hollywood are both in February and the entire world makes such a big deal about watching them, everyone's in a quandary. Hosts know what to dish up for the Super Bowl: wings, cheese dip, sandwiches the size of an Escalade, but what to serve at an Oscar-viewing party? Let an expert help. Hey, I wasn't the movie critic on *The Daily Show* all those years for nothing.

1. You can cook Veal Oscar, that mélange of veal, crab, asparagus, and hollandaise sauce. Truth be told, it was created in honor of a different Oscar, and, if you invite more than a couple of people over, you'll have to be the king of Sweden to afford the ingredients.
2. You can serve famous movie food like the enormous pasta drum called a timpano so lovingly prepared by Tony Shalhoub in *Big Night*, one of the greatest food movies ever, or put out the enormous spread of *Babette's Feast*. These options require a lot of cooking. Instead, you could make ratatouille, which is easier. But the movie *Ratatouille* was about rats; and if your kitchen's not spotless, no one will eat your version of the dish.
3. You could cook your boyfriend and serve him to your husband as Helen Mirren did in *The Cook, The Thief, His Wife, and Her Lover*. But honestly, that's just yucky—although people will talk about your Oscar party for many years after your incarceration.

Instead, I say go with a much safer bet for awards night. Serve a buffet of dishes using the recipes of some of the greatest Oscar-winning women of all time. Many of these broads navigated the ins and outs of the studio system;

surely they could find their way around a kitchen. Statue-whet your guests' appetites with such tasty tidbits as Claudette Colbert's Cheese and Olive Puffs, Edith Head's Chicken Casa Ladera, and Katharine Hepburn's famous Brownies. Let your guests stay overnight. Tell them to call in late for work and serve Bette Davis's Red Flannel Hash and Greer Garson's Capirotada the following morning. They'll be thrilled with the total Oscar immersion you've created. When the compliments for your all-night party come (and they will), you can paraphrase Sally Field and say, "You liked it! You really liked it!"

B ORN IN FRANCE BUT RAISED in New York City, Claudette Colbert started in the theatre, switched to film with the advent of talkies, and went on to become one of the highest paid actresses of her day. She won the Oscar for the 1934 comedy *It Happened One Night* and was nominated two more times for her dramatic turns in 1935's *Private Worlds*, set in a mental hospital, and the wonderful 1944 World War II weepy *Since You Went Away*, which featured Jennifer Jones and Shirley Temple. Among her other triumphs are her performances in the 1934 version of *Imitation of Life*, in which she markets her housekeeper's pancake recipe and makes a fortune, John Ford's 1939 Revolutionary War drama *Drums Along the Mohawk*, the 1942 Preston Sturges comedy *The Palm Beach Story*, and forty-five years later, the TV-movie version of the Dominick Dunne potboiler *The Two Mrs. Grenvilles*, opposite Ann Margret. Colbert spent much of her free time in Barbados, where she learned to make her Cheese and Olive Puffs. She's there permanently now.

CLaUDeTTe COLBerT'S CHeese anD OLive PUFFS

Add cheese and butter to bowl of a food processor and blend until smooth. Add flour, Tabasco, and Worcestershire sauce to form dough. Wrap each olive in a small amount of dough, completely covering the olive and forming a ball. Place on an ungreased cookie sheet and freeze. Transfer to a plastic bag and store in freezer until ready to use. To cook, place on a baking sheet and bake at 400° for 12 minutes or until crust is golden. Serve hot.

2 cups shredded sharp cheddar cheese, at room temperature

⅓ cup butter, softened

1 cup flour

¼ teaspoon Tabasco

Dash of Worcestershire sauce

2 (10-ounce) jars of pimento-stuffed green olives, drained and blotted dry

POST MorTem

A little more hot sauce greatly improves these bar snacks. Make sure the olives aren't flavored with say, vermouth, as this overwhelms the other flavors.

sandy Dennis 1937–1992

NOBODY PLAYED NEUROTIC BETTER THAN Sandy Dennis, who won the Academy Award for Best Supporting Actress in 1966 as Honey in the film version of Edward Albee's *Who's Afraid of Virginia Woolf?* Among her other notable films were *Splendor in the Grass, Up the Down Staircase, The Out of Towners,* which is based on the Neil Simon play, and the 1977 satire *Nasty Habits,* which is essentially Watergate with nuns instead of politicians. I have a soft spot for the 1982 Robert Altman film *Come Back to the Five and Dime, Jimmy Dean, Jimmy Dean,* based on Ed Graczyk's Broadway play. In it Dennis stars, along with Cher and Karen Black, as an odd woman who's convinced her son is James Dean's child. It's strange, in a good way, like Sandy Dennis herself.

anne Bancroft 1931–2005

TWO WORDS: MRS. ROBINSON. In the 1967 Mike Nichols comedy *The Graduate,* Anne Bancroft was the ultimate "cougar," decades before that awful term became popular. But her turn as the middle-aged seductress was only one amazing performance of many. A knockout beauty with a big enough sense of humor to be happily married to the madcap Mel Brooks for more than forty years, Bancroft gave hilarious performances in such comedies as *The Prisoner of Second Avenue* and *Fatso,* which she also wrote and directed, and searing performances in such dramas as *The Pumpkin Eater, The Turning Point, The Elephant Man,* and *Agnes of God.* She won her Oscar as Annie Sullivan, the teacher who opened the world to Helen Keller in the 1962 film version of *The Miracle Worker.* It was a role that had won her a Tony as well. A Method actor, she also won a Tony for *Two for the Seesaw* and a pair of Emmys. Bancroft was such a private person that even many of her friends were shocked by her passing. We all were. But, coo coo ca-choo, what a legacy she left!

sandy Dennis's Taramosalata

Toast the bread and trim off crusts.
Soak in water and then squeeze dry.
Place the roe in a blender and blend
at low speed until creamy. Add onions
and bread and blend slowly. Incorporate
olive oil and lemon juice while blending.
Increase speed to high and blend until
the mixture is light in color and creamy.
Serve as a dip with crackers and black
Greek olives.

Serves 8

7 slices white bread

1 (7-ounce) jar fish roe

2 tablespoons onion, grated

¾ cup olive oil

Juice of 2 lemons

anne Bancroft's Che-cha pasta

Drop tomatoes into boiling water for
about five seconds. Peel and chop. In
a bowl, mix tomatoes, basil leaves, and
garlic and cover. Let it sit at room temperature for at least 3 hours. Cook pasta
and drain. Add olive oil and pepper to
tomato mixture. Toss hot pasta with
tomato mixture. Serve.

Serves 4

14 Italian plum tomatoes

2 handfuls basil leaves, chopped

2 cloves garlic, chopped

10 ounces fusilli pasta

2 tablespoons olive oil

Fresh ground pepper, to taste

SHELLEY WINTERS 1920–2006

AS ZAFTIG GRANDMOTHER Belle Rosen in the 1972 disaster movie *The Poseidon Adventure*, Shelley Winters told a reluctant reverend played by Gene Hackman, "In the water, I'm a very skinny lady." The actress did all her own swimming in the picture. She was renowned for such chutzpah, willing to play a beauty or a beast, and she did both over her long career. Among Winters's stellar credits are the films *A Place in the Sun*, *The Night of the Hunter*, *Lolita*, and *Alfie*. She did some pretty groovy exploitation films in the '70s, too, like *Cleopatra Jones*, *What's the Matter with Helen?* and *Whoever Slew Auntie Roo?* Two TV guest shots have a special place in my heart. Winters played villainous Ma Parker on *Batman* in 1966—memorably riding a souped-up wheelchair with mad abandon—and she spoofed her own food issues as a compulsive-eating actress named Shelley Summers on *Here's Lucy* in 1968. Too much salad was not her problem. Winters was nominated for the Oscar four times and won twice, once for *The Diary of Anne Frank* and once for *A Patch of Blue*. Despite such plum parts, her tell-all memoirs, *Shelley: Also Known as Shirley* and *Shelley II: The Middle of My Century*, proved that being herself was her greatest role.

sHeLLey wiNters's caesar saLaD

1 head romaine lettuce

1 head iceberg lettuce

1 head Boston lettuce

2 eggs, at room temperature

½ cup red wine vinegar

½ cup olive oil

1 (2-ounce) can anchovies
in oil

1 tablespoon dry mustard

1½ teaspoons
Worcestershire sauce

Juice of 2 lemons

1 clove garlic, crushed

1 teaspoon fresh ground
pepper

1 cup croutons

½ cup Parmesan cheese

Tear lettuce into bite-sized pieces, wash and dry and refrigerate until ready to use. Coddle eggs by submerging them in simmering water and cooking for one minute. Crack coddled eggs into a blender and add vinegar, oil, anchovies, mustard, Worcestershire sauce, lemon juice, garlic, and pepper. Blend until ingredients are emulsified. Place lettuces in large wooden bowl. Pour dressing over all. Sprinkle with croutons and cheese. Toss and serve.

POST MorTem

The mélange of lettuces called for in this recipe don't really add much. All romaine would be just as tasty. The dressing is so delicious, in fact, that you can enjoy it on anything green. Well, within reason.

Joan Crawford 1905–1977

S O MAYBE SHE WASN'T MOTHER OF THE YEAR, but Joan Crawford was responsible for some of the most indelible performances ever put on film. The temptress Sadie Thompson in *Rain*, the other woman Crystal Allen in *The Women*, the manipulative domestic diva in *Harriet Craig*, the list goes on and on. Her role as the self-sacrificing restaurateur in *Mildred Pierce* won her the Academy Award for Best Actress, but she was great in so many others: *Daisy Kenyon, Sudden Fear, Queen Bee, Johnny Guitar, The Best of Everything, Whatever Happened to Baby Jane?* and even *Torch Song* in which she appeared (I kid you not) in black face. Hell, even her really bad films—*Strait-Jacket* and *Trog*—are fun. She's pretty terrific in the pilot for Rod Serling's *Night Gallery* TV series, too. Crawford was a terrific housekeeper. Anyone who saw *Mommie Dearest* knows she was mad at the dirt. Her cooking was as no-nonsense as she was. Get your hands on a copy of her legendary book *My Way of Life* and you may want to live yours by it. Here's her way with salmon. It's a start.

JOAN CRAWFORD'S
POACHED SALMON

Rinse and dry fish. Cut lemons in thin slices. Place slices on both sides of the fish. Wrap fish in a double thickness of cheesecloth and secure with kitchen string. Put water, onions, celery, parsley, bay leaves, crushed peppercorns, and salt in a fish poacher or on a rack in a deep saucepan. Cover and simmer 30 minutes. Place fish on rack in the kettle so that it is halfway submerged in the water. Cover and slowly simmer 40 minutes or until fish is barely done. Place fish on a heated platter. Remove cloth and lemon slices carefully. Combine mayonnaise, prepared mustard, and lemon juice; mix well and serve with fish. (Fish and dressing may also be served cold on a bed of lettuce.)

1 three-pound piece
   of fresh salmon

3 lemons

6 cups water

10 pearl onions, peeled

½ stalk celery with leaves

2 sprigs parsley

3 small bay leaves

12 peppercorns, crushed

2 teaspoons salt

Dressing:

2 cups mayonnaise

4 teaspoons prepared
   mustard

¼ cup fresh lemon juice

eDiTH HeaD 1897–1981

S HE WAS ALFRED HITCHCOCK'S FAVORITE costume designer and just perhaps the real-life model for Edna Mode in *The Incredibles*. Incredibly, Edith Head was nominated for the Oscar thirty-five times (a record for a costume designer and a woman) and took the little golden man home eight times (another record). Primarily working at Paramount and Universal, she won the awards for her work on such unforgettable films as *All About Eve*, *Roman Holiday*, and *The Sting*. She won for *Sabrina*, too, although Audrey Hepburn's "Parisian" clothes were designed by couturier Hubert de Givenchy, and many thought he deserved the prize. Some say she was a self-promoter at a time when that trait was frowned upon, unlike now, but there was no denying her talent. In Jay Jorgensen's gorgeous 2010 coffee table biography *Edith Head: The Fifty Year Career of Hollywood's Greatest Costume Designer*, though, Head herself downplays her abilities in the work room, but not in the kitchen. "I don't think I'm one of the greatest costume designers in the world," she is quoted as saying. "But I am one of the greatest cooks." You can win your own awards when you cook her Chicken Casa Ladera, named after her Beverly Hills home. It means "house on the side of the hill."

eDiTH HeaD'S CHiCKen casa LaDera

2 chicken fryers,
  cut up

1 good pinch salt

1 teaspoon paprika

1½ sticks butter

1 cup chicken broth

1 cup white wine

1 pound fresh mushrooms,
  sliced

1 pound chicken livers

2 tablespoons flour

½ bunch fresh chives

Season chicken pieces with salt and paprika, and then brown in one stick of butter. Place chicken in a casserole with broth and white wine, and cover. Cook at 300° for 40 minutes until tender. Sauté mushrooms in two tablespoons of butter. Next, in another pan, sauté chicken livers in two tablespoons of butter. Remove mushrooms and chicken livers and place on top of chicken on a serving plate. Combine liquid from mushrooms and chicken livers with pan drippings from chicken and add flour. Boil and when slightly thickened pour over chicken mixture and sprinkle with chives. Serve immediately.

POST MorTem

If this simple, rich, and delicious dish is any indication, Edith wasn't blowing her own horn about her abilities in the kitchen.

THE LAST OF THE TRUE MEGAWATT STARS of Old Hollywood, Elizabeth Taylor was, to quote *Doonesbury*, "a tad overweight but with violet eyes to die for." The stunningly beautiful but often deliciously profane actress bewitched movie fans for nearly seventy years, having begun her career at the age of ten. She made more than fifty films, captivating audiences from her earliest starring role in *National Velvet* in 1944 to her cinematic coming-of-age *A Place in the Sun* in 1951 to her last role in the camp-tastic TV movie *These Old Broads* in 2001. She won Oscars for *Butterfield 8* in 1960 and *Who's Afraid of Virginia Woolf?* in 1966, appeared on TV shows from *Here's Lucy* and *General Hospital* to *The Nanny*, and received the ultimate distinction of sorts when she was denounced by the Vatican. Like few other stars, Taylor always lived by her own morality and her life was as controversial off screen as on. Married eight times, including twice to her greatest love, the Welsh actor Richard Burton, Taylor lived in public. She famously stole another star's husband, had her favorite Chasten's chili flown in to the set of *Cleopatra*, flaunted diamonds so large they resembled skating rinks, and always bested the paparazzi at their own game. Late in her life, having built an empire as a fragrance queen, Taylor even hung out on occasion with a posse of worshipful gays at the West Hollywood bar called The Abbey. Her work as a tireless AIDS activist, prompted by the death of Rock Hudson, with whom she starred in *Giant* in 1956, may have been her greatest achievement. She thought so, anyway. As a founder of the American Foundation for AIDS Research, Taylor's outspoken advocacy began when it was hardly fashionable, and continues posthumously via her enormous estate. That, combined with her onscreen legacy, will keep Taylor's spirit among us for generations to come.

eLizaBeTH TaYLor's CHicken WiTH avocaDo anD MusHrooms

Sprinkle avocado with lemon juice. Cover and refrigerate. Season chicken with salt and pepper. In a large heavy skillet, over low heat, heat 3–4 tablespoons butter and sauté chicken until juices run yellow when it is pricked with a fork, about 35–40 minutes. Use two skillets if necessary, adding more butter as needed. Transfer cooked chicken to a serving dish. Cover loosely with aluminum foil. Keep warm in a 300° oven for 15 minutes, while preparing sauce. To make the sauce, add shallots to skillet. Cook over medium heat, stirring and scraping sides and bottom of pan with wooden spoon. Add 2 tablespoons of cognac and the wine and bring to a boil. Boil until mixture has almost evaporated. Add cream and boil 5 minutes longer. Add chicken stock to cream mixture. Cook over medium heat, stirring constantly, until thick. While sauce cooks, sauté mushrooms over high heat in butter. Add the mushrooms, remaining cognac, and avocado cubes to the thickened sauce. Stir until well blended. Pour over chicken. Sprinkle with parsley.

1 avocado, peeled and cubed

1 tablespoon lemon juice

2 (2½ pound) chickens, cut into serving pieces

Salt and freshly ground pepper

¼ cup butter, plus 3 tablespoons butter

3 finely chopped shallots

3 tablespoons cognac

⅓ cup dry white wine

1 cup heavy cream

1 cup chicken stock

2 cups sliced fresh mushrooms

Chopped fresh parsley, for garnish

KATHARINE HEPBURN 1907–2003

S HE WAS ONE OF THE ALL-TIME GREATS and as interesting a character in real life as any she played on screen, and Katharine Hepburn played plenty of characters in her sixty-year career. Whether as Eleanor of Aquitaine in *The Lion in Winter* or a loving wife to Henry Fonda in *On Golden Pond*, she was the embodiment of patrician womanhood. Hepburn held her own when starring opposite some of the most imposing men in film history: Cary Grant, Humphrey Bogart, and Henry Fonda among them. Her greatest pairing, onscreen and off, was with Spencer Tracy. Theirs was a legendary love affair, and their movies together—most notably *Woman of the Year, Pat and Mike, Desk Set*, and *Guess Who's Coming to Dinner*—are among the most beloved films of the twentieth century. Hepburn won four Oscars between 1934 and 1982. Her brownies are as legendary as she was.

Greer Garson 1904–1996

Y ES, SHE WAS THE WOMAN WHO NARRATED the stop-motion animated Christmas special *The Little Drummer Boy* in 1968. But movie lovers who knew Greer Garson's work from the 1930s and '40s remember her best for such films as *Madame Curie, Goodbye, Mr. Chips*, and *Random Harvest*. She took home the Oscar for playing the title character, opposite Walter Pidgeon, in the 1942 film *Mrs. Miniver*. (Some wags say that wherever she is, she's still giving her acceptance speech.) Garson was nominated six more times for the Academy Award, before and after her win; five of them were in a row. You can catch her in the 1978 TV movie of *Little Women*, which starred three of TV's most popular actresses of the day: Meredith Baxter, Susan Dey, and Eve Plumb. You won't remain little if you eat her Capirotada. But this French toast–like dish is worth the calories.

Katharine Hepburn's Brownies

Serves
8

Melt chocolate and butter in a heavy saucepan over low heat. Remove from heat and stir in sugar. Add eggs and vanilla and beat well. Stir in flour, salt and walnuts. Mix well. Pour into a buttered 8-inch square baking pan. Bake at 325° for 40 minutes. Cool and cut into squares.

2 (one-ounce) squares unsweetened baker's chocolate

1 stick unsalted butter

1 cup sugar

2 eggs

½ teaspoon vanilla

¼ cup flour

¼ teaspoon salt

1 cup chopped walnuts

Greer Garson's Capirotada

Serves
2

Combine sugar, water, and cinnamon in a saucepan and boil until sugar dissolves. When mixture begins to turn amber, immediately remove it from the stove. Place a layer of bread in a casserole. Add the cheese and raisins. Repeat until all ingredients are used. Pour the syrup over the mixture. Brush with the melted butter and bake at 375° until the bread absorbs the syrup and the capirotada is nicely browned.

8 ounces sugar

2⅛ cups water

1 teaspoon cinnamon

6 slices bread, toasted

6 ounces Longhorn Colby or Monterey Jack cheese, grated

5 ounces raisins

1 tablespoon butter, melted

vivien LeiGH 1913–1967

VIVIEN LEIGH WON THE OSCAR TWICE for playing two of the greatest female roles in all of movie history: Scarlett O'Hara in *Gone with the Wind* and Blanche DuBois in *A Streetcar Named Desire*. But those who knew her said her incredible beauty got in the way of the serious recognition she deserved. Her husband, Sir Laurence Olivier, contended critics failed to realize her true talents as an actress despite her awards, which included the Tony for *Tovarich* in 1963. On stage, Leigh was as adept at Shakespeare as she was at Noel Coward. However, she is remembered most for her movie career with credits in such pictures as *The Roman Spring of Mrs. Stone*, *Waterloo Bridge*, and *Ship of Fools*. If you don't like Leigh's recipe for Fruta Almina, well, frankly my dear, I don't give a damn.

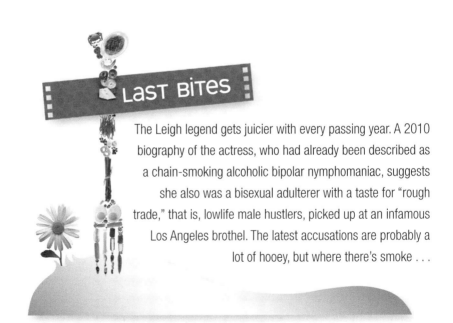

LaST BiTes

The Leigh legend gets juicier with every passing year. A 2010 biography of the actress, who had already been described as a chain-smoking alcoholic bipolar nymphomaniac, suggests she also was a bisexual adulterer with a taste for "rough trade," that is, lowlife male hustlers, picked up at an infamous Los Angeles brothel. The latest accusations are probably a lot of hooey, but where there's smoke . . .

vivien Leigh's Fruta aLmina

Combine water, corn syrup, salt, and vanilla in a pan and heat, stirring until it becomes a syrup. Peel and halve the pears and poach gently in the syrup until tender. Set aside to cool. Prepare a smooth creamy sauce by putting the egg yolks in a double boiler. Add the sugar and cornstarch and mix with a fork until well blended. Add milk slowly, stirring continuously. Then add orange rind. Continue cooking mixture slowly, stirring constantly until it thickens. Do not let it boil. When thick, remove from heat, add a dash of salt, and allow to cool. When cool, add cream, blending until smooth. Add the orange juice. Whip the remainder of the cream and add to the sauce to thicken it more. Chill in refrigerator briefly. Remove the cooled poached pears from liquid and pour chilled sauce over them. Sprinkle with nutmeg before serving.

⅝ cup water

4 tablespoons corn syrup

Dash salt

½ teaspoon vanilla

4–6 medium ripe pears
   (or bananas or peaches)

3 egg yolks, slightly beaten

3½ ounces extra-fine
   white sugar

¾ teaspoon cornstarch

⅓ cup milk

8 tablespoons cream

Juice and grated rind of
   ½ fresh orange

Nutmeg, for garnish

S HE WAS THE INSPIRATION FOR A LEGION of female impersonators
and the woman whose ocular divinity was immortalized in Kim Carnes's
biggest hit. But that's not the half of it. Bette Davis was, quite simply, one of
the greatest movie stars of all time. She won the Oscar in 1936 for *Dangerous* and in 1939 for *Jezebel*. But it's the movies for which she was nominated
but didn't win—*Dark Victory*, *The Little Foxes*, *Now, Voyager*, and *Whatever
Happened to Baby Jane?* among them—that remain seared into audiences'
memories. Even her bad movies are worth watching. I defy anyone not to be
entertained by *Hush . . . Hush, Sweet Charlotte*, *Burnt Offerings*, *The Nanny*,
or *Bunny O'Hare*; the last an obscure offering in which Davis played an aging
bank robber in hippie clothes, opposite Ernest Borgnine. Davis was pretty
darn good on a 1966 episode of *Gunsmoke*, too. Her gravestone says "She
did it the hard way," but she made it all look so easy. Her Red Flannel Hash
is worth the effort. But clean your apartment before your guests arrive. You
don't want anyone to walk in, roll his eyes and, in his best Bette, say, "What a
dump!"

LasT BiTes

Davis was famous for the line "What a dump!" from the 1949
film *Beyond the Forest*. But the exaggerated reading that most
people remember is actually Elizabeth Taylor doing an impression of Davis in 1966's *Who's Afraid of Virginia Woolf?* After
that film's success, Davis began doing the line Taylor's way,
much to the delight of anyone who heard her do it. "I
imitated the imitators," Davis explained.

Bette Davis's Red Flannel Hash

Chop all ingredients and combine in a large bowl. Season to taste and moisten mixture with cream. Place in a hot buttered heavy skillet. Stir and spread evenly in pan. Brown slowly over medium heat. Serve with poached eggs on top.

2 cups cooked corned beef

3 cups cold boiled potatoes

1½ cups cooked beets

Salt and pepper, to taste

½ cup or more of cream

½ stick butter

aFTer-Dinner viewing
oscars in THe KiTCHen

There is a feast of films featuring Oscar-winning actresses preparing all manner of food.

Katharine Hepburn's disastrous attempts at making breakfast for Spencer Tracy in *Woman of the Year* is a highlight of that frothy 1942 comedy, directed by George Stevens. Newswoman Tess Harding approaches the stove like an explorer venturing into deepest Africa and a drip coffee pot like a contraption so foreign it may as well have come from Mars.

In Frank Capra's 1934 classic *It Happened One Night*, Claudette Colbert plays an heiress who is much too highfalutin to know her way around a doughnut. But, on the run from her family, she learns to dunk from no less than Clark Gable.

Joan Crawford won her Oscar playing *Mildred Pierce*. In the classic 1945 noir, Crawford waits tables and bakes pies to keep a roof over her ungrateful daughter Veda's head. "My mother, a waitress," sniffs the little brat, the picture of entitlement as Ann Blyth played her. "Aren't the pies bad enough?"

But when it comes to over-the-top food moments, you really haven't seen it all until you've witnessed Bette Davis dish up a nightmare in the 1962 Robert Aldrich camp-fest *Whatever Happened to Baby Jane?* Davis serves her bedridden sister Blanche, played by Crawford in full-victim mode, what looks like a lovely meal. But when Blanche expectantly peers under the silver dome on the beautiful lunch tray before her, it's not what she ordered. It's a rat on a plate!

5
CHaracTers WeLcome

WHEN YOU ARE BORN WITH A CHARACTER ACTOR'S countenance, although you distinctly ordered a leading man's good looks, you develop a predilection for supporting players. You know the type. They're the funny-looking guys who make their entrances, deliver a few humdinger zingers, and then leave with a wake of laughs behind them. They have rarely become household names. Today, character actors receive more recognition. Think Seth Rogen and Michael Cera. But years ago, audiences rarely knew these guys' names. Their faces, though, were instantly recognizable. They were the kind of performers who'd show up on screen and the audience would think, *It's that guy, what's-his-name. I love him.* They may have been relegated to last-but-not-least billing. But, unlike many leading men, they worked their whole lives long. Funny always ages better than sexy. The character actors in this chapter are some of my favorites. They were gourmands one and all, by the way. Most of them made their mark on 1960s television. You may not recognize their names, but there is no denying that this ripe bunch of second bananas has tremendous—wait for it—appeal.

LOUIS NYE 1913–2005

OUIS NYE MADE A CAREER OF PLAYING the effete country club snob. His way-fey playboy character Gordon Hathaway on *The Steve Allen Show* would always greet the host with a lilting "Hi ho Steverino!" He was so scrumptiously fruity—I can say that, not you—that he did the same shtick when he was cast as the over-the-top rich fop Sonny Drysdale on *The Beverly Hillbillies*. In the 1960s and 70s, he made the rounds on variety shows and did guest shots on plenty of series. He was a regular on a short-lived sit-com set in the garment industry called *Needles and Pins* in 1973, too. Late in life, he played Jeff Greene's father on *Curb Your Enthusiasm*. Nearly ninety, he was as funny as ever.

LOUIS NYE'S STEAK TARTARE

Combine meat, mustard, salt, Worcestershire sauce, onion, and egg yolks. Mix well. Shape into loaf. Place on serving platter. Garnish with chopped eggs and onion. Serve with rye bread.

1½ pounds freshly ground lean beef

Serves 8–12 as an appetizer

1 tablespoon hot prepared mustard

1 teaspoon salt

½ teaspoon Worcestershire sauce

1½ cups finely chopped Bermuda or Spanish onion

3 egg yolks

2 hard-cooked eggs, chopped

1 tablespoon onion, chopped

Vincent Gardenia 1920–1992

H E WAS OSCAR NOMINATED TWICE: once for playing Cher's father in *Moonstruck* and once for his turn as the baseball manager in the male weepy *Bang the Drum Slowly*, and he memorably appeared as the flower shop owner whose plant eats him in the musical film version of *Little Shop of Horrors*. Vincent Gardenia played the hot-blooded Italian American as well as anyone ever has. He had recurring roles on such TV series as *L.A. Law* and *Breaking Away*, and did guest shots on shows as varied as *Voyage to the Bottom of the Sea* and *Love American Style*. But it was as Frank Lorenzo, Archie Bunker's neighbor after the Jeffersons moved out, on *All in the Family* in 1973, for which he is best remembered. Gardenia had a successful stage career as well. On Broadway, he won a Tony Award as a featured actor in the Neil Simon play, *The Prisoner of Second Avenue*. Among musical theatre lovers, he is beloved for his role as the married mailman who falls in love with a lonely widow in *Ballroom*. That legendary Michael Bennett musical version of *Queen of the Stardust Ballroom* opened in 1978. It wasn't a hit, but the score has many fans. To paraphrase that show's most famous song, I'd rather have "Fifty Percent" of Vincent Gardenia's Pasta Con Piselli than all of anybody else's at all.

Vincent Gardenia's Pasta con Piselli

Sauté bacon and onion in oil and cook slowly for 25 minutes. Cook pasta according to directions. Take 2 cups water from cooked pasta and add to sauce. Add pepper to taste. Let simmer for 5 minutes. Drain pasta. Warm up peas and mix them with the pasta. Serve pasta and pea mixture with sauce, topped with cheese.

2 slices of bacon, chopped

1 large onion, chopped

½ cup olive oil

1 pound pasta shells

2 cups water

Freshly ground pepper, to taste

1 large can green peas

Romano or Parmesan cheese, for garnish

POST MORTEM

Sure, you can use pasta water in the sauce for this refined cousin of *pasta e fagioli* (or what some of us always called "pasta fazool"). But two cups of low-sodium chicken stock would be even yummier. You can also use diced *pancetta* instead of bacon and frozen peas instead of canned ones. That would be really *delicioso,* as we used to say back in the old neighborhood.

VITO SCOTTI 1918–1996

V ITO SCOTTI WORKED STEADILY from the 1950s until right before his death, his credits running the gamut of classic TV shows from *Perry Mason* to *The Golden Girls*. If a chef or tailor or maitre d' had an accent and his name ended in a vowel, there's a good chance Scotti played him. Early in his career, he starred in the short-lived *Life with Luigi*, one of TV's earliest ethnic sitcoms. He had a recurring role on *The Flying Nun* as a suspicious police captain, played Sam Picasso on a few arty episodes of *The Addams Family*, and did half a dozen guest shots on *Columbo*. He played Mexican, Japanese, and Russian characters, but this Italian played his own heritage best. He notably played the baker Nazorine in *The Godfather*. His Linguini à la Carbonara is an offer you can't refuse.

BILLY De WOLFe 1907–1994

B ILLY DE WOLFE SPECIALIZED IN PLAYING the fussy, the flabbergasted, and the flamboyant. On *The Doris Day Show*, he appeared as the annoying (and frequently annoyed) neighbor, Mr. Jarvis, but in real life, he and the leading lady were the best of friends. De Wolfe also had recurring roles on *That Girl*, and two short-lived series, *Good Morning, World* and *The Queen and I*. He sadly didn't play the royal character in that last one. De Wolfe did play a character named Mrs. Murgatroyd as a comedy performer. She was a drag, but his Codfish Balls are anything but.

Vito Scotti's Linguini à la Carbonara

Boil the pasta according to package directions and drain, reserving some of the water. While the linguini is cooking, fry the bacon in the oil and butter until it becomes translucent but not crisp. Beat eggs in a bowl large enough to accommodate the pasta. Pour the cooked pasta into the eggs and stir. Pour the bacon and drippings, oil, and butter onto the pasta. To thin the sauce, add some pasta water. Sprinkle with pepper, parsley, and cheese. Serve immediately.

1 pound linguini

5 strips bacon, diced

2 tablespoons olive oil

¼ cup butter

2 eggs

Fresh ground pepper, to taste

1 cup chopped Italian parsley

2 tablespoons Parmesan, or to taste

Mr. Billy De Wolfe's Codfish Balls

Serves 4

Soak salt cod in cold water for 4 hours, changing water several times to remove saltiness. Peel the potatoes. Shred the fish. Add 1 cup of fish and potatoes to boiling water and cook until tender. Drain and mash. Mix melted butter, pepper, and egg with a fork and blend with the fish and potato. Shape the mixture into balls and deep fry in oil or sauté in butter.

½ pound dried salt cod

6 medium potatoes

1 tablespoon butter, melted

½ teaspoon pepper

1 well-beaten egg

Oil or butter for frying

James Coco 1930–1987

J AMES COCO HAD TWO FAILED SITCOMS, *Calucci's Department* and *The Dumplings,* under his large-size belt when he won the Emmy for a dramatic guest-starring role on a 1982 installment of *St. Elsewhere*, as a homeless man (opposite his real-life pal Doris Roberts, who also won an Emmy for the episode). His films included *The Cheap Detective* and *Only When I Laugh,* for which he was nominated for an Oscar. Both films were written by Neil Simon, with whom Coco previously had worked on stage to great acclaim in *The Last of the Red Hot Lovers.* Having lost weight in the '80s, Coco became something of a diet guru and a cookbook author. He also appeared on *Who's the Boss?* Here's his very boss recipe for his stuffed eggplant.

Last Bites

Coco was nominated not only for an Oscar for his performance as Marsha Mason's gay best friend in *Only When I Laugh,* but also for a Razzie, making him one of the few actors ever to be nominated as Best Supporting and Worst Supporting Actor for the same role. He didn't win either, which is really kind of sad if you think about it.

James coco's Stuffed eggplant

Serves 2

Preheat oven to 350°. Wash eggplant and cut in half lengthwise. Remove the pulp, leaving about ½ inch of the outer shell. Dice the pulp. Sauté mushrooms, onions, meat, diced eggplant pulp, and seasonings in margarine. Cook until the meat is slightly done. Transfer to mixing bowl and add bread crumbs, cheese, egg whites, and tomatoes. Mix well and spoon into the eggplant shells. Place on a greased baking dish. Bake 35 minutes. Garnish with parsley.

1 large eggplant

1 cup mushrooms, chopped

1 cup onions, chopped

4 ounces lean beef, chopped

4 ounces lean veal, chopped

1 teaspoon basil

½ teaspoon chervil

½ teaspoon pepper

2 tablespoons margarine

¼ cup bread crumbs

1 teaspoon Parmesan cheese

2 beaten egg whites

¼ cup cooked tomatoes

2 tablespoons chopped parsley

JOE FLYNN 1924–1974

I LOVE JOE FLYNN. He is best known as the frequently outfoxed Captain Binghamton on the classic TV series *McHale's Navy* in the 1960s. Besides playing "Old Leadbottom," as he was affectionately known for four seasons, Flynn guest starred on other series, memorably playing a dance instructor in cahoots with Catwoman on a very funny episode of *Batman*, for instance, and he lent his talents to a string of live-action Disney movies, including *The Love Bug, The Computer Wore Tennis Shoes*, and *Now You See Him, Now You Don't*. Make his Brisket of Beef. It's sure to disappear, too.

RICHARD DEACON 1921–1984

WHETHER PLAYING PRODUCER Mel Cooley on *The Dick Van Dyke Show*, Lumpy's dad on *Leave it to Beaver*, or Kaye Ballard's replacement husband on the second season of *The Mothers-in-Law*, Richard Deacon was best at playing the officious guy who is often tortured by the cutups around him. The prolific character actor played Tallulah Bankhead's butler in a memorable episode of *The Lucy-Desi Comedy Hour*, and had small roles in such classic films as *The Birds* and the original *Invasion of the Body Snatchers*. In real life, he was known as a gourmet chef, cookbook author, and an early authority on a device that would revolutionize home cooking, the microwave oven. His deliciously named dessert is quick and easy.

JOE FLYNN'S BELGIAN BRISKET OF BEEF

Season meat with salt and pepper, and place in roasting pan with onions and celery. Pour chili sauce on top. Put ¼ inch of water in bottom of pan. Bake at 325°s for 3 hours uncovered. Baste often. Add beer, cover, and cook for 2 more hours.

5 pounds brisket of beef

2 teaspoons salt

¼ teaspoon pepper

2 onions, sliced thick

4 whole celery stalks

1 cup chili sauce

1 can beer

RICHARD DEACON'S BITTER AND BOOZE

Melt the chocolate chips in the microwave for 1½ minutes in a 1-cup measure. Beat until smooth. Set aside to cool. Whip the cream until stiff. Fold in the brandy, salt, and chocolate. Spoon into dessert glasses and chill in the refrigerator.

1 six-ounce package of semi-sweet chocolate chips

½ pint whipping cream

2 jiggers of brandy

¼ teaspoon salt

aFTer-Dinner viewing

unexpecTeD DeLiGHTS

Vincent Gardenia played the recurring role of next-door neighbor Frank Lorenzo on *All in the Family*, but he'd previously played two other one-shot characters on that classic series. His second appearance was his most colorful. He played half of a wife-swapping couple in the third-season episode, "The Bunkers and the Swingers." Rue McClanahan, whose cheesecake recipe appears in Chapter 25, played the hot-to-trot wife whose personal ad Edith Bunker (Jean Stapleton) inadvertently answers. The dingbat thinks the couple has come for coffee . . . but doesn't know what besides her Cupid's Delight pie they're after. Thanks to the guest stars, the episode is as poignant as it is funny.

Vito Scotti has a hilarious bit in the all-but-forgotten Debbie Reynolds and James Garner 1968 comedy *How Sweet It Is!* that finally came out on DVD in 2010. He plays a chef so Italian—that is, so horny—the sight of the middle-aged leading lady in a bikini sends him into a fit of stomach kissing. Tammy would have been shocked at such behavior, but you'll laugh.

Christmas isn't Christmas without the classic 1969 animated special *Frosty the Snowman*. Billy De Wolfe plays the villain of the piece, but he's so much fun as the klutzy prestidigitator Professor Hinkle that, Frosty be damned, you almost want him to get his magic hat back. The Rankin/Bass cartoon is a great showcase for one of De Wolfe's comic signatures: repeating a word or phrase three times with increasing emphasis. In *Frosty*, we get not only his famous "Busy! Busy! Busy!," we get a "Messy! Messy! Messy!" and a "Think nasty! Think nasty! Think nasty!" You can't ask an evil magician for more than that, especially around the holidays.

Louis Nye guest stars in one of *The Munsters'* best episodes, "Zombo," about a fright-wigged horror show host whose biggest fan is Eddie Munster (Butch Patrick). That is, until the little boy realizes he's not a real zombie. In full horror makeup, Nye does a commercial for Crumble Creature Crackers that's a scream.

In the 1976 Neil Simon mystery spoof *Murder by Death*, James Coco plays Inspector Milo Perrier, a send-up of Agatha Christie's Hercule Poirot. "I'm not a Frenchie, I'm a Belgie," he says. Whatever his nationality, Coco gets to utter the classic, "This entire murder has been . . . catered!"

No one believes me when I say this, but *McHale's Navy* on DVD is so much more entertaining than you'd ever imagine. Any chance to see Joe Flynn utter his oft-repeated line, "I could just scream!" is worth taking. Foodies can start with the season-one episode, "The Captain Steals a Cook."

He had so many brilliant moments as the target of everyone's insults on *The Dick Van Dyke Show*, but Richard Deacon really shines when his long-suffering producer character has finally had enough of his boss' disrespect in the episode "The Bottom of Mel Cooley's Heart." What happens when Mel finally stands up for himself in this season-five episode? He gets fired, of course, but even his nemesis Buddy Sorrell (the brilliant Morey Amsterdam) has to admit he's going to miss the big lummox. The DVD also includes a featurette in which the cast remembers the actor they called "Deac."

6

I LUNCH LUCY

F OR LUCILLE BALL, THE PREPARATION OF food and drink was an endless font of side-splitting physical shtick. Whatever series she was doing, *I Love Lucy*, *The Lucy Show*, or *Here's Lucy*, Ball found herself in the kitchen making a hilarious mess.

When Lucy Ricardo, the showbiz-hungry '50s housewife she immortalized on *I Love Lucy*, tried candy dipping, she ended up with a blouse full (and hat full and face full) of chocolate. An attempt at winemaking ended in an actual grapes-to-the-face brawl with an Italian fruit stomper who'd been hired to play one. Much to her husband Ricky's dismay, Lucy threw dinner rolls like baseballs through a pass-through kitchen window, dressed a giant cheese up as a baby to get it home from Europe on a plane, wrestled a totem pole-sized loaf of bread protruding from her oven, nearly froze to death in a meat freezer, and ran her own salad dressing company, right into the ground.

As the widowed '60s housewife Lucille Carmichael on *The Lucy Show*, she tried her hand at being a soda jerk and a kiddy-party caterer, opened a doomed restaurant in the middle of nowhere, proved just how lousy a pie baker she could be, lost a contact lens in chocolate frosting, battled popover batter, and wreaked more havoc with baked beans than Ann-Margret did in the movie *Tommy*. As Lucille Carter on *Here's Lucy*, she swept through a supermarket like a hurricane and bought into a frozen custard franchise resulting in pure frozen chaos.

She and food just didn't get along.

Ball wasn't much of a cook in real life, by all accounts, although as a struggling actress she worked as a waitress. Actor Jim Brochu, in his heartfelt memoir *Lucy In the Afternoon*, said Ball could even botch up store-bought frozen lemonade by using too little water and more artificial sweetener than an army of lab rats could stand. In 1970, she offered one possible explanation for her aversion to the culinary arts when, in a voice that by then sounded like hot gravel on a Palm Springs driveway, she told talk-show pioneer Virginia Graham, "I just don't care about food. I only eat what I need." Once Lucy was done with breakfast, she said she didn't want to hear about food the rest of the day.

Others in their remembrances of life with Lucy have let it slip that Ball did have a weakness for franks-and-beans, and spaghetti and meatballs in her older years, and that she adored blintzes, to which her second husband Gary Morton claimed to have introduced her.

But on that day when Graham, whose Coffee Toffee Pie recipe is among Chapter 1's recipes, asked Lucy to name what she'd want for her final meal on earth, Ball replied, "Even on the last day, you're not going to catch me cooking." Ball employed long-term a personal chef named Willie Mae Williams, whose specialty was said to be Ball's favorite. It was a one-pot main course, a "Chinese-y thing" that the comedienne called in the somehow acceptable patois of the day, "Chinkee Goodee." (Insert one of Lucy's signature "spider noises" here.)

Graham described the dish as "served with a spicy sauce . . . that keeps improving as it gets older, like many wines and a few women." Actually, the recipe really improves if you use fresh peapods and bean sprouts, and substitute shredded bok choy, bamboo shoots cut into tiny strips, sliced fresh mushrooms, some oyster sauce, and a little sesame oil for the canned Asian-style veggies! Then you can call it "Chop Lucy" and no one is offended.

Ball was also partial to chopped chicken livers. She liked goulash, which she recommended for casual Sunday evenings; and she enjoyed tropical fruit salad, apple John, and persimmon cake. For someone who didn't care much about food, she left behind a batch of recipes.

LUCILLE BALL'S "CHINESE-Y THING"

Melt butter. Add garlic, green onions, celery, and pepper and sauté 10 minutes, stirring constantly. While this is cooking, mix cornstarch in a little cold water. Boil remaining water, add cornstarch mixture, and stir well. Add sautéed ingredients to this sauce, together with all other ingredients except the meat. Cook over low heat for 30 minutes. Add meat and cook 10 minutes longer. Serve over rice.

POST MORTEM

Even with the addition of fresh ingredients, Lucy's "Chinese-y Thing" is bland compared to the Asian food we're accustomed to eating today. But this chow mein–like dish certainly brings back memories of the days when canned Asian foods helped Chinese food "swing American."

4 tablespoons butter

2 cloves garlic, minced

2 small bunches green onions, chopped

2 stalks celery, chopped

1 large green pepper, diced

6 cups water

½ cup cornstarch

1 can Chinese water chestnuts

1 can bean sprouts

1 package frozen pea pods

1 large can Asian-style vegetables

½ cup beef broth

Soy sauce to taste

4 sirloin tip steaks, medium thick, cut into very thin strips

LUCILLE BALL'S CHOPPED CHICKEN LIVERS

Serves 8
as an
appetizer

¼ cup chicken fat

½ pound chicken livers, quartered

1 medium onion, finely minced

½ teaspoon salt

¼ teaspoon freshly ground pepper

2 hard cooked eggs, yolks and whites minced separately

Melba rounds or whole wheat toast

Melt chicken fat in a large skillet. Cook livers in hot fat about 8 minutes. Do not overcook. Remove from pan, drain, and cool to room temperature. Chop livers with a sharp knife to the size of cornmeal. Cook half the onion until golden in the same fat. Add sautéed onion, remaining raw onion, salt and pepper to chopped livers. Mix well. Add more chicken fat if necessary to make mixture spreadable. Arrange chopped liver on small serving dish. Put chopped egg white in center of separate dish; arrange yolks around white. Serve with garnish on thin Melba rounds or toast.

LUCILLE BALL'S SUNDAY NIGHT GOULASH

2 bunches green onions, chopped

2 large green peppers, chopped

½ clove garlic, chopped

2 pounds ground beef

1 large can solid packed tomatoes

½ pound small egg noodles

Sauté onions, green pepper, and garlic until tender. Brown meat in butter, then add sautéed ingredients. Add tomatoes with juice and simmer slowly. Add salt and pepper to taste. During last 30 minutes of cooking, add cooked, strained egg noodles.

LUCILLE BALL'S TROPICAL TREAT

1 head lettuce

1 can pineapple rings

2 bananas, thinly sliced

1 tablespoon half-and-half

½ cup mayonnaise

½ cup finely chopped nuts

4 maraschino cherries

Line the bottoms of four individual salad bowls with lettuce leaves; lay in several pineapple rings, then a layer of sliced bananas. Mix half-and-half with mayonnaise and stir into a thick creamy mixture. Spoon the dressing over the salad, sprinkle with chopped nuts, and top each with a cherry.

Lucille Ball's Apple John

Toss together apples, ½ cup sugar, nutmeg, cinnamon, lemon peel, lemon juice, and water. Place in a greased two-quart casserole. Cover and bake at 375° for 1 hour or until apples are tender. Remove from oven and raise temperature to 450°. Combine biscuit mix, and remaining 2 tablespoons sugar, and then quickly stir in melted butter and milk. Drop by rounded tablespoonfuls around top edge of casserole and one in the center. Bake uncovered about 12–15 minutes or until biscuits are golden and done. Cool slightly. Serve warm with vanilla ice cream on top of each serving.

8 cups thinly sliced, pared cooking apples

½ cup, plus 2 tablespoons, sugar

½ teaspoon ground nutmeg

¼ teaspoon ground cinnamon

1 tablespoon grated lemon peel

2 tablespoons lemon juice

¼ cup water

2 cups packaged biscuit mix

2 to 3 tablespoons butter, melted

½ cup milk

Lucille Ball's Persimmon Cake

Mix all ingredients and bake in two large buttered loaf tins or 4 small ones for 1½ hours at 300°.

Serves 12

2 cups sugar

3 tablespoons butter

2 cups persimmon pulp

2 cups chopped walnut meats

1 cup seedless raisins

1 cup dates, chopped fine

Rind of one orange, grated

1 cup milk

4 cups sifted cake flour

2 teaspoon cinnamon

½ teaspoon cloves

½ teaspoon allspice

½ teaspoon nutmeg

4 teaspoons baking soda

3 teaspoons baking powder

2 teaspoons vanilla extract

after-Dinner viewing

LUCY'S TOP 10 FOOD Fiascos on DVD

1. "Job Switching." Two words: candy factory. A second-season episode of *I Love Lucy* that's second to none.

2. "Lucy's Italian Movie." Wine-making in Italy leads to a grape-stomping brawl during the season-five European tour of *I Love Lucy*.

3. "Lucy Does the Tango," and breaks dozens of eggs in the process on a fine season-six *I Love Lucy* show.

4. "Lucy, the Camp Cook." A vat of frozen popover batter crashes through the floor and later explodes out of an oven in this season-three episode of *The Lucy Show*.

5. "Return Home from Europe." Lucy dresses an enormous cheese in swaddling and sneaks it aboard an airplane on this season-five *I Love Lucy* episode.

6. "The Freezer." Lucy-cicle anyone? Frigid fun from the first season of *I Love Lucy*.

7. Selling salad dressing sounds like "The Million Dollar Idea" on a season three *I Love Lucy* episode but, of course, it's not.

8. "Lucy's Schedule." A fast-motion dinner party from season one of *I Love Lucy*.

9. "Lucy and Viv Open a Restaurant" and nobody comes on this season-two episode of *The Lucy Show*.

10. "Lucy's Contact Lenses" prove problematic when one ends up in the frosting of one of fifteen cakes during this season-three episode of *The Lucy Show*.

7

Burning a Torch for Tiki

I T STARTED, AS SO MANY OBSESSIONS DO, in my teenage years. In the summer of 1976, Bette Midler's "Live at Last" concert was on HBO twenty-three times. Eight PM, 3 AM, weekends, weekdays, I watched the show every time it was on. And I mean every time. This was in the days before VCRs and DVRs tamed the television, and it was wild. I loved Midler's nose-thumbing banter and her raw-throated blues numbers, but I was particularly fascinated by the titian-haired Divine Miss M's naughty rendition of the "Hawaiian War Chant." She would lead the audience, Cleveland, this crowd was from, through the song's ribald chorus about getting lei-ed, telling them first and foremost, "This is real Polynesian, you understand." This dirty ditty was truly fabulous, genuinely exotic, but real Polynesian? Not on your life.

It's okay, though. Midler's Polynesia is the one that everyone who isn't from Polynesia likes best. It's the Polynesia of our pop-culture dreams, the far-off land where Trader Vic, Don the Beachcomber, and the casts of *Gilligan's Island* and *Hawaiian Eye* share mai-tais under one giant fringed straw umbrella. It's the magical land of tiki mugs and exotic fire dancers and lounge music playing on a never-ending loop. *Brigadoon* in grass skirts. I realize now that when I visited the real Hawaii for the first time in the early '90s, I was actually looking for the fake one. The night after I flew home from Honolulu on a red eye, I celebrated my thirtieth birthday at Trader Vic's in the Plaza Hotel in Manhattan.

I liked Honolulu, but I LOVED Trader Vic's.

In the years since my happy birthday hukilau, I have pushed the idea that "tiki is chic-y" in every publication that would let me, including *Martha Stewart Living* and the *New York Times*. I like to think my articles, as trumped up as they were, helped the tiki trend along. In the last decade or so, hipsters actually have rediscovered the allure that our grandparents found at places like the Tonga Room in San Francisco or the Kahiki in Columbus, Ohio, or the Hawaii Kai in Times Square, New York. Unlike my interest, the interest of these cool kids wasn't sparked in time to save the thatched-ceilinged joints of yore, where Asian waiters served those cream-cheese- and seafood-filled wontons called Crab Rangoon to patrons who got snockered on fruity drinks like the Sufferin' Bastard or the Maiden's Downfall. But all is not lost. New, albeit less ambitious tiki places have begun to pop up in places like, oh, Brooklyn, New York. It may not be chic-y, but Tiki is most definitely cool again.

The four men who share their recipes in this chapter contributed more, via their music and TV appearances, to the pop culture image of Hawaii than anyone . . . well, anyone this side of Bette Midler. Cook their favorite dishes, even Don Ho's Pig Foot Soup, if you dare, and you'll be transported to a far-off place. It may not be Hawaii, but it'll definitely offer a change of scenery on your dinner table.

Don Ho 1930–2007

DON HO WAS MORE THAN JUST THE good-looking guy who sang "Tiny Bubbles." He was Hawaii's ambassador to the world ... or at least to the world of American pop culture. In the '60s and '70s, the Waikiki showroom headliner was Hollywood's go-to islander, appearing on TV shows from *Batman* to *The Brady Bunch*. He even had his own TV variety show for a while. When his *Don Ho! Greatest Hits* album was certified gold, Ho became the first Hawaiian singer to hold that distinction. Anyone visiting the fiftieth state had to include one of Ho's shows in his plans. To those of us who saw him perform, he embodied Hawaii. Like the islands, he was exotic but familiar, laid back but exciting. His pigs' feet soup? Well, that might be a little daunting for most. But intrepid eaters will certainly want to say "Aloha" to at least one bowl.

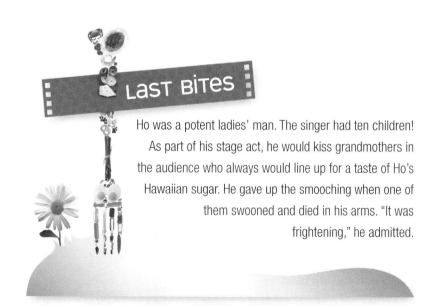

Last Bites

Ho was a potent ladies' man. The singer had ten children! As part of his stage act, he would kiss grandmothers in the audience who always would line up for a taste of Ho's Hawaiian sugar. He gave up the smooching when one of them swooned and died in his arms. "It was frightening," he admitted.

DON HO'S SOUP

Put pigs' feet, ginger, and Hawaiian salt in a large pot with water to cover. Bring to boil, and then reduce heat, add salted turnip and orange peel, and slowly simmer for 2½ hours. Toss in fresh turnips and watercress or cabbage and cook for another 15 minutes or so. Correct seasoning. Serve in large soup bowls.

Serves 6

3 pounds pigs' feet

8 slices ginger

1 teaspoon Hawaiian salt

1 small bunch salted turnip (available at Asian grocery stores)

1 orange peel

5 fresh turnips

1 bunch watercress, Chinese cabbage, or mustard cabbage

Jack Lord 1920–1998

FOR 12 ACTION-PACKED SEASONS—okay, eleven action-packed seasons and that last one that nobody really liked—Jack Lord was Steve McGarrett, the no-nonsense detective heading up *Hawaii Five-O*. He and the series, it is said, did more for Hawaiian tourism than anyone but Don Ho. Before *Five-O*, Lord appeared in the 1958 big-screen comedy *God's Little Acre* and the 1962 James Bond film *Dr. No*. He did guest shots on numerous TV shows and starred in his own short-lived 1962 western series called *Stoney Burke*, in which he played the title character, a rodeo rider. Besides acting, Lord was an accomplished painter whose work is included in various museum collections. On an island where people came to "hang ten," he hung paintings. Interesting guy. Yummy soup.

Jack Lord's watercress soup

1 large bunch watercress

1½ cups cold water

1¾ pounds baking potatoes

3 cups water

½ cup whole milk

Salt and white pepper,
   to taste

Croutons, for garnish

Wash watercress thoroughly, and separate leaves from stems. Put leaves aside. In blender, combine stems with cold water and puree. Strain liquid through a sieve, into a pitcher. Boil potatoes in salted water. Remove potatoes (reserving water) and peel. Blend, in small amounts, potato water, potatoes, watercress liquid, watercress leaves. Add whole milk for medium consistency. Before serving, season with salt and white pepper and heat thoroughly but do not boil. Serve with croutons.

A S THE GODFATHER OF THE LOUNGE MUSIC subgenre known as "exotica," composer, pianist, and occasional actor Martin Denny was a tiki god in the 1950s and '60s. His albums, boasting such intoxicating titles as *Afro-Desia*, and *Hypnotique*, are the soundtrack to a smoking jacket-clad bachelor's dreams, the aural equivalent of a high-proof potion in a skull-head mug, a beaded curtain shimmering in the breeze, and a gorgeous blonde poised atop a leopard skin rug. "Quiet Village," an island tune, was his biggest hit, but Denny put his own tropical spin on songs from Broadway shows and Hollywood musicals, too. Living in the real Hawaii while adding to the glamour of a mythical one, he performed into his 90s and happily lived long enough to see his music embraced by the "hep cats" of a whole new century. His corn pudding, like his music, is timeless.

Martin Denny's Corn Pudding

Mix all ingredients well and pour into two-quart casserole. Bake at 350° for 35–45 minutes, or until firm.

3 eggs, beaten well

1 (17 ounce) can corn, drained

1 green pepper, diced

1 onion, diced

4 slices crisp cooked bacon, diced

2 tablespoons bacon fat

POST Mortem

Denny's Corn Pudding is almost a baked frittata. For a more pudding-y corn pudding, use this recipe but add a box of corn muffin mix, a cup of sour cream, a can of creamed corn, and half a stick of melted butter. (A half-cup of grated mild cheddar and a couple of splashes of hot sauce wouldn't hurt, either.) Mix well and bake in a greased casserole until puffed and slightly brown.

James MacArthur 1937-2010

J AMES MACARTHUR DIDN'T REALLY HAVE A CHOICE when it came to being an actor. He was the adopted son of Helen Hayes who was the so-called First Lady of the American Theater and the playwright Charles MacArthur; and silent film megastar Lillian Gish was his godmother. It may not have been in his blood, but that was only a technicality. MacArthur was making movies (including Disney's *Swiss Family Robinson*) in his teens, appearing on Broadway (opposite Jane Fonda) in his early twenties, and working on such TV series as *Bonanza, Wagon Train,* and *Gunsmoke* shortly after that. His best known films were *Battle of the Bulge* and the Clint Eastwood picture, *Hang 'Em High*. His impressive performance in the latter landed MacArthur the part that would immortalize him: Dan "Danno" Williams on *Hawaii Five-O*. For eleven seasons, audiences couldn't wait for McGarrett (Jack Lord) to say, "Book 'em, Danno." Although he grew up in Nyack, New York, and worked in Hollywood, MacArthur would always be associated with Hawaii, and the series that made so many of us want to visit there. The recipes he left behind, like this one, were anything but island fare. Still, we say, "Cook 'em, Danno!"

James MacArthur's Beef à la Deutsch

Serves 4

Sauté beef, mushrooms, green pepper, and onion in butter until onion is soft. Add stock and simmer until the meat is tender. Mix flour with ½ cup sour cream and add to meat. Season with salt and pepper, and cook until mixture has thickened. Add remaining sour cream and pimiento and heat until boiling. Remove from heat and keep warm for 15 minutes before serving.

1½ pounds top sirloin, cut into 1-inch strips

1 cup sliced fresh mushrooms

½ cup sliced green pepper

½ cup diced onion

2 tablespoons butter

4 cups beef stock

¼ cup flour

1½ cups sour cream, divided

Salt and pepper, to taste

¼ cup chopped pimiento

POST Mortem

Hearty fare like MacArthur's German beef tastes better once the flavors have had a chance to mingle. Try making this recipe the day before, refrigerating it overnight, and then reheating it when it's time to serve.

AFTER-DINNER VIEWING

ALOHA STYLE

Most every baby boomer is familiar with Don Ho's appearance on *The Brady Bunch*. But Hawaii's favorite son really shines on a 1967 season-three installment of *I Dream of Jeannie* called "Jeannie Goes to Honolulu." It's a terrible episode of a not-very-good show, but Ho, backed by the Alii's, performs "Ain't No Big Thing" and "The Days of My Youth." The latter is shot like a music video and seems stuck in this sitcom for no good reason.

The best thing about Jack Lord, the original Steve McGarrett, is that his hair never moved in twelve seasons of *Hawaii Five-O*. Any episode with the villainous Wo Fat is worth watching, if only to listen to Lord say, "Wo Fat." To hear the humorless detective say his classic catchphrase "Book him, Danno" for the first time, watch the season-one episode "Twenty-Four Karat Kill."

As for Martin Denny, Hollywood must have decided he was better heard than seen. His most notable appearance was in the 1959 film *Forbidden Island*, but that's out of print. You can hear his music on the soundtrack for director Alan Rudolph's big-screen 2000 adaptation of the Kurt Vonnegut novel *Breakfast of Champions*.

8

SUPPER UNDER THE STARS

MADISON AVENUE PROMISED US back in the 1960s that we'd all be drinking Tang and eating Space Food Sticks by now. Our televisions, the same sets upon which we watched a man walk on the moon, told us it would be a strange new culinary world in the future, a place where foods that were actually grown would be outmoded. Well, that turned out to be baloney.

Thanks guys. I guess I'm never getting that jet pack, either.

But the writers of the classic TV series *Star Trek* had it right. The foods of the future that they envisioned wouldn't be anything so fake. The crew of the starship Enterprise may have used a synthesizer to create their meals in the twenty-third century, but they used it to make dishes we recognized in the twentieth. When half-Vulcan, half-human First Officer Mr. Spock (Leonard Nimoy) went into heat—you can call it "pon farr" if you must—in the episode "Amok Time," Nurse Chapel (Majel Barrett-Roddenberry) made him soup. Yes, it was Plomeek soup, and yes, an uncharacteristically bitchy Spock threw it at her, but it was soup. Plain old Vulcan soup.

There were other food moments on the original (and best) *Star Trek*. Those furry Tribbles ate all the super-duper wheat on the ship in "The Trouble with Tribbles," and Saurian brandy led to many a bar fight on the show. But Spock's broth hurling remains the most memorable instance. It seems only fitting that the show's best food moment would have been written by a man named Theodore Sturgeon.

For a bunch of space travelers, the cast of *Star Trek* dishes up recipes that are decidedly terrestrial. But they make a Trektacular supper under the stars. Serve these homey dishes outside on a warm summer night, then lie back on the grass, and stare up at the heavens. If you look beyond the stars, you just might see Nurse Chapel dodging a bowl of soup right this very minute.

DeForest Kelly 1920–1999

T HEY SAY DEFOREST KELLEY PREFERRED ACTING in westerns to science-fiction adventures, and he certainly starred in plenty. Before landing the role of Dr. Leonard "Bones" McCoy on *Star Trek*, he appeared in such TV tumbleweeds as *Gunsmoke* and *Rawhide* in the 1950s, and *Bat Masterson*, *The Virginian*, and *Bonanza* in the 1960s. But it was as a Southern gentleman in space that the Georgia-born actor was immortalized. Dr. McCoy reacted to the future with the same trepidation that many in the audience would have. He hated, for instance, such modern "conveniences" as the transporter, never quite believing that a man's molecules were supposed to be taken apart, beamed to a new location, and put back together again. When Kelley died, at least one obituary began with McCoy's most-fitting catchphrase, "He's dead, Jim." Kelley's cheesy casserole lives on, even though he's been transported to the great beyond.

DeForest Kelley's Swiss Cheese Potato Casserole

Boil potatoes in their skins until half-cooked. Chill, preferably overnight. Peel potatoes and grate into a bowl. Place a layer of potatoes in a well-buttered 2-quart shallow baking dish. Sprinkle with a layer of cheese. Dot with butter. Sprinkle with salt and pepper. Repeat layers and sprinkle top with paprika. Bake at 350° for about an hour.

Serves 8

3 pounds potatoes

1½ pounds Swiss cheese, shredded

½ cup butter

Salt and pepper, to taste

Paprika, to taste

James Doohan 1920–2005

ALTHOUGH HE HAD APPEARED ON numerous American TV series from *Peyton Place* to *Voyage to the Bottom of the Sea*, Canadian actor James Doohan hit it big only when he affected a Scottish accent to become Chief Engineer Montgomery Scott on the original *Star Trek* in 1966. With a mischievous twinkle in his eye, and the acting ability to convince audiences that he really was holding that starship's engines together by sheer force of will, he turned "Scotty" into not just a job, but a cultural phenomenon. For the rest of his life, fans wanted him to beam them up. The series, which ended its initial run in 1969, was only the beginning of Doohan's "Trek." He supplied voices for the animated version of the series in the '70s, and then went on to appear in half a dozen or so Star Trek movies from 1979 to 1994. After his death, some of Doohan's ashes were blasted off into space. As the story goes, the rocket was lost—at least for a while. Surely, that never would have happened if Scotty had been alive and kicking. Here's his twist on a classic Italian dish.

POST Mortem

This super-tasty dish is as comforting as tuna noodle casserole, but more dressed up, and it tastes great as leftovers. When I cooked half a pound of lasagna, I had three noodles left over, so I ended with a layer of those, and then sprinkled an extra cup of mozzarella cheese, along with the Parmesan, on top. It worked out great. You might want to "Doohan" the same.

James Doohan's Chicken Lasagna

Serves 8

In a medium pan, melt the butter and blend in the flour, salt, and oregano. Stir in the chicken broth and cook, stirring, until thickened and boiling. Remove from heat and add the diced chicken. In a small bowl, beat the egg. Add the cottage cheese, making it a spreadable mixture. Lightly grease the baking pan. Place one-third of the chicken mixture in the bottom of the pan. Layer with one half of the noodles, one half of the cottage cheese mix, one half of the spinach and one half of the mozzarella. Repeat ending with the last third of the chicken mixture. Sprinkle the grated Parmesan on top. Bake at 375° for 45 minutes.

½ cup butter

½ cup flour

½ teaspoon salt

½ teaspoon oregano

3 cups chicken broth

2½ cups chicken, diced and cooked

1 egg

2 cups creamed cottage cheese

½ pound lasagna noodles, cooked and drained

1 (10-ounce) package frozen chopped spinach or broccoli, thawed and squeezed dry

¼ pound mozzarella cheese, shredded

¼ cup grated Parmesan cheese

Gene RODDENBERRY 1921–1991

F EW CAN SAY THEY CREATED SOMETHING AS enduring as *Star Trek*. But that series—one that writer and producer Gene Roddenberry often described as a *Wagon Train* to the stars—was only part of his legacy. A dedicated futurist, he showed the world a better tomorrow and, in so doing, inspired would-be scientists and adventurers (not to mention legions of sci-fi geeks) to dream big. Roddenberry, who went on to marry Majel Barrett, was also responsible for such projects as the TV series *Andromeda* and *Earth: Final Conflict*, both produced after his death, and the fondly remembered TV movies *Genesis II* and *Planet Earth*. His infamous foray into the world of sexploitation with the film *Pretty Maids All in a Row* was released on DVD in 2010. To some it may be more "out of this world," than any of his science-fiction offerings. His recipe, though, is truly earthy.

Gene Roddenberry's Lima Beans and Ham

1 pound dried lima
  beans

2 ½ pounds of ham

1 bunch celery, chopped

2 large onions, chopped

3 cups raw long-grain rice

1½ teaspoons salt

¾ pound sharp cheddar
  cheese, grated

Put lima beans in a large pot with 5 cups of water. Bring to a boil and then turn down the heat to a gentle simmer. Cook the beans for about 5 hours, adding another cup or two of water to keep the beans moist. Once the beans begin to cook, put the ham in a saucepan and add 3 cups water. Cook ham about 3½ hours. After the beans have cooked for 4 hours, add the ham, celery, onion, and some of the liquid from the ham. Continue to cook ham and beans while making the rice. Cook the rice in six cups of water to which 1½ teaspoons salt have been added. Cook until the water is absorbed and the rice is tender. To serve, sprinkle cheese in serving bowls, add rice and top with ham and beans.

after-dinner viewing

THE NOT-SO-FINAL FRONTIER

Star Trek II: The Wrath of Khan, is the best Trek movie ever. James Doohan and DeForest Kelley and the gang are all in it, not to mention Ricardo Montalban, whose Carne Asada recipe appears in Chapter 23. But if you really want to show your guests something unexpected, there's *Trek Stars Go West,* a 2010 DVD compilation of Star Trek actors making appearances on Westerns. Kelley gets beaten up pretty bad in a 1949 episode of *The Lone Ranger.* But Doohan is on the other end of the fist in a 1957 episode of *The Last of the Mohicans.* In a long wig, he plays a paleface-hating Indian with an itchy quiver finger, who'll stop at nothing to take charge. As one of his more levelheaded tribesmen predicts, "Tonkawa make bad chief." But it okay. Doohan make good chief engineer.

9

Make Room For Dinner

FATHER MAY HAVE KNOWN BEST on classic TV shows, but never in the kitchen. The breadwinner was never the bread baker in the '50s and '60s. Maybe TV was just reflecting the gender roles of the day, but cooking was usually a woman's job. You didn't see Howard Cunningham (Tom Bosley) at the stove on *Happy Days*. That was Mrs. C's bailiwick. (The show premiered in the 1970s, I know, but it was set in the 1950s.)

If a family was lucky, or a wife was liberated, food preparation was the domestic's duty. Mike Brady (Robert Reed) and his wife Carol (Florence Henderson) had Alice (Ann B. Davis) to whip up pork chops and applesauce on *The Brady Bunch*. Danny Williams (Danny Thomas) charged Louise (Amanda Randolph) with making everything from lasagna to matzo ball soup on *Make Room for Daddy*. And Mrs. Livingston (Miyoshi Umeki) saw to it that Eddie (Brandon Cruz) and Mr. Eddie's Father (Bill Bixby) didn't starve on *The Courtship of Eddie's Father*.

If you didn't want to hire someone, you could always play the widower card and rook a relative into kitchen duty. Steve Douglas (Fred MacMurray) and his *Three Sons* not only had Bub (William Frawley), but when he split, they got Uncle Charlie (William Demarest) to cook for them.

Off screen, though, TV dads did cook. The men whose recipes appear in this chapter were secure enough in their manhood to don an apron, grab a spatula, and do it. If they can, so can you, Daddy-O.

Fred MacMurray 1908–1991

TV LOVERS REMEMBER HIM AS THE soft-spoken father on *My Three Sons*, but filmgoers know him best cast as the insurance agent in on the con in *Double Indemnity*. Working from the late 1920s to the late 1970s, MacMurray appeared in such varied fare as *The Absent-Minded Professor* and its sequel *Son of Flubber*, the stylish sex comedy *The Apartment*, and the killer-bee disaster movie, *The Swarm*. He is said to have valued time spent with his own family so much that he made sure all of his scenes for *My Three Sons* were shot first. That may have made life hell for his cast mates, but he sounds like a pretty good real-life dad. His pot roast is enough for three sons or more.

Fred MacMurray's Flemish Pot Roast

In a heavy Dutch oven, brown meat in oil, turning to brown both sides. In a separate pan, sauté onions until pale golden color. Sprinkle with flour and cook 2 minutes. Pour in beer and bring to a boil, stirring. Then pour over meat. Add brown sugar, vinegar, bay leaf, garlic, and salt. Cover and simmer 2 hours, or until juices are slightly thickened. Strain juices into a bowl. Spoon onions into a vegetable bowl. Carve meat. Pass sauce and onions at the table with the meat.

Serves 6

4–5 pound beef chuck roast

1 tablespoon oil

4 medium onions, sliced

2 tablespoons butter

2 tablespoons flour

1 (12-ounce) can of beer

1 tablespoon brown sugar

1 tablespoon vinegar

1 bay leaf

2 cloves garlic

1½ teaspoons salt

2 tablespoons parsley

Danny Thomas 1912–1991

AS DANNY WILLIAMS, THE NIGHTCLUB COMIC and father on the long-running sitcom popularly known as *Make Room for Daddy*, Danny Thomas was a fixture on television for more than a decade, surviving one wife (Jean Hagen), getting another (Marjorie Lord) and, for a while, even playing pop to an Italian exchange student portrayed by Annette Funicello. He was dapper and funny and loud; and no one has ever done a better spit take. Behind the scenes, he was an executive producer on such TV series as *The Mod Squad*, *The Andy Griffith Show*, and *The Dick Van Dyke Show*. As a real-life dad, he had an effect on television, too, by producing three children, two of whom, Marlo and Tony, went on to work in the business. Marlo starred in the early feminist sitcom *That Girl*, while Tony executive produced *The Golden Girls*. Danny Thomas's greatest accomplishment, though, was probably his founding of the St. Jude Children's Research Hospital, a legacy to which his children dedicate themselves today. He was a proud Lebanese-American and his recipe for *fatayer* reflects that.

Last Bites

Thomas liked to make cameo appearances on the series he produced. His most famous was on *The Dick Van Dyke Show* in an episode called "It May Look Like a Walnut!"—a sci-fi spoof featuring a closetful of walnuts and written by series creator Carl Reiner. Thomas played Kolak, an alien from the planet Twilo, in the 1963 installment of the classic comedy.

Danny Thomas's Fatayer

Serves
12
or more

Combine flour, oil, salt, dissolved yeast, and water and mix well. Knead until smooth. Cover and let rise in a warm place for 1½ hours. While dough is rising, combine lamb, onions, lemon juice, yogurt, pine nuts, and spices. Roll dough thin and cut out in 3-inch rounds. Fill dough patties with meat mixture. Shape into half moons, and score a vent for steam to escape. Place on a greased baking sheet, brush tops with oil and bake in a 375° oven for one hour.

8 cups flour

3 tablespoons oil

1 tablespoon salt

1 packet cake yeast, dissolved in 2 tablespoons warm water

2½–3 cups lukewarm water

3 pounds lamb, coarsely ground

4 medium onions, chopped fine

1–2 cups fresh lemon juice

⅔ cup plain yogurt

¾ cup pine nuts, sautéed lightly in butter

Salt, pepper, and allspice, to taste

TOM BOSLEY 1927–2010

H E MAY HAVE BEEN THE POIROT OF THE PRIESTHOOD on *Father Dowling Mysteries*, and a sure-footed sheriff on *Murder, She Wrote*, but Tom Bosley will always be Howard Cunningham on *Happy Days* to those of us who spent many happy nights watching that hit 1970s sitcom set in the era of *American Graffiti*. As the father of Richie (Ron Howard) and Joanie (Erin Moran) and even the mysteriously disappearing Chuck (Gavan O'Herlihy), Bosley was the dad everyone wanted to be his own, and that included the too-cool-for-school Arthur "Fonzie" Fonzarelli (Henry Winkler). Bosley's paternal quality served him well both before and after *Happy Days*. Two of his other notable roles were dads. He voiced the title character in the animated series *Wait Till Your Father Gets Home*, which was sort of the *Family Guy* of 1972. And, after winning the Tony Award for playing the title role in the musical *Fiorello!* in 1960, he played Belle's father in the Broadway stage version of *Beauty and the Beast* in 1994. But

Mr. C is the dad we like best. Make Bosley's red clam sauce after the kids are in bed. After a meal this delicious, you—like Howard Cunningham—may want to get "frisky."

TOM BOSLEY'S
Linguine With
Red Clam Sauce

Serves
4

Heat oil in large pot. Add garlic and onion and cook until softened. Add tomatoes, spices, and salt and pepper. Simmer 15 minutes, stirring occasionally. Add clams and simmer another 5 minutes. Meanwhile, cook linguine according to package directions. Spoon sauce on top and sprinkle with Parmesan.

2 tablespoons olive oil

1 clove garlic, minced

¼ cup chopped onion

2 ½ cups crushed tomatoes
    with juice

½ teaspoon dried oregano

¼ teaspoon dried basil

2 tablespoons chopped
    fresh parsley

Salt and pepper, to taste

1 cup canned baby clams,
    drained and minced

1 pound linguine

¼ cup freshly grated
    Parmesan cheese

ROBERT REED 1932–1992

OTHER PEOPLE PLAYED THEIR PARTS. But to millions and millions of TV viewers who grew up watching *The Brady Bunch,* and every subsequent reiteration of it from *The Brady Bunch Hour* in 1977 to *The Bradys* in 1990, Robert Reed was Mike Brady. With a perm or without, he was the understanding patriarch of TV's first "blended family" and an architect who never built anything but inspired legions of viewers to choose that profession. Today he seems like the most modern dad ever on television: he not only had a combined family long before they were commonplace, he was secretly gay! Okay, Mike Brady wasn't gay, but Reed was. That may be why his 1975 portrayal of a doctor undergoing sexual reassignment surgery on *Medical Center* was more sensitive than previous portrayals of LGBT characters. Then again, it may just have been that he was a damn good actor and handsome to boot. Speaking of boots, his beef and biscuit casserole should get you to kick up yours.

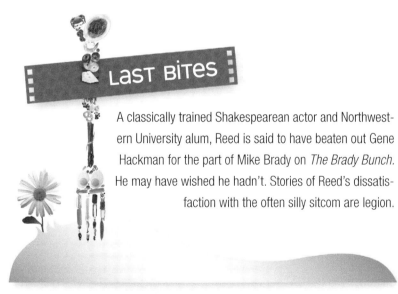

Last Bites

A classically trained Shakespearean actor and Northwestern University alum, Reed is said to have beaten out Gene Hackman for the part of Mike Brady on *The Brady Bunch.* He may have wished he hadn't. Stories of Reed's dissatisfaction with the often silly sitcom are legion.

ROBERT REED'S BEEF AND BISCUIT CASSEROLE

Preheat oven to 375°. Brown ground beef, chopped onion, and diced green chilies in pan; drain grease. Stir in tomato sauce, chili powder, garlic salt, and minced onion. Simmer. Separate refrigerated buttermilk biscuits into 10 biscuits, then separate again into 20 half-biscuits. Place 10 of the half-biscuits into bottom of 8- or 9-inch square glass baking dish. Combine ½ cup shredded Monterey jack and cheddar cheese with sour cream and egg, mix well. Remove meat from heat, stir in sour cream mixture. Place other 10 biscuits on top of meat mixture. Sprinkle remaining 1 cup of cheese on top of dough. Bake at 375° for 30 minutes until golden brown.

1–1¼ pounds ground beef

½ cup chopped onion

¼ cup diced green chilies

1 (8-ounce) can tomato sauce

2 teaspoons chili powder

¾ teaspoon garlic salt

3 tablespoons dried minced onion

1 (8-ounce) can refrigerated buttermilk biscuits

1½ cups shredded Monterey jack and cheddar cheese

½ cup sour cream

1 egg, slightly beaten

H E WAS HANDSOME, HE WAS QUIET, and, unlike almost every TV dad before him, he talked to his son as an equal. Bill Bixby wasn't just Eddie's father on *The Courtship of Eddie's Father*, he was his best friend. The theme song told us so! Bixby came to that show having starred in *My Favorite Martian* opposite Ray Walston, so we loved him already. He went on, of course, to become David Banner on *The Incredible Hulk*, so we loved him after *Eddie* as well. And let's not forget his one season as *The Magician*, a crime drama with sleight-of-hand that deserved a lot more love than it got in 1973. I loved him in the 1975 Disney movie *The Apple Dumpling Gang*, too. Okay, I'll say it. I love Bill Bixby. You'll love his zucchini bread almost as much.

BILL BIXBY'S ZUCCHINI BREAD

Preheat oven to 350°. Combine flour, cinnamon, baking powder, and salt and set aside. In a large mixing bowl, using an electric mixer, beat eggs and sugar until foamy. At low speed, blend in zucchini, oil, and vanilla. Add flour mixture a third at a time, beating just until blended. Stir in nuts. Spoon batter into a greased loaf pan. Bake for one hour or until a toothpick inserted in the center comes out clean. Cool in pan for 10 minutes. Remove to wire rack and cool completely.

1½ cups all-purpose flour

2 teaspoons cinnamon

2 teaspoons baking powder

1 teaspoon salt

2 eggs

1 cup sugar

1 cup vegetable oil

2 cups coarsely grated zucchini

1 teaspoon vanilla extract

1 cup coarsely chopped walnuts

POST MORTEM

This quick bread is as soothing as Bixby's voice and tastes even better the next day and the day after that. Some raisins tossed in would make it extra nice.

aFter-Dinner Viewing
FAMILY FOOD

On *Make Room for Daddy*, Kathy Williams (Marjorie Lord) almost loses a $10,000 donation to Danny's favorite charity by refusing to write down dinner appointments in the 1958 "Take a Message" episode from season six. Relax, the dough does come through, but only after Danny is forced to eat three lasagna dinners in one evening.

When Potsie (Anson Williams) finds a bone in his meat loaf on the 1976 season-four "Muckrakers" episode of *Happy Days*, budding journalist Richie not only exposes a "meat fraud" in the school cafeteria, but discovers that Fonzie's Kryptonite is liver.

On season three of *The Brady Bunch*, Peter (Christopher Knight) begins doing impressions of famous stars when he realizes he's not exactly "The Personality Kid." His Humphrey Bogart may have been hacky even in 1971, but "pork chops and applesauce" became a time-honored catchphrase.

For something truly special, there's the Thanksgiving 1960 episode of *My Three Sons* in which Bub sings "She's only a bird in a gilded cage" to an uncooked turkey. Called "Chip's Harvest," this season-one holiday offering involves an indigent Indian, a hot science teacher, and a broken stove.

Finally, the 1964 season-one "Shake Well and Don't Use" episode of *My Favorite Martian* shows what can happen when an earthling dinner guest is fed Martian spices. He moves in slow motion.

a. RiNG-a-DiNG-DiNG RaT PacK BBQ

WHEN FRANK SINATRA SANG the Johnny Mercer and Hoagy Carmichael standard "In the Cool, Cool, Cool of the Evening," he meant every word. A wienie bake was fine, even boiled ham was okay, as long as Sinatra was there when the party was "a-getting a glow on." The man liked a good barbecue. It was a way of life in California year round, he liked to boast. But that didn't mean, of course, that the gang back in Hoboken couldn't fire up the grill every summer. Those sausages weren't going to cook themselves!

As the leader of the "Rat Pack"—as his posse of macho guys and their good time gals will always be known—Sinatra knew how to have fun. With Dean Martin and Sammy Davis Jr. by his side, he made every party they attended together, from New York to Vegas to Hollywood, swing in the '50s and '60s.

Modern day glamour-pusses—Mr. Pitt and Mr. Clooney, you know who you are—can only hope to imitate their original swagger. But that hasn't stopped legions of neo-hipsters from trying. The "Rat Pack" spirit is alive and well. There are Rat Pack–themed restaurants around the country. Any book about cocktails that's worth its salt rim mentions the gang's antics. And the Internet is flush with Rat Pack–party ideas. But to really capture their brio, you have to cook what they did. And that's where these recipes come in. Follow the Chairman of the Board's grilling advice, and let the spirits flow as his pal Dino advises, and you'll be following in some very cool footsteps . . . all the way out to the patio.

And don't forget Sammy's salad. You can't live on meat and booze alone!

H E WAS THE CHAIRMAN OF THE BOARD, New Jersey's favorite son (other than me), Nancy's dad, and perhaps the greatest interpreter of the American popular songbook ever to have lived. He was a heartthrob (although my mother always said he was so skinny he had to leave the hangers in his jackets to have shoulders) and he was a serious actor—anyone who saw him in *The Man with the Golden Arm* can attest. He took home the Oscar for *From Here to Eternity* in 1954 and gave memorable performances in the musicals *On the Town* and *Guys and Dolls*. But it is Sinatra's music that endures. If you don't love his albums *Frank Sinatra Sings for Only the Lonely, Come Fly with Me, September of My Years*, and the samba record *Francis Albert Sinatra & Antonio Carlo Jobim*, you just don't get it. In fact, if you don't like those records, you don't deserve his lamb recipe.

Frank Sinatra's Barbecued Lamb

Combine oil, vinegar, garlic, and salt to make a marinade. Place lamb skin-side up in a shallow pan and pour the marinade over it. Slather mustard on skin side. Cover and let marinate over-night. To cook, place lamb mustard-side down on a very hot grill, five inches from flame. When brown on one side, turn. Cook about one hour total, checking for doneness at 45 minutes. Slice thinly to serve.

1 (7-pound) leg of lamb, boned and butterflied

Serves 6
or more

1 cup olive oil

8 tablespoons wine vinegar

2 cloves garlic, crushed

1 teaspoon salt

½ cup prepared mustard

sammy Davis Jr. 1925–1990

H E DANCED. HE SANG. HE ACTED. HE KIBITZED. He conk-conk-a-chonked his way into our hearts. Was there anything Sammy Davis Jr. couldn't do? Other than check into certain hotels back in the day, probably not. He was the consummate entertainer, and he had the Emmy and Grammy awards to prove it. Starting out in vaudeville as a kid, Davis went on to become a Broadway sensation in the shows *Mr. Wonderful* and *Golden Boy*, appeared in not only the Rat Pack movies but the noteworthy *A Man Called Adam* and *Sweet Charity*, and delivered one of the world's most famous kisses on a 1972 episode of *All in the Family*. When Davis, playing himself, realized what a bigot Archie Bunker (Carroll O'Connor) really was, he asked for a picture with him and then hit him with a buss. Davis was Archie's biggest nightmare: a triple minority. As a one-eyed African-American Jew, Davis was a tireless (and sometimes controversial) equal-rights activist. But like the "Candy Man," whom he immortalized in song, he made the world taste good. His salad will do the same.

THE DeaD CeLeBriTY COOKBOOK

sammy Davis Jr.'s salad

Rub the inside of a large wooden salad bowl with a garlic clove. Discard garlic. Wash and dry lettuce. Place in bowl. Add tomatoes, wheat germ, and olives. Blend all dressing ingredients in a jar, cover and shake well. Toss salad with dressing. Garnish with green pepper rings.

Salad:

1 clove garlic

1 head romaine lettuce

2 tomatoes, quartered

3–4 tablespoons wheat germ

6 ripe olives, pitted and sliced

2 green peppers, cut in rings

Dressing:

¼ cup salad oil

¼ cup red wine vinegar

½ teaspoon Worcestershire sauce

½ teaspoon lemon juice

½ teaspoon salt

⅛ teaspoon fresh ground pepper

Dean Martin 1917–1995

WHETHER HE WAS PLAYING STRAIGHT MAN to Jerry Lewis in the movies, crooning "Everybody Loves Somebody" on the radio, or presiding over a celebrity roast on television, Dean Martin played the role of the ultimate party boy with charm and ease. Who else could say, "You're not drunk if you can lie on the floor without holding on," and make it seem like sober advice? The old chestnut about "women wanted him, men wanted to be him" was never truer than in Martin's case. He was a suave-but-funny leading man, which suited him in the more than fifty films he made including *Bells Are Ringing*, *Rio Bravo*, and *The Young Lions*. Hell, Martin was even good in *Airport*. I always liked him best as Matt Helm, the James Bond-esque super-spy he played in four films that now are classified as Martini Movies. He had fans from the *Cannonball Run* pictures, too. (Those would be Jack Daniels movies.) I loved him for his TV work as well. *The Dean Martin Comedy Hour* and The Dean Martin Celebrity Roasts always seemed like parties to which all of America was invited. And while his singing was overshadowed by his proximity to Sinatra, Martin's brilliant catalog of music will live on for generations. Some of us like his music better than—gasp!—Sinatra's. "That's Amore" for you. Martin's burgers and bourbon may not seem like much of a recipe, but they're appropriately easygoing.

Dean Martin's Burgers and Bourbon

1 pound ground beef

¼ teaspoon salt

8 ounces bourbon, chilled

Preheat a heavy skillet and sprinkle with salt. Shape beef, handling as little as possible, into four patties. Cook over medium-high heat for 4 minutes, flip and cook another 4 minutes. Pour two ounces of bourbon in each of four shot glasses. Drink with burgers.

POST MORTEM

Dean's daughter Deana told me her father's favorite drink was not bourbon but Scotch whiskey. "He liked J&B," she said. "He said it stood for 'Just Booze.'" Personally, I'd rather have an ice-cold Maker's Mark Manhattan, served straight up, with my burger. But who are you going to listen to, me or Dean?

AFTER-DINNER VIEWING

LIVE AND SWINGIN'

This may sound like blasphemy, but the Rat Pack movies are more fondly remembered than they are good. Have you tried watching *Robin and the 7 Hoods* lately? If you're mad for Frank, Dino, and Sammy, you can have a fine time watching *Ocean's 11*. But for a real look at what made the boys so ring-a-ding-ding, pick up a CD/DVD combo pack called *The Ultimate Rat Pack Collection: Live and Swingin'*. Play the CD during dinner and then settle in with the DVD after. The disc preserves a 1965 charity concert from St. Louis that captures the spirit of their legendary Vegas gigs. Sinatra, Martin, and Davis cut-up, carouse, and sing up a storm, as only they could.

READER/CUSTOMER CARE SURVEY

HEFG

We care about your opinions! Please take a moment to fill out our online Reader Survey at **http://survey.hcibooks.com.**
As a **"THANK YOU"** you will receive a **VALUABLE INSTANT COUPON** towards future book purchases
as well as a **SPECIAL GIFT** available only online! Or, you may mail this card back to us.

(PLEASE PRINT IN ALL CAPS)

First Name _____ MI. _____ Last Name _____

Address _____ City _____

State _____ Zip _____ Email _____

1. Gender
❏ Female ❏ Male

2. Age
❏ 8 or younger
❏ 9-12 ❏ 13-16
❏ 17-20 ❏ 21-30
❏ 31+

3. Did you receive this book as a gift?
❏ Yes ❏ No

4. Annual Household Income
❏ under $25,000
❏ $25,000 - $34,999
❏ $35,000 - $49,999
❏ $50,000 - $74,999
❏ over $75,000

5. What are the ages of the children living in your house?
❏ 0 - 14 ❏ 15+

6. Marital Status
❏ Single
❏ Married
❏ Divorced
❏ Widowed

7. How did you find out about the book?
(please choose one)
❏ Recommendation
❏ Store Display
❏ Online
❏ Catalog/Mailing
❏ Interview/Review

8. Where do you usually buy books?
(please choose one)
❏ Bookstore
❏ Online
❏ Book Club/Mail Order
❏ Price Club (Sam's Club, Costco's, etc.)
❏ Retail Store (Target, Wal-Mart, etc.)

9. What subject do you enjoy reading about the most?
(please choose one)
❏ Parenting/Family
❏ Relationships
❏ Recovery/Addictions
❏ Health/Nutrition
❏ Christianity
❏ Spirituality/Inspiration
❏ Business Self-help
❏ Women's Issues
❏ Sports

10. What attracts you most to a book?
(please choose one)
❏ Title
❏ Cover Design
❏ Author
❏ Content

TAPE IN MIDDLE; DO NOT STAPLE

|ı.||ıı.||ı.|ıı.|ı|ıı.|ıı.|ı|ı|ı|.|ıı.|ı.|ı|ıı.ı.|ı|ı.|ı|ı|

FOLD HERE

Comments

a GaY BaSH

FOR THE LAST TWENTY-THREE YEARS, there's only one place I've wanted to be on the last Sunday in June and that's my neighborhood in New York City. I've never lived farther than half a block from the annual Gay Pride Parade, and I've attended all but one. Don't get me started on the wedding that took me away from it in the summer of 1997. I still haven't forgiven that darn bride.

When I lived on Fifth Avenue, I would always throw a brunch—the official gay meal, in case you had any doubt—and then make blender drinks and head down to the street in front of our building with a gaggle of overly exuberant, well-lubricated revelers. I liked to think of myself as the Perle Mesta of Lower Fifth. One year I encountered the British actor Stephen Rea in my elevator. He had no idea it was Pride Sunday in New York, he was just coming to see a friend. But I had my own *Crying Game* moment right there in my lift. One of my neighbors screamed when she saw him as if she'd just won the showcase on *The Price Is Right*. I told him, "I was going to do that, too, but then I thought better of it."

What made me scream, year after year, was how to top myself, so to speak. *You* try and keep a discerning, some would say evil, group of friends coming back for more. I know now that the answer to the ultimate gay pride celebration is to cook dishes originally prepared by some very nifty nellies. If you make in your kitchen what, say, Wayland Flowers made in his, they can't complain about your muffins. You may be just you, but he was the man behind Madame, for God's sake!

The men and trans woman whose recipes appear in this chapter were not only fabulously talented (or at least terrifically charismatic), they were pioneers. They came out of the closet long before others had the courage to do it. I salute them. They're some of the shoulders upon which the LGBT community now stands.

I hope that thanks to *The Dead Celebrity Cookbook*, others can come out of the pantry, too.

William Haines 1900–1973

WILLIAM HAINES WASN'T THE ONLY homosexual in Hollywood in the 1930s, but he was perhaps the first to refuse to hide in the closet. In the late '20s and early '30s, Haines was a box-office champion with such silent films as *Little Annie Rooney*, opposite Mary Pickford, and *Show People*, with Marion Davies. He made the leap to talkies successfully, but when his homosexuality was found out he was told he had to enter a "lavender marriage" with a woman or be fired from MGM. He chose the man rather than the sham and, with his lover, became a highly successful interior decorator instead. Their clients over the years included Joan Crawford, Gloria Swanson, Carole Lombard, George Burns, George Cukor, and Ronald and Nancy Reagan. Since 1998, he's been the subject of two books and a film documentary, and hailed as Hollywood's first out and proud star. Haines's furniture designs are still in production and look as glamorous as ever. Although he had to give up his film career, he made the right choice. Haines and his partner Jimmy Shields were together for their entire lives. Bachelor, my foot.

WILLIAM HAINES'S BACHELOR OMELET

½ teaspoon milk

1 teaspoon flour

3 eggs, separated

3 tablespoons butter

¼ cup boiled ham, finely chopped

½ teaspoon parsley, chopped

Whisk together milk and flour until smooth. Beat egg yolks until creamy, add milk and flour mixture and beat well. In a separate bowl, beat egg whites until stiff, and then gently add to yolk mixture. Melt butter in skillet and then add eggs. When omelet starts to set, sprinkle ham and parsley over all. Bake in hot oven three minutes to finish. Fold and serve.

Leonard Frey 1938–1988

"TURNING!" WITH THAT ONE WORD, Leonard Frey achieved immortality, at least in gay circles, as the bitter birthday boy Harold in *The Boys in the Band*, Mart Crowley's landmark off-Broadway play and the subsequent film version directed by William Friedkin. Frey was subsequently nominated for a Best Supporting Actor Oscar for his role as Motel the tailor in the film version of *Fiddler on the Roof*. He'd been in the Broadway version in another role. His TV work included guest shots on shows as disparate as *Mission: Impossible* and *The Mary Tyler Moore Show*, and he was a regular on a couple of short-lived series, including the 1981 cowboy comedy *Best of the West* and a show about a talking orangutan with a ridiculously high I.Q. that worked as a political adviser in Washington called *Mr. Smith*. His Scotch Eggs are a lot tastier than his TV work.

Christine Jorgensen 1926–1989

BEFORE CHRISTINE JORGENSEN, no one knew a transsexual. After Christine Jorgensen came back from Denmark, everyone did. When the *New York Daily News* ran the headline FORMER GI BECOMES BLONDE BEAUTY, she became the world's first transgender celebrity. Jorgensen went on to perform as a nightclub entertainer. "I Enjoy Being a Girl" was part of her act, and she was the subject of the 1970 film *The Christine Jorgensen Story*. The poster for the movie asked, "Did the surgeon's knife make me a woman or a freak?" Jorgensen herself had a healthy attitude about it all. When comedians kidded her that she went abroad and came back one, she laughed it off. Schlockmeister Ed Wood claimed she was the inspiration for his film, *Glen or Glenda?* As an activist with a sense of humor, Jorgensen was an inspiration for a lot more than just that one laughable film.

Leonard Frey's Scotch Eggs

Peel hard-boiled eggs and set aside. In a bowl, combine sausage, pepper, lemon rind, and sage, and mix well. Divide into four portions. Enclose each peeled egg in the seasoned meat mixture, then dip in beaten egg and coat in bread crumbs. Fry in oil until crisp and golden. Serve whole.

Serves 4

4 hard-boiled eggs

3 ounces mild-flavored fresh pork sausage

Few gratings freshly ground pepper

¼ teaspoon finely grated lemon rind

Pinch dried sage, thyme, or savory

1 egg, beaten

1 cup fine bread crumbs

Vegetable oil, for frying

Christine Jorgensen's Pineapple-Apricot Preserves

In a medium saucepan, gently simmer apricots and sugar in water for 20 minutes or until tender. While cooking, drain pineapple tidbits. In a blender, food processor, or food mill, puree apricots and cooking water with lemon juice and salt until smooth. Return mixture to saucepan, stir in pineapple and simmer gently for 5 minutes, stirring occasionally. Remove from heat, cool and refrigerate.

Makes about 2 cups

4 ounces dried apricots

½ cup sugar

1 cup water

1 (8-ounce) can pineapple tidbits

1 tablespoon lemon juice

Dash salt (optional)

WAYLAND FLOWERS 1939–1988

WAYLAND FLOWERS GAVE THE WORLD MADAME, the saucy, man-hungry puppet who liked to say that it didn't matter that Flowers wasn't much of a ventriloquist because she was "no f#@%ing dummy." The naughty old girl and her right-hand man found success in Las Vegas and in clubs across America with jokes like: "These are my summer diamonds. Some are diamonds. Some are not!" They scored on television as the center square on *The Hollywood Squares*, as guests on various specials (including one starring Bea Arthur, whose Vegetarian Breakfast recipe appears in Chapter 25), and as the centerpiece of the fondly remembered series, *Madame's Place*. Flowers gave life to other puppet characters too: Jiffy, Crazy Mary, Baby Smedley, but it was Madame who was the star. Their appearance in the film *Norman . . . Is That You?* was one of the few performances that you can actually get your hands on. His estate is working to see that Flowers' popularity blooms again, posthumously. As fans, we wait and munch his muffins.

wayland flowers's muffins

Preheat oven to 350°. Mix dry ingredients. Add orange rind, apples, raisins, and pecans. Set aside. In a separate bowl, beat eggs. Blend in honey, molasses, vanilla, and oil. Add orange juice and buttermilk to the egg mixture. Mix dry ingredients with egg mixture using as few strokes as possible to incorporate ingredients. Fill 24 muffin cups fitted with paper liners. Bake for 20–25 minutes.

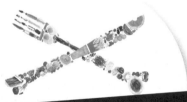

POST MORTEM

Made with mashed bananas and without paper liners, these are morning glorious and freeze quite well. Your family will love them. If you don't wake her too early, Madame will definitely approve, too.

Serves 24

2 cups whole wheat flour

1½ cups wheat bran

½ teaspoon salt

1¼ teaspoon baking soda

½ teaspoon nutmeg

1 tablespoon grated orange rind

1 apple, chopped (or 4 ripe bana.1as, whipped)

1 cup raisins

1 cup chopped pecans

2 eggs, beaten

½ cup molasses

⅓ cup honey

1 teaspoon vanilla

2 tablespoons cooking oil

Juice of one orange plus

Buttermilk to make 2 cups liquid

A S THE AUTHOR OF SUCH WORKS AS *Other Voices, Other Rooms*, *Breakfast at Tiffany's*, and *In Cold Blood*, Truman Capote was one of the greatest writers who ever put pen to paper, and he knew it. He had no patience for those he considered of lesser talents. "That's not writing, that's typing," Capote said of Jack Kerouac's *On the Road*. As his books scaled the best-seller lists and were made into movies, Capote became the toast of New York society. Eventually, being Truman Capote became his full-time job. But even at that, he excelled. Capote's 1966 Black and White Ball, held in honor of *Washington Post* publisher Katharine Graham, is considered to have been THE party of the twentieth century.

Capote, though, maintained that he didn't really like to give parties. "But if I'm going to do it, I really do it," he said. Later in his life, his so-called friends turned their backs on him, feeling their confidences had been betrayed in a series of articles he'd written. (These became the basis of his unfinished novel *Answered Prayers*.) Near the end, there were drunken talk show appearances and Capote became a caricature of himself. He was very funny, though, sending up his own swishiness as the mysterious Lionel Twain in the spy spoof *Murder by Death*. Capote also had a cameo in *Annie Hall*, playing a passerby whom Woody Allen calls "the winner of the Truman Capote look-alike contest." His fettuccine is the real thing.

Truman Capote's Fettuccine

1 pound fettuccine
  noodles

½ cup diced prosciutto

½ cup diced lean bacon

2 egg yolks

½ cup hot heavy cream

Salt, to taste

Freshly ground pepper,
  to taste

½ cup finely grated Gruyere
  or Parmesan cheese

Cook noodles in boiling salted water until al dente, about 8–9 minutes. Drain in colander and keep warm. Meanwhile, cook prosciutto and bacon over low heat until crisp and brown. Pour off half the fat. Toss noodles with prosciutto/bacon mixture. Add egg yolks, one at a time, tossing quickly. Add hot cream, season with salt and pepper, and toss. Sprinkle with grated cheese. Serves 2 or more.

NOTE: As with all traditional recipes for Fettuccine Alfredo, this dish contains a raw egg yolk "cooked" by only the heat of the pasta. If you don't want to eat raw egg, substitute a dollop of cream cheese.

peter aLLen 1944–1992

H E WAS KNOWN AS "THE BOY FROM OZ" and, for a time, "Mr. Liza Minnelli," because, yes, Australian singer/songwriter Peter Allen actually did have Judy Garland for a mother-in-law. But the tireless entertainer was too flamboyant even for that family. Allen sang about being "Bicoastal" at a time when that innuendo was actually provocative. The man co-wrote some amazing songs, including "I Honestly Love You," "Don't Cry Out Loud," "I'd Rather Leave While I'm in Love," all hits for other singers, and "Arthur's Theme (Best That You Can Do)," which was a smash for Christopher Cross and won Allen and his colleagues Oscars. He conquered Broadway in his own 1971 concert extravaganza *Up in One*, but his book musical *Legs Diamond* was a flop. As a singer, Allen didn't really have an impact on the United States charts. But his versions of "I Go to Rio," sort of a theme song for him, and "Everything Old Is New Again," which is featured in the film *All That Jazz*, are terrific. His snapper isn't so bad, either.

LasT BiTes

Allen made cameo appearances in a 1985 episode of *Miami Vice* and the 1978 film *Sgt. Pepper's Lonely Hearts Club Band*. His role in a 1982 British TV version of *Pirates of Penzance* was larger—he played the Pirate King. Shiver those timbers!

Peter Allen's Baked Snapper

Brush fish, inside and out, with lime juice, sprinkle lightly with salt, and chill for at least 4 hours before cooking. Place fish in a well-greased baking dish. Combine nuts, cheese, garlic, and onion. Add milk and mix to form a stiff paste. Season with salt and cayenne pepper. Stir in nutmeg, bay leaves, and sherry. Spread paste on fish, covering well. Sprinkle with bread crumbs and dot with butter. Bake in a 350° oven, basting occasionally, until browned and fish flakes easily with a fork.

1 whole five-pound red snapper, cleaned

Juice of 3 limes or 1½ lemons

½ teaspoon salt

3 cups chopped cashews, almonds, Brazil nuts, hazelnuts, or pecans

1 cup grated mild cheese

1 small clove garlic, crushed

1 small onion, grated

1 cup milk

Cayenne pepper, to taste

½ teaspoon grated nutmeg

2 bay leaves, finely crushed

¼ cup sherry or Madeira wine

1 cup dry fine bread crumbs

6 tablespoons butter

WHILE ANDY WARHOL DIDN'T LIVE into the twenty-first century, he knew exactly where our fame-obsessed culture was headed in it. A pop art painter and a pop culture philosopher, Warhol was more than just the guy who silkscreened celebrity portraits and painted soup cans, more than just the consummate collector of everything from cookie jars to Fiesta Ware, more than just the man who predicted that "in the future, everyone will be world-famous for fifteen minutes."

He embodied every decade in which he lived and worked. To fans like me, he was New York, even when he wasn't in it. I had lunch with Warhol once in Detroit, when he was there promoting his photo book *America*. I asked him how he'd managed to stay on the forefront of the avant-garde for thirty years. He said, "I don't know." Next question. I thought all was lost, but then we gossiped for an hour about everything from AIDS to Madonna's wedding to Sean Penn. It was my brush with greatness or at least with great gossip. Next time you find yourself in Pittsburgh, visit his museum. Until then, try making his stuffed cabbage. Warhol liked to make it for Halloween. He called it "ghoulish goulash." You'll call it "just great."

anDY WarHOL's STUFFeD caBBaGe

Remove core from cabbages. Separate six of the largest leaves from each head and wash under running water. Blanch cabbage by plunging leaves into a pot of boiling salted water. Cover and cook three minutes. Remove to a paper towel to drain. Mix together beef, rice, egg, parsley, lemon juice, salt, pepper, and ginger. Place 2–3 tablespoons of the meat-rice mixture in center of each leaf. Fold in corners to form a rectangle; roll up and secure with toothpicks or string. Repeat until all blanched leaves are filled. Brown cabbage rolls in butter and place in casserole. Stir broth and tomatoes into pan drippings and bring to a boil. Stir in sour cream. Pour sauce over cabbage rolls. Cover and bake in a preheated 350° oven for 1 hour. Serve immediately.

2 medium heads red cabbage

½ pound lean ground beef

2 cups cooked rice

1 egg, beaten

2 tablespoons chopped parsley

2 tablespoons fresh lemon juice

1 teaspoon salt

Freshly ground black pepper, to taste

½ teaspoon ground ginger or ¼ teaspoon finely grated ginger root

4 tablespoons butter

½ cup beef broth

2 cups ripe, fresh tomatoes, peeled

½ cup (or more) sour cream

Dirk Bogarde 1921–1999

H E WAS A MATINEE IDOL in Britain in the 1950s and made some very good (*Victim*) and some very silly (*Modesty Blaise*) films in the 1960s. But international actor Dirk Bogarde really assured his legacy when he took on some of the most challenging roles in some of the most controversial cinema of the late 1960s and early '70s. He most famously played a German industrialist in *The Damned*, an ex-Nazi in *The Night Porter*, and a lovesick composer with an eye for a certain young boy in *Death in Venice*. Some say his career would have been even greater if he'd done more to conceal his homosexuality. To hell with that! Bogarde made bold choices when it came to picking roles. Add *Darling* and *The Servant* to the list of his must-see films. And he had a second successful career as a memoirist. He left behind a lot, not the least of which is his paella recipe.

Last Bites

Bogarde became a star playing Dr. Simon Sparrow in a series of light comedies that were huge at the British box office. The 1954 film *Doctor in the House* was such a smash it spawned numerous sequels including *Doctor at Sea*, *Doctor at Large*, and *Doctor in Distress*. All four were released on DVD in 2011.

Dirk Bogarde's Spanish Paella

Cut the chicken and pork into small serving pieces. Fry the meat in hot oil and butter in a large shallow pan until golden brown, and then add the garlic and the onion. Allow to brown and then add the tomatoes, peppers, and the rice. Fry for about 2 minutes, and then add the boiling stock with the saffron and other seasonings. Chop the lobster into slices, but do not shell, and add to the dish with the prawns. Bring to boil, cover, and either cook on the top of the stove or in a hot oven (450°) for 20 minutes until the rice is tender, by which time all the stock should have been absorbed.

1 large young chicken

8 ounces lean pork

2 tablespoons olive oil

4 ounces butter

1 large clove garlic, crushed

1 large Spanish onion, finely chopped

3 large tomatoes, peeled and chopped

1 green pepper, chopped

1 sweet red pepper, chopped

1 pound medium grain rice

3¾ cups boiling chicken stock

½ teaspoon saffron

2 bay leaves

Salt and pepper, to taste

1 medium-size lobster

2½ cups shelled and deveined shrimp

M OST AMERICANS FIRST LAID EYES ON German countertenor Klaus Nomi when he sang backup for David Bowie in space drag on *Saturday Night Live* in 1979. It was not the kind of appearance one could easily forget. Combining opera, punk, new wave, '60s kitsch, and Weimar cabaret traditions, Nomi created a wholly original body of work in the late '70s and early '80s. His biggest songs, *hits* is too strong a word, were "Total Eclipse," a catchy ditty about nuclear holocaust, a très gay remake of the Lesley Gore single "You Don't Own Me," and a version of "Ding Dong! The Witch Is Dead" that would've knocked the striped socks off the Wicked Witch of the East. In Andrew Horn's 2005 documentary *The Nomi Song: The Klaus Nomi Odyssey*, fans learned that Nomi was an accomplished baker. His renowned lime tart, some say, was even tastier than his music.

Klaus Nomi's Lime Tart

To make the crust, combine crumbs, sugar, and melted butter in a bowl and mix until well blended. Press firmly into 9-inch pie pan and chill. To make the filling, beat egg yokes in a medium bowl. Then add milk and beat. Pour in lime juice and beat until it thickens like pudding. In a separate bowl, beat egg whites until stiff and then fold into the above mixture. Pour into pie shell. Garnish with thin strips of lime zest. Chill in refrigerator overnight and serve.

Crust:

1¼ cups fine graham cracker crumbs

⅓ cup brown sugar

¼ cup melted butter

Filling:

4 eggs, separated

1 can sweetened condensed milk

½ cup lime juice

AFTER-DINNER VIEWING

A GAY OLD TIME

Leonard Frey's performance as the self-described "Jew fairy" in *The Boys in the Band* drips with self-loathing, but it, like the movie, is something to behold. To enjoy Wayland Flowers and Madame on video, you've got to dig out the VCR and pick up a VHS copy of the comedy *Norman . . . Is That You?* starring Redd Foxx, whose spaghetti sauce recipe is in Chapter 19. Christine Jorgensen is the subject of a 2006 *Biography* installment available on DVD. Truman Capote's appearance in *Murder by Death* is a bloody scream. The documentary *Peter Allen: The Boy from Oz* gives you a good glimpse at the fabulousness of the man. Andy Warhol's legendary appearance on *The Love Boat* sadly isn't out yet, but you can learn plenty by watching *Andy Warhol: A Documentary Film*, narrated by Laurie Anderson. There's a ton of Dirk Bogarde movies to enjoy; *Death in Venice* will blow your mind. Finally, for fans of Klaus Nomi, the music documentary *Urgh! A Music War* is required viewing for anyone who ever worried about the effects of the atom bomb on looking fabulous.

a PSYCHO SHOWER

MOTHER WARNED YOU NOT TO FEED HER. "You won't be appeasing her ugly appetite with MY food!" she said. But Norman, you did it anyway. First you brought Marion a nice sandwich and a cold pitcher of milk, told her she ate like a bird, and then, when she least expected it, you sent a whole lot of chocolate sauce swirling down her bathtub drain. Norm, you all but ruined taking a shower, not to mention enjoying Hershey's Syrup, for anyone who has ever seen *Psycho*, which is, or should be, everyone!

The classic 1960 film, which defied movie conventions by killing off the star early on, still has the power to unnerve audiences. As Roger Ebert said, "No other Hitchcock film had a greater impact." The film is truly warped. The shick-shick-shick of the windshield wipers in the rain. The taxidermy. The reet-reet-reet of the Bernard Herrmann music underscoring the murder scene. The swinging light bulb casting shadows in Mother's eyes. Martin Balsam. Together it's enough to ruin a girl's appetite. Certainly Marion Crane wouldn't be eating any more sandwiches after her night at the Bates Motel.

Is it just me or wouldn't it be fun to throw a *Psycho*-themed shower? You'd have to thrown it for the right person, of course—say your kookiest, horror movie–loving gal-pal—and it would have to be done right. Otherwise everyone would think *you're* the psycho. Here's what you can do: rent out every room of a decrepit motel in the desert, decorate the rooms with taxidermy, pray for rain . . . wait a minute, that's just too involved. Here's another plan: invite the dear and some of her friends over to your house; fix the recipes of the film's stars, and Mr. Hitchcock's famous quiche, too; and pop a copy of the movie into your player. It's much simpler and the film is killer on Blu-ray.

anthony perkins 1932–1992

W HAT DOES IT SAY ABOUT AN ACTOR who is perfectly cast as the sexually fractured serial killer Norman Bates? Anthony Perkins spent his career and three sequels to *Psycho* trying to figure that out. A successful Broadway actor, Perkins was both desirable and creepy, which made him irresistible to audience members (and fellow cast members). He's great in the TV productions *Evening Primrose*, a Stephen Sondheim musical out on DVD for the first time in 2010, and *How Awful About Allan*, and in the theatrical films *Desire Under the Elms*, starring Sophia Loren, *Pretty Poison* with Tuesday Weld, and *Mahogany*, opposite Diana Ross. He's great in *The Life and Times of Judge Roy Bean* and *Murder on the Orient Express*, too. And if you thought his Norman Bates was weird, you have to see Perkins as the voyeuristic, poppers-sniffing reverend in Ken Russell's kinky thriller *Crimes of Passion*, with Kathleen Turner in the lead. Norman was a delight in comparison.

anthony perkins's tuna salad

Place tuna into a salad bowl and break up with a fork. Add celery, onion, and mayonnaise and gently mix to combine. Season with black pepper. Squeeze lemon juice over all and mix thoroughly. Serve on lettuce leaves.

1 can chunk white tuna, drained

Serves 2

1 stalk celery, chopped fine

¼ onion, minced

2 heaping tablespoons mayonnaise

Black pepper, to taste

Juice of half a lemon

Lettuce leaves

aLFreD HiTCHCOCK 1899–1980

I N MORE THAN HALF A CENTURY OF FILMMAKING, Alfred Hitchcock gave moviegoers more scares (and more subsequent laughs) than perhaps any other filmmaker. His many classic pictures read like a history of suspense in the movies: *The 39 Steps, North by Northwest, Rear Window, Vertigo, Rope, The Man Who Knew Too Much, The Trouble with Harry, The Birds, Psycho.* The roly-poly Brit made cameo appearances in his films, and much was made of his corpulence. "I'm not a heavy eater," Hitch once said. "I'm just heavy and I eat." His love of food and his love of mayhem came together best in a 1958 episode of *Alfred Hitchcock Presents* called "Lamb to the Slaughter" in which a wife (Barbara Bel Geddes) murders her philandering husband with a frozen leg of lamb, then cooks the murder weapon and serves it to the policemen investigating the crime. It was written by Roald Dahl, but it's classic Hitchcock. Stick with Hitch's quiche at home, though, it's safer.

POST MOrTem

My chief taster lamented the lack of cheese and called this quiche no better than "bacon and eggs in a pie shell." But as brunch-by-the-slice, it's pretty delicious, and not even Norman Bates will kill you for using a store-bought crust.

aLFreD HiTCHCOCK'S QUiCHe Lorraine

To make the crust, work together pastry flour, butter, egg yolk, salt, and cold water. Chill dough 1 hour, or until needed. Roll out half the dough to line a 10-inch pie pan. Crimp edges and prick crust with a fork. (Reserve rest of dough for another use.) For filling, scatter diced ham on the crust. Sauté onions in butter until they are soft, but not brown. Spread over ham. In a saucepan, beat 4 eggs with salt, cayenne, and nutmeg. Gradually add 2 cups hot milk, beating with a wire whisk. Continue to beat the mixture over a low heat until the custard begins to thicken. Pour it into the pastry shell and bake at 375° for 30 minutes or until the custard is set and the top is golden.

Serves 6

Crust:

2 cups pastry flour

½ cup butter

1 egg yolk

1 pinch salt

¼ cup cold water

Filling:

2 or 3 slices ham, diced

2 onions, chopped

4 eggs

Pinch salt

Pinch cayenne

Pinch nutmeg

2 cups hot milk

G ORGEOUS AND TALENTED JANET LEIGH is best remembered for her role as the thieving Marion Crane in *Psycho*, but she made very fun pictures in a variety of genres. She appeared in the musicals *My Sister Eileen* and *Bye Bye Birdie*, the thrillers *Touch of Evil* and *The Manchurian Candidate* and the horror films *The Fog* and *Halloween H20: Twenty Years Later*, the last two with her daughter from her marriage to Tony Curtis, Jamie Lee Curtis. Leigh was considered Hollywood's "No. 1 glamour girl" for a time in the late '40s. But the unglamorous role of murder victim in *Psycho* gave her cinematic immortality. Leigh wrote a couple of memoirs, *There Really Was a Hollywood* was a bestseller in the '80s; and she did her share of guest shots on such TV shows as *Columbo*, *Murder, She Wrote,* and *Fantasy Island*. In any role, her beauty was as golden as her gâteau.

Janet Leigh's Gâteau Doré

Serves 8

½ cup butter

1 cup sugar

4 egg yolks, lightly beaten

1 teaspoon vanilla

½ cup milk

2 cups cake flour

3 teaspoons baking powder

Preheat oven to 350°. Cream butter well, then add sugar, and continue beating. Add yolks and vanilla and mix thoroughly. Then add milk alternately with the flour and baking powder mixture. Beat until smooth. Pour into greased and floured loaf pan. Bake 35–45 minutes. Serve with ice cream.

POST MORTEM

There's no reason not to further gild this golden *gâteau.* Despite the fancy name, it is just a yellow cake. Serve slices not only with vanilla ice cream on the side but also with some fruit—Clementine sections are a sunny accompaniment—and drizzle it all with warm caramel sauce.

after-dinner viewing

all *PSYCHO*, all night

If your hunger for Norman Bates runs deep, you can spend the night with him if you dare. He's a character in about ten hours of *Psycho*, its sequels, and its remake, all available on DVD. His saga starts with Hitchcock's 1960 masterpiece *Psycho*, which was based on a novel by Robert Bloch. Twenty-three years later Norman Bates (and Anthony Perkins) returned in *Psycho II*, which proved that more than two decades of therapy weren't enough to cure this sick puppy. There's still trouble at the Bates Motel in 1986's *Psycho III*, which Perkins not only starred in but also directed. Diana Scarwid of *Mommie Dearest* is the female lead. Then there was the 1990 TV movie, *Psycho IV: The Beginning*, in which Henry Thomas, so cute in *E.T.: The Extra-Terrestrial*, plays a young Norman Bates. Finally, almost forty years after the original, there's Gus Van Sant's shot-for-shot remake starring Vince Vaughn (who's not nearly pansexual enough) and Anne Heche (who would have made a better Norman). It's a curiosity worth watching if only to say you have seen it.

aLL-DAY
TV TraY

I T'S A FANTASY. Calling in sick to work and lounging on the couch in footy pajamas all day, watching television from morning til night, a snack tray at the ready for every meal that comes my way. There is no dog to walk in my dream. No e-mails to answer. No phone to ring. It's just me and my classic TV, and course after course of delicious food. What would I eat on my all-day TV tray? I'd start with a Beverly Hills (by way of the Ozarks) breakfast: delicately rendered eggs with a side of country cornbread. A few hours later, I'd pop in on a certain ad man's wife—her relatives are always doing that so she won't mind—and have some elegant edibles. Next, I'd set off on a three-hour tour of the tropics aboard a tiny ship, breaking bread with a millionaire and his wife. And, because I'd be hungry again after awhile—that was one long three-hour tour—I'd wind up my day down on the farm for, surprise of surprises, a European dinner with a gentleman farmer, his glamorous Hungarian wife, and one very smart pig named Arnold. The calories wouldn't count either. I *told* you this is my fantasy. If it's yours too, these recipes will help. But the bit about the calories not counting? Don't bet on it.

ALL-DAY TV TRAY

BUDDY EBSEN 1908–2003

ACTOR AND HOOFER BUDDY EBSEN DANCED in vaudeville with his sister Vilma and was so good that he made the leap to motion picture musicals. He almost was the Tin Man in the classic 1939 version of *The Wizard of Oz*, but his allergic reaction to the aluminum dust in his silver makeup made him quit. Instead, after a stint on the TV series *Disneyland* as Davy Crockett's sidekick, Ebsen's break came when he was cast as Jed Clampett, the poor mountaineer who struck it rich when he found oil, "black gold, Texas tea," as the theme song said, on his property on *The Beverly Hillbillies*. The rural '60s sitcom ran for nine seasons, pulling in some of the highest ratings episodic television has ever known. Ebsen followed that up in the 1970s with eight seasons of crime drama as the elderly, milk-drinking detective Barnaby Jones. In a strange twist, he made a cameo as Barnaby Jones in the 1993 big-screen version of *The Beverly Hillbillies*. He made a noteworthy film appearance as Doc, the rural veterinarian who comes looking for his estranged wife Holly Golightly in the big-city world of *Breakfast at Tiffany's*. Whoa doggies, was Ebsen good in that!

BUDDY EBSEN'S CHIFFON EGGS

2 eggs

2 tablespoons butter

1 pinch garlic salt

Beat two eggs with whisk. Heat butter in a non-stick skillet. When the skillet is hot, pour eggs in and sprinkle with garlic salt. With a plastic spatula, gently and continuously stir the eggs so the inside remains soft. Do not let the eggs harden. As soon as they're cooked just enough that they can be removed from the pan, transfer the eggs to a hot plate and serve.

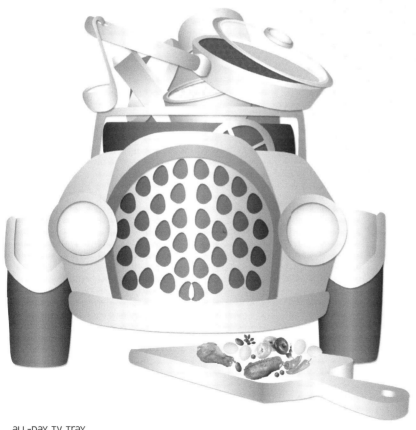

ALL-DAY TV TRAY

I RENE RYAN FOUND SUCCESS IN VAUDEVILLE (doing a double act with her first husband), on radio (with Bob Hope), in film, and on television before hitting paydirt as Granny on *The Beverly Hillbillies*. She may have been little, but she was big enough to push that galoot Jethro (Max Baer Jr.) around, and still find time to make moonshine out behind her mansion. So identified with Granny Clampett, Ryan took that role to two other series as well, playing the character on both *Mister Ed* and *Petticoat Junction*. Her other big role was on Broadway in the 1973 Stephen Schwartz musical *Pippin*, starring Ben Vereen and directed by Bob Fosse. If theatre lore is correct, she had a stroke during a performance of that musical. She was nominated for but didn't win a Tony Award that year. After her death, she left a million dollars to a foundation that created a scholarship for theatre students in her name. Granny Clampett lives on, and so does her Spicy Corn Bread recipe.

Irene Ryan's Spicy Corn Bread

Preheat oven to 400°. In a large bowl, mix all ingredients together until well blended. Pour into a greased 8-inch-square baking pan and bake for 40 minutes or until lightly browned.

1 cup white or yellow corn meal

1 can creamed corn

2 eggs, beaten

¾ cup milk

½ cup grated cheddar cheese

1 onion, chopped fine

1 tablespoon taco sauce

½ cup melted butter, plus more to grease the pan

1 teaspoon baking powder

1 teaspoon salt

POST MORTEM

Granny Clampett never used Sriracha sauce to lend heat to hers, but I did. These vittles will keep guests coming back for more, so make enough. If you want to cut some of the fat, leave out the butter. Jethro will never know the difference.

S HE HAD THE BEST EYE MAKEUP on '60s television, but the brilliant character actress Agnes Moorehead was so much more than Endora, the mischievous mother-in-law in Cleopatra's mascara on *Bewitched*. Moorehead did *The Shadow* and other classic programs on radio, then in the 1930s, became a compatriot of Orson Welles and his Mercury Theatre. Welles cast her in his infamous radio play *War of the Worlds* and in the classic films *Citizen Kane* and *The Magnificent Ambersons*. Later she appeared in such well-regarded melodramas as 1944's *Since You Went Away* and the Douglas Sirk gems *Magnificent Obsession* and *All That Heaven Allows* in the '50s. Her dialogue-free performance on the 1961 *Twilight Zone* episode "The Invaders,"

as an old woman tormented by little men from another planet, is genius. And you really do need to see her in *The Singing Nun*, *Hush ... Hush, Sweet Charlotte*, and *What's the Matter with Helen?* too. None of Moorehead's stellar performances really needs a nosh to go with it, but a mousse with this pedigree couldn't hurt.

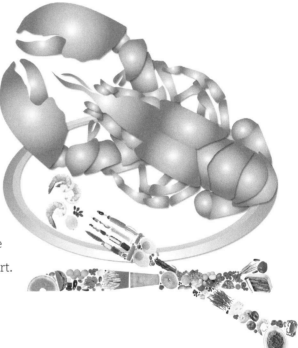

agnes moorehead's lobster mousse

Put lobster meat in a food processor and process until smooth. Sprinkle
lightly with lemon juice. Place in a bowl
and season to taste with salt, white
pepper, and nutmeg. Gradually beat in
cream and sherry with wire whisk. In a
separate bowl, beat egg whites until stiff
but not dry. Gently fold in egg whites
to lobster mixture. Butter a large deep
mold. Turn lobster mixture into mold
and place in a pan filled with hot water.
Garnish with whole peeled shrimp. Bake
in a preheated 350° oven for 20 minutes
or until firm. Let cool a few moments
before turning out on to a large heated
platter. Garnish with parsley and lemon
wedges.

1 pound fresh lobster meat

Few drops fresh lemon juice

Salt, to taste

White pepper, to taste

Pinch of nutmeg

¾ cup heavy cream

2 tablespoons dry sherry

3 egg whites

Butter (to grease mold)

12 peeled shrimp

Handful parsley sprigs

Lemon wedges

eLizaBeTH MonTGomerY 1933–1995

THE DAUGHTER OF ACTORS Robert Montgomery and Elizabeth Bryan Allen, Elizabeth Montgomery appeared on lots of TV shows in the '50s and '60s: *Alfred Hitchcock Presents, Thriller,* and *The Untouchables,* before finding the role that would become synonymous with her name: housewife, mother, and witch Samantha Stephens on *Bewitched.* She survived eight seasons, two Darrins, and more annoying aunts and uncles than anyone should ever have to deal with, and always looked great doing it. And don't forget, Montgomery played both the blonde beauty Samantha and her bad-girl brunette cousin Serena. After *Bewitched,* Montgomery conquered the TV movie form with such '70s tele-films as *A Case of Rape, The Legend of Lizzie Borden,* and an update of the Bette Davis classic *Dark Victory.* She continued working in the genre right up until her death, notably playing real-life journalist Edna Buchanan in *The Corpse Had a Familiar Face* and *Deadline for Murder.* A statue of Samantha Stephens stands in Salem, Massachusetts. This dish would feel right at home there.

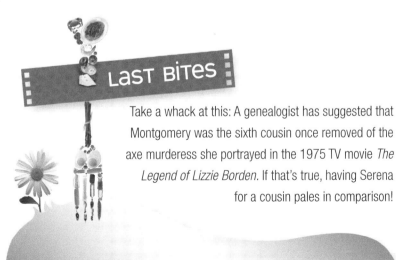

LaST BiTes

Take a whack at this: A genealogist has suggested that Montgomery was the sixth cousin once removed of the axe murderess she portrayed in the 1975 TV movie *The Legend of Lizzie Borden.* If that's true, having Serena for a cousin pales in comparison!

eLiZaBeTH MOnTGOMeRY'S POTTeD SHrimP

Serves 6
as an
appetizer

1 pound cooked
   bay shrimp

½ pound butter, softened

1 tablespoon lemon juice

½ teaspoon ground mace

Pinch cayenne

Pinch black pepper

Pinch salt

Toast triangles, for serving

Chop half the shrimp and reserve. Place the other half of the shrimp in a food processor. Add half the butter and the lemon juice and puree to a paste. Stir the reserved shrimp into the paste and add seasonings. Press the mixture into a 3-cup mold or serving dish. Melt the remaining butter and pour into the mold. Refrigerate until the butter is firm. Unmold or not and serve with warm toast triangles.

Dick Sargent 1930–1994

A LTHOUGH HE WAS SAID TO HAVE BEEN the first choice for the role of the advertising man married to a witch, Dick Sargent became the second Darrin Stephens when he replaced Dick York in 1969. Lanky and likeable, Sargent had done some decent films like *Operation Petticoat* and *That Touch of Mink* and some deliciously dreadful ones like *Billie* and *The Ghost and Mr. Chicken* before achieving true stardom on *Bewitched*. In the decades that followed, he did one-offs on series from *Ellery Queen* to *Vegas* to *Family Ties*. Playing a sleazeball in Paul Schrader's 1979 film *Hardcore*, which starred George C. Scott, garnered him good notices. Late in life, he came out as a gay man, calling himself a "retroactive role model" in the fight for equality. He and Elizabeth Montgomery were the grand marshals of the Los Angeles Gay Pride Parade in June 1992. His Chinese Chicken Salad would work quite nicely at your next pre-parade brunch, gay or otherwise.

Dick Sargent's Chinese Chicken Salad

Combine oil, vinegar, sugar, and pepper, shaking well to mix. Set aside. Deep fry rice sticks until light brown. Combine chicken, lettuce, nuts, cilantro, green onions, sesame seeds and rice sticks just before serving. Toss with dressing, and add salt and pepper to taste.

¼ cup oil

2 to 3 tablespoons vinegar

2 tablespoons sugar

½ teaspoon pepper

2 ounces rice sticks

½ pound cooked and shredded chicken breast

1 small head of lettuce, shredded

2 tablespoons toasted almonds or peanuts

2–3 tablespoons chopped cilantro

4 green onions, chopped

2 tablespoons toasted sesame seeds

Salt and pepper, to taste

POST Mortem

Feel free to use peanut oil for a more Asian flavor and substitute a blend of finely shredded Napa and red cabbage for the lettuce. In your own kitchen, you definitely outrank a Sargent.

NaTaLie schaFer 1900–1991

S HE HAD BEEN TYPECAST AS FUSTY AND WELL-TO-DO, playing
charm school teacher Phoebe Emerson on *I Love Lucy,* for instance, long
before she was cast as the millionaire's wife Lovey Wentworth Howell on *Gilligan's Island*. But for Natalie Schafer, that sitcom's "three-hour tour" gone
awry became her life's work. Schafer reprised her signature role not only in
such TV movies as 1981's *The Harlem Globetrotters on Gilligan's Island*, but
also in animated form on 1982's space-age redo *Gilligan's Planet*. That's dedication! A successful Broadway and film actress before *Gilligan*, Schafer was
a supporting player in *The Snake Pit* with Olivia de Havilland, *Female on the
Beach* with Joan Crawford, and *Anastasia* with Ingrid Bergman. After the TV
show that immortalized her, Schafer appeared in two films I adore, *40 Carats*
and *The Day of the Locust*. Many remember her from a guest shot on *The
Brady Bunch*, as a client of Mike's who is mistaken for a talent scout. Schafer
never did answer the burning question: where did Lovey get all those clothes
if she was only supposed to be gone a few hours? She took that secret to her
grave. She left her tuna salad recipe, though.

Natalie Schafer's Tuna Salad

Mix all ingredients and spread thickly on lightly toasted bread that has been spread on one side with mayonnaise. Put under broiler until slightly brown and heated through. Any leftover mixture can be used as a salad.

1 (8 ounce) can tuna

Mayonnaise, for spreading

2 chopped hard-boiled eggs

1 green pepper, finely chopped

Few green onions, finely chopped

Worcestershire sauce, to taste

4 slices white sandwich bread, lightly toasted

Jim Backus 1913–1989

HOW'S THIS FOR BEING A POP CULTURE GIANT? Not only did Jim Backus play Thurston Howell III on *Gilligan's Island* and its many reincarnations, he was also the voice of the very nearsighted Mr. Magoo on a long-running series of cartoons. Backus's other regular TV roles included Judge Bradley Stevens on *I Married Joan*; Mr. Dithers, Dagwood's boss, on a sitcom remake of *Blondie*; and the star of his own show, *Hot Off the Wire*. He appeared in some classic movies: *Rebel Without a Cause, Pat and Mike,* and *It's a Mad, Mad, Mad, Mad World,* as well as in such cult favorites as *Myra Breckenridge, Crazy Mama, Friday Foster,* the musical remake of *The Women* called *The Opposite Sex,* and the children's picture *Pete's Dragon.* But for all he did, Backus will be remembered best as the shipwrecked millionaire with a taste for the finer things in life. Off screen, his tastes were more common, like his favorite chili.

Last Bites

Margaret Hamilton who played the Wicked Witch of the West in *The Wizard of Oz* was Jim Backus's grade school teacher. If she'd taught him how to ride a broom, he might have gotten off that island a lot sooner!

Jim Backus's Chili

Serves 4

Brown onion, peppers, garlic, and meat in bacon fat until brown and crumbly. Add tomatoes, beans, salt, cloves, bay leaf, and chili powder. Bring to a boil. Then cook over very low heat for about 2½ hours, stirring occasionally. To thicken, leave the lid off until it reaches desired thickness. Serve with saltines and sour cream.

1 pound ground round

1 medium onion, chopped

1 large green pepper, chopped

2 cloves garlic, minced

3 tablespoons bacon fat

1½ cans kidney beans, drained

1½ cans whole tomatoes

1½ teaspoons salt

3 whole cloves

1 bay leaf

3 tablespoons chili powder

H E WAS THE GILLIGAN OF *Gilligan's Island*, of course, but Bob Denver already had a place in TV history before he was marooned. He was the beloved beatnik Maynard G. Krebs for four seasons on the Dwayne Hickman sitcom *The Many Loves of Dobie Gillis* from 1959 to 1963. In the 1970s, he starred in two fondly remembered (but really quite terrible) series about being lost, *Dusty's Trail* (which was basically *Gilligan's Island* set on a wagon train in the Old West), and *Far Out Space Nuts* (a Saturday morning comedy from the *H. R. Pufnstuf* guys Sid and Marty Krofft). But so synonymous with Gilligan was Denver that he played the bumbler in the bucket hat not only in sequels to the original *Gilligan's Island*, but also on a handful of other series including *Baywatch* and *ALF*. Late in his life, he was charged with marijuana possession. Maybe he was more like Maynard than Gilligan in real life. In any case, his beans will get you through a case of the munchies.

BOB Denver's Denver Beans

Drain beans but reserve juices. Mix all ingredients, except the bean juices and the oil. Refrigerate the mixture (and the reserved juices) overnight. A half hour before serving, toss with the vegetable oil and 2 cups of the reserved juices.

1 can kidney beans

1 can French-cut green beans

1 can garbanzo beans

1 can yellow wax beans

1 purple onion, thinly sliced

¾ cup cider vinegar

¾ cup sugar

1 teaspoon soy sauce

1 teaspoon celery salt

½ teaspoon salt

½ teaspoon pepper

¼ cup vegetable oil

POST Mortem

I'm with Denver all the way to *Gilligan's Island*, but the thought of adding canned bean juice to the dish right before serving leaves me seasick. Leave it out—Mom always did—and you'll be fine.

eva GaBor 1919–1995

S HE WAS KNOWN AS "THE GOOD GABOR," but really she was the best, which makes it especially sad that Eva Gabor bought the farm before her two sisters. Before she was the gorgeous blonde (and wig magnate) on her friend Merv Griffin's arm, Gabor played the delightfully ditzy Lisa Douglas on *Green Acres*, the most surreal (and thus most timeless) of the CBS rural comedies of the 1960s. Lisa would have preferred Park Avenue, but the New York socialite with the Budapest accent was a dutiful wife so she took her leopard print couch and followed her gentleman farmer husband to Hooterville. She guest-starred on episodes of *Beverly Hillbillies* and *Petticoat Junction*, too. Other TV work included appearances on both the '60s and '90s versions of *Burke's Law*, and a very funny turn on *Here's Lucy*. For someone with a sister who's famous for being famous (and slapping a cop), Eva Gabor had an impressive resume. She did Broadway and appeared in some movies—*The Last Time I Saw Paris*, *My Man Godfrey*, and *Gigi*, among them—and she was a voice actor in three Disney classics. She was deliciously feline in *The Aristocats* and played the adorable, adventurous mouse Miss Bianca in both *The Rescuers* and *The Rescuers Down Under*. Her goulash will transport you.

eva GaBor's HunGarian GouLasH

In a large covered casserole or Dutch oven, melt lard over medium heat. Add the onions and cook until transparent, about 5 minutes. Add the meats and continue cooking until no longer pink, about 10 minutes, stirring often. Remove from heat and set aside. Crush the garlic and grind in a food processor with the caraway seeds and salt until a thick paste is formed. Add to the meat and stir in the paprika. Put the pot on medium heat, add the water, and bring to a simmer. Lower the heat and slowly cook until the soup has thickened, about 1 hour. Add the tomatoes, peppers, and potatoes to the pot, season with salt to taste and continue cooking until the potatoes are tender, about 20 more minutes. Add water if necessary, to obtain the consistency of a hearty soup. To make the dumplings, combine the egg, flour, and salt in a small bowl. Mix with a fork until a soft dough forms. Just before serving, spoon the mixture into the boiling soup, ¼ teaspoon at a time. Cook for 2–3 minutes, then ladle into warmed bowls and serve immediately.

2 tablespoons lard

2 medium onions, chopped

2½ pounds beef chuck or round, cut into ¾-inch cubes

½ pound beef heart, cut into ¾-inch cubes

1 garlic clove

½ teaspoon caraway seeds

¼ teaspoon salt

2 tablespoons imported sweet Hungarian paprika

2½ quarts water

1 medium tomato, peeled and diced

2 green or Italian frying peppers, cored and sliced

3 to 4 medium potatoes, peeled and diced

Salt, to taste

Dumplings:

1 egg

3 tablespoons flour

Pinch salt

EDDIE ALBERT BEGAN WRITING FOR AND ACTING on television in the dawn of the medium in the 1930s. Throughout his very long career, he hosted radio programs, starred on Broadway in such shows as *The Boys from Syracuse*, *The Seven Year Itch*, and *The Music Man*, and made plenty of movies including *Oklahoma!*, *The Longest Day*, and *Roman Holiday*, for which he was nominated for an Oscar. Albert became a household name in the '60s when he was cast as attorney-turned-farmer Oliver Wendell Douglas on *Green Acres*, suffering the fools of Hooterville none too gladly. After *Green Acres*, he made the film *The Heartbreak Kid* and received his second Academy Award nomination. In 1975, he began his second hit series *Switch*, a light-hearted crime drama opposite Robert Wagner and featuring Sharon Gless. His handsome son Edward was an accomplished actor himself, but sadly died at fifty-five shortly after his father did. The elder Albert shared one thing with his *Green Acres* character: they both loved nature. *TV Guide* once called the environmentally concerned actor "an ecological Paul Revere" for his activism. Serve his flan outdoors, if you like.

eddie aLBert's FLan

6 tablespoons sugar

4 tablespoons water

5 eggs

1 cup water

1 teaspoon vanilla

1 can (14 ounces) sweetened
condensed milk

Make caramel by cooking sugar and water over moderately high heat, stirring occasionally, until it reaches a light nut-brown color, about 3–4 minutes. Line a warm, lightly greased 9- or 10-inch pie plate with caramel, working quickly using a swirling motion to coat dish evenly. Set aside. In a large bowl, beat eggs, and then add water and vanilla and beat well. Add condensed milk and beat again. Pour this mixture into caramel-coated dish. Place the pie plate in a larger pan, half filled with hot water. Bake at 350° for 1 hour 15 minutes, or until set. When cool, turn flan over onto a serving plate.

aFTer-DInner VIeWInG

IncreDIBLe IneDIBLes

The last Thursday in November at the Clampett mansion is anything but traditional. In "Turkey Day," a season-two episode of *The Beverly Hillbillies*, the turkey becomes a pet named Herman instead of, as Granny says, "Thanksgiving vittles."

Be careful what you nosh for. In the *Bewitched* season-five episode "Samantha's French Pastry," Uncle Arthur (played by Paul Lynde, whose beef stew recipe appears in Chapter 19) conjures up Napoleon Bonaparte instead of the layered dessert named for the French general.

Gilligan was just fishing when he hooked a floating case of garden seeds in the season-three episode of *Gilligan's Island* called "Pass the Vegetables, Please." Trouble is that the seeds are radioactive and not only grow at an enormous rate but also give those who eat the veggies super powers.

Don't go to *Green Acres* looking for dessert, unless it's Eddie Albert's flan. In the season-one episode "Lisa Bakes a Cake," the dizzy Hungarian tries to make a twenty-pound cake, using a hammer to separate the eggs and a scissors to divide the dough.

sitcom moms really cook

EVERY TRUE TV LOVER HAS A SITCOM MOM—the mother who most reminds him of his own. Whether it's the guilt-inducing half-pint Ida Morgenstern of *Rhoda* or the supersized-but-sensible Mabel "Mama" Thomas on *What's Happening!!*, there is always a TV stand-in for the woman who brought a fellow into this world. My sitcom mom was always Lily Munster, the matriarch of *The Munsters*. Not only did the actress who played her, Yvonne De Carlo, have a last name similar to mine, she had a certain other-worldly glamour that my mother possessed. My mother owned a beauty parlor. When Lily went into business in my favorite episode "The Most Beautiful Ghoul in the World," what did she open? You guessed it, a salon. The goings on behind the ghastly gargoyle door knockers at 1313 Mockingbird Lane were like watching home movies for me. In the kitchen, my real mom and my sitcom mom shared one trait for better or worse. Both women were family-pleasing cooks, but they took shortcuts. It was the '60s and everyone did in those days, I guess. When Lily made a tossed fruit salad, she did so not by cutting up fresh fruit, but by hurling it whole into a huge bowl across the room. My mother never tried that—she just opened a can of fruit cocktail—and as best I can remember, my mother's popovers never popped all over the dining room the way Lily's did. (But there was a French dressing incident that left our kitchen looking like a Jackson Pollock painting.) In any case, this chapter is a salute to the women who raised us on TV. Any of their recipes would be a fabulous Mother's Day treat for your real mom.

Nancy Walker 1922–1992

N O ONE, NOT EVEN MOLLY GOLDBERG, made a better Jewish mother on television than Nancy Walker did on *The Mary Tyler Moore Show* and *Rhoda*. As Ida Morgenstern, she could play the guilt card like a pro, and cut anyone down to her size, which actually was very little for such a big presence. The daughter of a vaudevillian, Walker was a hit on Broadway in such shows as *On The Town,* famously singing "I Can Cook, Too!" as the horny cabdriver, and was twice nominated for the Tony Award. Besides her role as Rhoda's mother, Walker played the housekeeper on *McMillan & Wife* and was equally well-known as Rosie, the diner waitress who raved about the strength of Bounty paper towels, the so-called "quicker picker-upper." Two attempts at her own sitcom, *The Nancy Walker Show* and *Blansky's Beauties*, were failures, but Walker endured. Her strangest credit? She directed the Village People movie, *Can't Stop the Music*. Only God could stop Nancy Walker.

Nancy Walker's Chicken à La Nancy

Blanch asparagus in boiling water for five minutes, then drain. Place asparagus in a buttered oblong baking dish. Place chicken breasts on top of asparagus, and cover with cream, butter, and mushrooms. Season with salt and pepper, and sprinkle cheese over all. Put a dash of paprika on top. Bake at 350° for 40 minutes, or until chicken is cooked through.

Serves 6

2 bunches fresh asparagus

6 boneless chicken breasts

1 cup cream

4 tablespoons butter

1 cup fresh sliced mushrooms

Salt and pepper, to taste

½ cup grated Parmesan cheese

Dash of paprika

Y VONNE DE CARLO WAS SO BEAUTIFUL playing Moses' wife Sephora in *The Ten Commandments* that they named a chain of makeup boutiques after her. Okay, that's not true. But De Carlo was about as glamorous a B-movie queen as there ever was. Before the Canadian-born actress was immortalized as Lily, the drop-dead gorgeous mother of TV's *The Munsters*, she appeared in such memorable films as *Brute Force* and *Criss Cross*, both starring Burt Lancaster, *Sea Devils*, opposite Rock Hudson, *Band of Angels*, featuring Clark Gable, and *McLintock!* with John Wayne. After *The Munsters* was cancelled following its second season, De Carlo's movie options were rel-

egated to such cult fare as *Blazing Stewardesses*, *Satan's Cheerleaders*, and *American Gothic*. But on stage, she had a major triumph. Cast as Carlotta Campion in the original Broadway cast of *Follies*, she sang Stephen Sondheim's classic ode to survival, "I'm Still Here." De Carlo's not here anymore. But happily, her recipe for Exotic Chicken Ecstasy endures.

yvonne De carlo's exotic chicken ecstasy

Serves 4

Sprinkle chicken with salt and pepper. Heat oil in a Dutch oven and sauté chicken until golden brown. Top the chicken with celery, cabbage, chop suey vegetables, and drained pineapple. Cover and simmer for 25 minutes. Place cornstarch, ginger powder, and chutney powder in a mixing bowl. Combine pineapple juice, water, soy sauce, and sherry wine, and gradually add to dry ingredients in mixing bowl, stirring constantly until cornstarch is dissolved. Pour cornstarch mixture over chicken and vegetables in casserole. Stir, cover tightly and simmer for another ten minutes; serve at once over hot steamed rice.

1 (2½ pound) chicken, cut into 10 pieces

5 tablespoons vegetable oil

1 stalk celery, sliced

¼ cup Chinese cabbage, shredded

1 can chop suey vegetables

½ can pineapple tidbits (drained, juice reserved)

2 heaping teaspoons cornstarch

1½ cups water

¼ teaspoon ginger powder

2 tablespoons chutney powder

1½ teaspoons salt

½ teaspoon white pepper

3 tablespoons light soy sauce

¼ cup sherry

Carolyn Jones 1930–1983

S HE WAS A KNOCKOUT, WEARING mod clothes and dripping with jewels, as Marsha, Queen of Diamonds on *Batman*. She almost took the Caped Crusader to the altar in one episode! She also played Hippolyta, mother of Wonder Woman on the 1970s superhero series starring Linda Carter. But it was as Morticia Frump Addams, the macabre mother to Wednesday and Pugsley, and passionate wife of Gomez, on *The Addams Family* that Carolyn Jones will always be remembered. The actress, Academy Award–nominated for *The Bachelor Party* in 1957, appeared in such movies as *House of Wax*, with Vincent Price, *King Creole*, with Elvis Presley, the 1956 horror classic *Invasion of the Body Snatchers*, and *The Opposite Sex*, the musical version of *The Women*. But the TV series eclipsed all that. How could it not? No one ever looked more bleakly beautiful than Jones did, dressed in black tatters, sitting in a fan-back chair, snapping along to *The Addams Family* theme song. Her recipe for That Fish Thing has nothing to do with the disembodied hand known as Thing on that show.

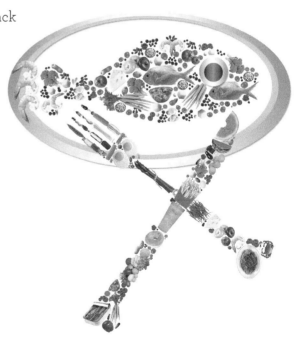

carolyn Jones's
That Fish Thing

Lay the filet flat, then take the mush-room caps, chopped pimento, fresh dill, bay shrimp, and a tiny bit of garlic salt and put them on the fish. Then roll the fish up like a blintz and anchor with toothpicks. Place in a baking dish. Mix the mushroom soup with the water and white wine and pour over fish. Bake in a 350° oven for about 25 minutes.

Serves 2

1 pound fresh filet of sole

1 pound bay shrimp

1 medium jar mushroom caps

1 small jar pimentos

½ teaspoon fresh dill

Pinch of garlic salt

1 can condensed mushroom soup

½ can white wine

½ can water

N O ONE IS MORE IDENTIFIABLE AS A SITCOM MOM than Harriet Nelson. On radio and then on screen as the star of *The Adventures of Ozzie and Harriet* and off, she was the wife of Ozzie and the mother of Ricky and David. No one, except the Nelsons themselves, knew where the show ended and their real lives began. Nelson's most notable film was the 1936 Fred Astaire and Ginger Rogers musical *Follow the Fleet*. And after the long run of *Ozzie and Harriet* ended in 1966, and a failed attempt to revive their characters on a sitcom called *Ozzie's Girls*, Nelson did guest shots on *Love Boat*, *Fantasy Island*, *Happy Days*, and *Father Dowling Mysteries*. Her favorite chicken recipe is as comforting as one would expect.

LaST BiTes

For its first five years on radio, *The Adventures of Ozzie and Harriet* used child actors to play David and Ricky. In 1949, the boys began playing themselves.

THE DeaD CeLeBriTY COOKBOOK

Harriet Nelson's Favorite Chicken

Serves
6

6 to 8 chicken breasts

1 can cream of chicken soup

1 can cream of mushroom soup

1 can cream of celery soup

½ cup light cream

½ stick butter, melted

1½ cups uncooked rice (not Minute Rice)

Salt and pepper

Paprika

Combine soups, cream, melted butter, and rice. Pour into buttered baking dish. Lay chicken breasts on top. Sprinkle lightly with salt and pepper, and generously with paprika. Dot with butter. Bake covered for 1½ hours at 325°.

POST MORTEM

This easy-to-make recipe is so creamy and rich that it can't possibly be good for you. But who cares? It's exactly the kind of comfort food you'd expect from the Nelson kitchen. Dee-lish!

I SABEL SANFORD CAUGHT HOLLYWOOD'S ATTENTION playing the maid in 1967's *Guess Who's Coming to Dinner* and appeared in such films as *Lady Sings the Blues*, *Up the Sandbox*, and *Love at First Bite*. But the world will always know her as the long-suffering wife of George Jefferson (Sherman Hemsley), Archie Bunker's next door neighbor on *All in the Family*. When Louise "Weezy" Jefferson and her successful dry-cleaner husband moved on up to the East Side of Manhattan for ten seasons of *The Jeffersons*, America went with them. Sanford looked so young and was so adept at physical comedy on both shows that no one had any idea that she was so much

older than she appeared. Playing Louise Jefferson typecast her, but she made the best of it, gamely appearing with her costar Hemsley in commercials for such chains as Old Navy and Denny's. Fittingly, the plaque on Sanford's mausoleum reads "Weezy."

Isabel Sanford's Boston Chicken

Wash chicken and potatoes and set aside. Preheat oven to 300°. In a bowl, combine the salad dressing, preserves, onion soup mix, grated onion, and cinnamon to form a paste. Spread the pieces of chicken in a single layer in a greased shallow baking dish. Slice the potatoes in half and place around the chicken. Completely cover the chicken and potatoes with the sauce. Cover with aluminum foil and bake for 40 minutes. Remove foil, turn up heat to 375°, and bake for 15 minutes more or until chicken and potatoes have a golden brown glaze.

8 pieces of chicken

4 whole large potatoes

1 cup Russian or Thousand Island salad dressing

½ cup apricot preserves

½ cup pineapple preserves

1 package instant onion soup mix

¼ cup grated onion

1 dash cinnamon

POST MORTEM

Everyone who grew up watching *All in the Family* and *The Jeffersons* when they were first on television seems to remember eating a version of this dish as kids. Like so many foods from our childhoods, Boston Chicken is better remembered than it is eaten as adults. It's not a hit today.

Donna Reed 1921–1986

DONNA REED SO EMBODIED the suburban housewife and mother of the 1950s on *The Donna Reed Show* that not everyone remembers she won an Oscar playing a prostitute in *From Here to Eternity*. Her movies included *The Human Comedy*, with Mickey Rooney, *The Picture of Dorian Gray*, and *They Were Expendable*. Her best-loved movie role was Mary Bailey in the classic Frank Capra film *It's a Wonderful Life* opposite Jimmy Stewart. In 1984, Reed replaced Barbara Bel Geddes as Miss Ellie on *Dallas* for one season, but when the original actress decided to return, Reed was out the door. As the story goes, Reed sued for breach of contract and reportedly settled for more than one million dollars. That's at least enough to buy Bisque Tortoni for everyone on the Southfork Ranch.

Mabel King 1932–1999

ANY CHAPTER ON SITCOM MOMS would have to include actress and gospel singer Mabel King who played Mabel "Mama" Thomas on the first two seasons of the popular 1970s series *What's Happening!!* King also made a huge impression—she was a big woman—as Evillene, the witch who sings "Don't Nobody Bring Me No Bad News" in both the Broadway and film versions of *The Wiz*. She was in *The Bingo Long Traveling All-Stars & Motor Kings* and *Scrooged*, too. But her most famous film role, strangely enough, was probably playing Steve Martin's mother in *The Jerk*. King's banana fritters will make you say, "Hey, hey-hey." Rerun must have loved them.

Donna Reed's Bisque Tortoni

Mix ½ cup macaroons with cream, sugar, and salt. Stir and then let stand for 1 hour. Beat heavy cream until thick, and then gradually add macaroon mixture. Add vanilla and almond extract. Divide among four molds and freeze 3 hours. Unmold and sprinkle with additional macaroon crumbs and serve.

½ cup crushed dry macaroons

½ cup light cream

¾ cup sugar

Few grains of salt

½ pint heavy cream

1 teaspoon vanilla

Few drops almond extract

Mabel King's Banana Fritters

Cut each banana crosswise into 3 chunks, each about 2 inches long. Sprinkle with lemon juice and confectioners' sugar. Let stand 20 minutes. Meanwhile, mix biscuit mix with sugar, egg, and milk. Dip each banana piece into batter to coat completely. Fry banana chunks in hot oil until brown. Serve with maple syrup.

4 medium firm bananas

Juice of ½ lemon

2 tablespoons confectioners' sugar

½ cup biscuit mix

1 tablespoon sugar

1 egg

1 cup milk

Vegetable oil for deep frying

AFTER-DINNER VIEWING

MOTHERS DAZE

Two suggestions for food-oriented fun on *The Munsters*: Lily packs a lunch of boar's head knockwurst and bat's milk yogurt for herself and the tall mysterious stranger with whom she's working at the shipyard to earn extra money to buy an anniversary present in "Happy 100th Anniversary." Little does she know that she's welding next to and flirting with her own husband. Speaking of that hubby, watching a starving Herman eat an olive pit with a knife and fork, while Lily, Marilyn, and Eddie tuck into a sumptuous feast in "A House Divided" is a scream. Both episodes are from season two.

Dining on *The Addams Family* always meant indulging in such delicacies as baked eye of newt, puree of aardvark, and roast yak. "Salt, pepper, or cyanide?" Morticia would ask her guests. But when French pen pal Yvette (Peggy Mondo) announces she's coming to visit Uncle Fester (Jackie Coogan) in the season-two episode "Fester Goes on a Diet," it's reducing time for the baldest Addams. With the help of Jack LaLanne, Fester begins an exercise program and not a moment too soon. As LaLanne says, "I've seen people let themselves go, but you're almost gone." Fester doesn't lose much weight and is panicked. "Perhaps she'll love you for your soul," Morticia says. "Well, that's even fatter!" Fester confesses. It turns out that Yvette's a chubby chaser and Fester is too thin for her. Oh well.

On the season-six episode of *The Adventures of Ozzie and Harriet*, "Tutti Frutti Ice Cream," the Nelsons get a craving for their favorite flavor and go on a major search for it in every market around. Not only does that prove frutti-less, they end up lost. It's out on a "best of" DVD compilation.

On the season-two episode of *The Jeffersons* called "Louise's Cookbook," Weezy is asked to turn her grandmother's soul food recipes into what George calls "a ghetto cookbook." George (Sherman Hemsley) loves Weezy's possum stew. She makes it with rabbit, thank heaven, but George can't deal with his wife's success. "Do you want to be my wife, or Aunt Jemima?" he grouses.

A Jewish mother and her food should never be parted. So when Ida Morgenstern gets mugged on the subway in the two-part episode "Five for the Road" during the fourth season of *Rhoda*, it's a crying shame. The thief makes off with Ida's brisket—her Tupperware still had a burp in it—but not her handbag because, as she says, nobody gets her purse.

What's Happening!! was lousy with fat jokes. The season-one episode "The Maid Did It" includes Shirley calling Rerun an elephant, shortly before he runs off to eat a mixture of barbecue and ice cream, which he calls "chicken ala mode." Rerun tells Shirley she has a heart of gold and a body like Fort Knox. When Mama is fired from her maid job, by Alice Ghostley (see Chapter 20), she threatens to jump out the window and cause an earthquake. Meanwhile, even thin little Dee is solving her "if-Johnny-had-six-apples" word problems by eating her way through a houseful of fruit.

When the charity dance she hosted doesn't raise enough money, Donna Stone decides to make up her twenty-seven-dollar share of the deficit by selling her greatest culinary triumph in "Pickles for Charity," a season-two episode of *The Donna Reed Show*. When the dilled cukes don't fly off the shelves, Donna's husband secretly buys the lot and gives them away. One thing's for certain: no one ever looked as chic as Reed did grocery shopping for 150 pounds of cucumbers.

15

TV TWOSOMES AT THE TABLE

THANK HEAVEN FOR YOUTUBE. With it, a TV lover can watch things he never knew existed. Along with the unaired pilot episodes (who knew Bette Davis had a failed sitcom?) and the outtakes, there are archival TV clips that are just plain weird. The one that takes the cake for me is a spot for Jell-O and Dream Whip starring the cast of *Hogan's Heroes* and, wait for it, Carol Channing. With no explanation why she's in Germany during World War II, the Broadway legend climbs out of a trap door in the floor of Stalag 13, looks around, and observes, "My, how the General Foods kitchens have changed!" The prisoners are just finishing their latest gourmet meal prepared for them by their resident French chef Louis LeBeau (Robert Clary). Channing joins them for Jell-O. Two minutes later, even Nazi officers Colonel Klink (Werner Klemperer) and Sergeant Schultz (John Banner) are enjoying a jiggling dessert with fake whipped cream on top. They're so into their dessert, in fact, that they don't even notice Carol standing there. Maybe this is why we won the war. The recipes that follow celebrate two of the stars of *Hogan's Heroes*, plus two other terrific twosomes of television. They're strange bedfellows, one and all. But oh are they adorable together!!!

a *Hogan's Heroes* Meat-up

B OB CRANE, WHO PLAYED Colonel Robert E. Hogan, and John Banner, who played Sergeant Hans Georg Schultz, on *Hogan's Heroes* had more fun together than any P.O.W. and Luftwaffe guard ever had behind "frenemy" lines. The handsome Hogan used his looks and his wiles to get what he wanted. The bumbling Schultz had neither, but the series' most noted catchphrase, "I know nothing! Nothing!" was all his. Before landing the title role on the show, Crane had done some guest shots on such series as *Alfred Hitchcock Presents* and *Twilight Zone*, and was a regular on *The Donna Reed Show*, playing Dr. Dave Kelsey. Banner had roles in numerous movies and TV shows including *Father Knows Best*, *Adventures of Superman*, *Hazel*, and *Voyage to the Bottom of the Sea* before being immortalized as a regular on six seasons of *Hogan's Heroes*. Crane was murdered, and his story became the subject of the 2002 film *Auto Focus*, starring Greg Kinnear. Banner, whose last role was on *The Partridge Family*, retired to France. He was visiting friends in Vienna when he died on his sixty-third birthday. Odd endings, but long live Crane's kebabs and Banner's flambéed chicken!

BOB CRane's
LamB KeBaBS

Trim excess fat from lamb. Mix together olive oil, vinegar, onion, and seasonings in a large bowl and place meat in marinade. Cover and refrigerate several hours or overnight, turning meat occasionally. Arrange lamb on skewers alternately with vegetables. Brush lightly with marinade. Cook on an outdoor grill over coals or under the broiler. Turn and baste frequently with marinade while cooking for 15 minutes or until meat is done. Remove cooked lamb and vegetables from skewers onto plate.

Serves
8

4 cups deboned leg of lamb, cut into 2-inch cubes

⅓ cup olive oil

1 cup wine vinegar

1 medium yellow onion, sliced

⅛ teaspoon garlic salt

1½ teaspoons salt

½ teaspoon freshly ground pepper

¼ teaspoon dried oregano

¼ teaspoon thyme

1 large green pepper, cut in pieces

8 large or 16 small mushroom caps

2–3 tomatoes, cut in quarters

1 onion, peeled and cut in pieces

1 small jar whole drained pimentoes

Salt and pepper, to taste

JOHN BANNER'S FLAMBÉED CHICKEN

11 tablespoons butter

1 broiler-fryer chicken, quartered

Salt, to taste

Freshly ground black pepper, to taste

4–5 cooking apples, peeled, cored, and cut in thin slices

1 tablespoon sugar (optional)

½ pound mushrooms, cleaned and chopped

3 ounces calvados or apple brandy

½ cup heavy cream

2 egg yolks

Melt 4 tablespoons butter in skillet. Brown chicken quickly on all sides; season with salt and pepper. Set aside. Melt 4 tablespoons butter in separate skillet. Sauté apple slices until soft but not mushy. Set aside. (If apples are tart, add about 1 tablespoon sugar.) Melt 3 tablespoons butter in large saucepan. Sauté mushrooms in butter; cover, and simmer 5 minutes. Pour calvados or brandy over chicken; touch with a lighted match. When the flaming stops, transfer chicken to saucepan containing mushrooms, but reserve skillet and its drippings. Continue cooking chicken in saucepan over low heat until done. Remove chicken and mushrooms to heated serving plate. Add cream beaten slightly with egg yolks to skillet in which the chicken was cooked. Stir over low heat until thickened. Do not boil. Pour sauce over chicken. Serve with sautéed apple slices.

Brian Keith 1921–1997 and Sebastian Cabot 1918–1977

a Real Family Affair

FAMILY AFFAIR WAS ABOUT WEALTHY New York playboy Bill Davis (Brian Keith) and his butler Mr. Giles French (Sebastian Cabot), whose lives were disrupted when his late brother's three children moved in. I think of them as the first gay family on television. Hey, you watch *Family Affair* your way, I'll watch it mine. However you imagine their relationship, Brian Keith and Sebastian Cabot had enough chemistry to give this show longevity. Acting was in Keith's blood. His parents were both actors, and he made his film debut at age three. The man worked until he died. Besides *Family Affair*, he's known for the film *The Russians Are Coming, The Russians Are Coming*, the TV miniseries *Centennial*, two seasons as a pediatrician on *The Brian Keith Show* and three as a tough-as-nails judge on *Hardcastle and McCormick*. Cabot started acting in his teens and made numerous appearances in TV and films including playing a British criminologist in the early '60s detective series *Checkmate*. He famously lent his voice to the Disney classics *Jungle Book* (as the panther Bagheera) and *The Sword in the Stone*, and narrated several Winnie the Pooh films. You can decide who has the better recipe: the man of the house or the man servant.

Brian Keith's
Good Chicken Gus

Serves
4

Season chicken liberally with salt and pepper. Melt butter and olive oil in a heavy skillet over low heat. Add garlic and chicken and cook uncovered over low heat, turning chicken until it is done. Remove pieces to a heated casserole. Add parsley and sauterne to skillet. Cover and boil one minute. Pour pan drippings over chicken in casserole and serve.

1 (3-pound) chicken, cut into 8 pieces

Salt and pepper, to taste

2 tablespoons unsalted butter

2 tablespoons olive oil

1 clove garlic, minced

¾ cup parsley, chopped

¾ cup dry sauterne

POST Mortem

This dish is simple and tasty, but a little plain for intense flavor-cravers. Hey, Uncle Bill never said it was Great Chicken Gus! Leftovers are yummy at room temperature, though, and even better, if you ask me, right from the fridge.

sebastian cabot's avocado surprise

Start by making the crepe batter. Sift dry ingredients together. Beat whole eggs and yolks until frothy. Add eggs and milk to dry ingredients. Stir until smooth. Add melted butter. Stir until well combined. Set aside for 2 hours. While the crepe batter rests, make the guacamole. Cut avocado in half. Remove pit. Spoon out pulp and mash. Add remaining guacamole ingredients. Whip into fine paste. Cover and refrigerate until needed.

After two hours of resting the batter, make the crepes. Heat 1 teaspoon of sweet butter over moderate heat in a 5- or 6-inch frying pan until the butter foams. Pour 1½ tablespoons batter into pan. Rotate pan quickly to spread batter as thinly and evenly as possible. Cook crepe 1 minute on each side. Stack crepes on top of each other until all are done.

Then make the cheese sauce. Place cream over hot water in double boiler. When hot, gradually add cheese, stirring constantly. When completely melted add equal amount of hot mixture to eggs and mix well. Add egg mixture to cheese mixture. Add salt and pepper and blend well. Cook until thickened, approximately 5 minutes, stirring constantly. Remove immediately from heat.

Preheat broiler. To assemble the crepes, place 1 slice lox and 1 tablespoon guacamole on each crepe. Roll and tuck in ends. Arrange one layer in a 9-inch-square greased glass casserole. Pour cream sauce over crepes. Broil 4 inches from heat 4–5 minutes or until bubbly and golden brown. Garnish with leftover guacamole.

Serves 8

Crepes:

½ pound thinly sliced Nova lox

⅔ cup flour

1 tablespoon sugar

Pinch salt

2 eggs

2 egg yolks

1¾ cups milk

2 tablespoons melted butter

Guacamole:

2 large very ripe avocados

¼ cup grated onion

1 tablespoon fresh lemon juice

1 teaspoon salt

4 to 6 drops Tabasco

Cheese sauce:

3 cups half-and-half

1 cup (4 ounces) finely shredded Cheddar cheese

3 egg yolks, beaten

¾ teaspoon salt

⅛ teaspoon white pepper

eLLen corBY 1911–1999 anD WiLL Geer 1902–1978

Bake SaLe on WaLTon's MounTain

THE ACTORS WHO PLAYED ESTHER AND ZEBULON WALTON— that's Grandma and Grandpa Walton to you, me, and all those kids— led fascinating lives long before they found themselves under a crazy quilt of Americana on *The Waltons*. Ellen Corby was an Atlantic City chorine, an RKO script girl, and a screenwriter before becoming an actress. The hit TV series made her famous and earned her three Emmy Awards, but Corby had had roles in some other very cool earlier projects. She appeared in the camp favorites *Caged* and *Hush . . . Hush, Sweet Charlotte*, the underappreciated Joan Crawford melodrama *Harriet Craig*, and the classic films *Sabrina, Vertigo*, and *Shane*. Her TV work ran the gamut from *The Andy Griffith Show*, on which she played the thieving Myrt "Hubcaps" Lesh, to *The Addams Family*, which saw her cast as the gargantuan Lurch's mother.

Will Geer was a folksinger, a radical, a communist, a lover of Harry Hay (the man considered the founder of the modern gay rights movement), a husband and a father before he was cast as the grandfather on *The Waltons*, And, oh yes, he was a terrific actor who appeared on Broadway and in such movies as *In Cold Blood, Jeremiah Johnson*, and *Bandolero!,* and such TV shows as *Mayberry R.F.D., Hawaii Five-O, Columbo*, and *Medical Center*. He even played George Washington on *Bewitched*.

Together, Corby and Geer were the best thing about *The Waltons* this side of John-Boy's mole. Their recipes would be right at home on Walton's Mountain. A swig of the Baldwin Sisters' "recipe" wouldn't hurt while you're baking them, either.

ellen corby's apple cake

4 slices dry white bread

2 cups applesauce

1 tablespoon brown sugar

1 tablespoon melted butter

Whipped cream for topping

Tear up bread into small pieces and process in food processor to make crumbs. In a 1-quart baking dish, make a layer with half the bread crumbs, then top with applesauce. Sprinkle with sugar and then remaining crumbs. Press mixture together with spoon and pour butter over it. Bake for 30 minutes in a 350° oven. Serve lukewarm with ice-cold whipped cream.

will geer's walton's mountain muffins

1 cup whole bran ready-to-eat cereal

1 cup mashed ripe bananas (about 2 medium)

¼ cup skim milk

¼ cup margarine or butter, melted

1 egg

1 cup flour

2 teaspoons baking powder

½ teaspoon salt

¼ cup brown sugar, lightly packed

Combine bran, milk, and bananas in a medium bowl and let soften. Add egg and melted margarine or butter, and beat well with electric mixer. With a whisk, stir flour, baking powder, salt, and sugar in a small bowl together until well mixed. Add flour mixture to banana mixture. Stir only enough to dampen dry ingredients. Do not over mix. Line muffin tin with paper muffin cups and then fill each two-thirds full with batter. Bake in a 400° oven for 30 minutes, or until wooden pick inserted in center comes out clean.

aFTer-Dinner viewing

everyone's in a "jam"

LeBeau (Robert Clary) makes a mean Crepes Suzette, even in a Nazi prison camp. But the fiercely patriotic French chef is persuaded to pop a few pies in the oven to win over a visiting Italian officer (Hans Conreid) in "The Pizza Parlor," a season-one episode of *Hogan's Heroes*.

On the *Family Affair* episode called "Marmalade," an advertising executive drafts Mr. French to be a commercial spokesman for Dunholt Marmalade. He's so popular that the company wants Mr. French to be its goodwill ambassador. But when he actually tries a spoonful of the product, the jam hits the fan.

In "The Calf," a first season episode of *The Waltons*, it's a case of pet or meat when Chance, the family cow, gives birth to a bull. The kids are thrilled by the blessed event. (They don't have much in the way of real excitement on Walton's Mountain.) But their father John (Ralph Waite) sells the little fellow to pay for truck repairs. It gets worse: when Jim-Bob (David Harper) and Elizabeth (Kami Cotler) learn the calf is to be slaughtered for beef, they calf-nap him. Spoiler alert: a deal is brokered and the calf lives.

16

Dance This Mess around

TRUE STORY: MY HUSBAND AND I were invited in 2004 to a small dinner party in one of the most beautiful homes in Greenwich Village. The hostess had originally invited another same-sex couple, but when they dropped out at the last minute, she went on a frantic search for two well-dressed, articulate gays. We were the best she could do on short notice. Not to namedrop, but among the guests at that intimate soirée was the dancer and choreographer Twyla Tharp. Twyla didn't say much during dinner, but when she was offered dessert, her words were loud and clear.

"GOD, no!" Tharp said. It was as if the hostess had asked, "Would you like my monkey to fling poop at you?" Tharp's response made extremely apparent her feelings about eating unhealthy foods. Clearly, Twyla is not someone you take to Dairy Queen for a Peanut Buster Parfait.

The dancer/choreographer's outburst shouldn't have surprised anyone. Despite all the dinner-dances my parents went to while I was growing up in the 1960s and '70s, dancing and indulgent eating really don't go well together, at least not professional dancing. That line of work is all about rigor, not rigatoni, although diet guidelines do say that dancers are supposed to get half their calories from carbohydrates. There are some dance companies that welcome all body types. For example, Mark Morris, no waif himself, has always been big on such diversity, although most dancers are purely muscle in motion. If you saw the movie *Black Swan*, you know how crazy dancers can be about what they eat. (Mila Kunis, this includes you.)

Stringent dieting doesn't mean, of course, that some dancers aren't as good whirling around the kitchen floor making a signature dish as they are on the dance floor performing signature works. The recipes in this chapter—with the exception of Gwen Verdon's cardboard, I mean, crazy-good muffins—are not going to keep the weight off you. But they will keep a smile on your face, particularly Moira Shearer's Apricot Pudding, which is lovely served during a screening of *The Red Shoes*. One taste of her sweet concoction and you'll be as happy as a dessert eater can be. Twyla Tharp be damned.

Gwen Verdon 1925–2000

RED-HEADED DYNAMO Gwen Verdon overcame childhood illness to become one of the greatest dancers the Great White Way has ever seen. She was renowned for her work in such landmark Broadway musicals as *Sweet Charity*, *Damn Yankees*, and *Chicago*, which were all choreographed by her husband, the legendary choreographer Bob Fosse. Verdon won four Tony Awards and a Grammy over her long career. She recreated the role of Lola in the film version of *Damn Yankees* in 1958. Subsequent film and TV work paled in comparison. But at '60, she appeared in the hit *Cocoon*. A few years later, Verdon also played Mia Farrow's mother in the Woody Allen film *Alice*. Her muffins may not be her greatest work, but they are slimming. In fact, you may not even want to eat them.

Ann Miller 1923–2004

THE REASONS TO BE CRAZY ABOUT Ann Miller are plentiful. She appeared in the musical films *Kiss Me Kate*, *Easter Parade*, and *On the Town*, wowed Broadway audiences with *Sugar Babies* opposite Mickey Rooney in 1979, and knocked "I'm Still Here" out of the park in her last stage performance in the 1998 Paper Mill Playhouse revival of *Follies*. But here are the reasons I loved her: She had enormous lacquered hair long after women had abandoned the bouffant. She once tap-danced on a giant aluminum can for a legendary TV commercial for Great American Soups. Her 1982 episode of *The Love Boat*, costarring Carol Channing, Ethel Merman, Della Reese, Van Johnson, and Cab Calloway, is the second best *Love Boat* episode ever. (Only the Andy Warhol episode is better.) She appeared in the David Lynch movie *Mulholland Drive* when she was pushing eighty. And, I repeat, she had enormous lacquered hair. Her bouffant was as rich and timeless as her Fettuccine Alfredo.

GWen verDon's MUFFins

Put oats in blender and blend until coarse flour forms. Mix with other dry ingredients in a bowl. Add all the wet ingredients except the egg whites. Mix thoroughly and then fold in beaten egg whites. Stir in raisins. Put paper liners in muffin pan. Spoon batter into muffin cups and bake at 425° for 17 minutes. Remove from oven, leave in pan 2 minutes, then transfer to rack to cool.

Makes a dozen or more

1¼ cups oats (not instant)

1¼ cups whole bran

2 packages artificial sweetener

2 teaspoons baking powder

1¼ cups skim milk

1 tablespoon vegetable oil

1 teaspoon cinnamon

1 teaspoon vanilla

4 egg whites, beaten until stiff

½ cup raisins

ann MiLLer's FeTTuccine aLFreDo

Cook noodles according to package directions. Drain. While noodles are cooking, beat yolk lightly with a fork and add cream. Melt butter. Place drained hot noodles in a warm serving bowl and pour the egg and cream mixture, the melted butter, and about half the grated cheese. Toss until well blended, adding the rest of the cheese a little at a time. Serve immediately.

Serves 4

1 package egg noodles

1 stick unsalted butter

1 egg yolk, preferably from an organic egg

⅓ cup light cream or sour cream

½ cup grated Parmesan cheese

POST MorTem

Quick and easy to throw together with ingredients on hand in most kitchens, Miller's pasta dish is rich but also comforting in its simplicity. Certainly, it's worth adding to your repertoire.

B EFORE HE WAS THE LEADING MAN in such hits as *Ghost, Red Dawn,* and *Point Break,* and a leading lady of sorts in *To Wong Foo, Thanks for Everything, Julie Newmar,* Patrick Swayze was a classically trained dancer whose mother was a choreographer. The 1987 film *Dirty Dancing* made him a superstar. Johnny Castle's gracefully masculine moves were the reason the film made the leap from pleasant diversion to cultural touchstone. "Nobody puts Baby in the corner" remains one of Hollywood's greatest quotes. *People* magazine put Swayze on the cover in 1991 and named him the Sexiest Man Alive. But more than just sexy, Swayze was a truly beloved performer. Stumble upon *Dirty Dancing* while you're channel surfing on a lazy afternoon and I dare you to turn it off. You won't. Make his Chicken Pot Pie and you, too, will have the time of your life.

patrick swayze's chicken pot pie

Bring first seven ingredients to a boil in a large pot. Reduce heat to low and simmer, partially covered one hour. Remove chicken. Tear off meat, and place in bowl. Strain and reserve two cups broth.

Bring broth to boil in a large saucepan. Add diced carrots and celery, reduce heat, and simmer five minutes. Add pearl onions, pepper, mushrooms, and peas, and simmer one minute. Remove vegetables from broth and put in the bowl with the chicken. Reserve broth.

Melt butter in a saucepan over medium-high heat. Add flour and cook, whisking one minute. Whisk in reserved chicken broth, milk, Worcestershire sauce, salt, and hot pepper sauce. Simmer five minutes, whisking. Add to chicken mixture and stir to combine.

Preheat oven to 425°. Spoon mixture into four single-serving baking dishes. Cut pastry to fit over dishes. Crimp edges and brush with beaten egg. Bake on a cookie sheet until golden brown, about 25 minutes.

Serves 4

1 chicken

1 carrot, sliced

1 rib celery, sliced

1 medium onion, halved

10 cups water

1 bay leaf

¼ teaspoon freshly ground pepper

½ cup diced peeled carrot

½ cup diced celery

1 cup frozen pearl onions

1 red pepper, diced

8 ounces fresh mushrooms, quartered

½ cup frozen peas

3 tablespoons butter

3 tablespoons flour

½ cup milk

1 teaspoon Worcestershire sauce

½ teaspoon salt

Dash red pepper sauce

2 sheets frozen puffed pastry, thawed according to package directions

1 egg, lightly beaten

JULieT Prowse 1936–1996

THE EXOTICALLY BEAUTIFUL South African dancer Juliet Prowse was almost six feet tall, and more than half of that were her incredible legs. In 1960, she appeared with Frank Sinatra, with whom she was romantically linked, in *Can-Can*, and opposite Elvis Presley in *G.I. Blues*. Prowse's pairing with Kermit the Frog on the first episode of *The Muppet Show* in 1976 made a lot of baby boomers just as happy. After performing a black-lit dance dressed in diaphanous chiffon and accompanied by green gazelle puppets, Prowse got up close and personal with Kermie, calling him "the Robert Redford of frogs." In that spirit, the dish that follows is the Juliet Prowse of moussaka.

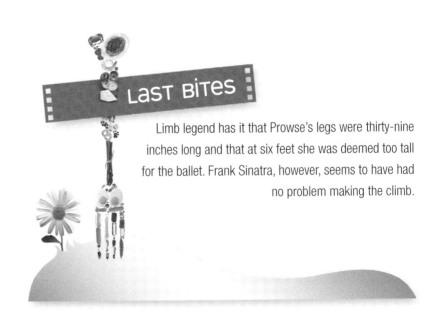

LasT BiTes

Limb legend has it that Prowse's legs were thirty-nine inches long and that at six feet she was deemed too tall for the ballet. Frank Sinatra, however, seems to have had no problem making the climb.

JULiET Prowse's Moussaka

Slice eggplant into ½-inch rounds and sprinkle with salt. Let stand for ten minutes, and then pat dry. Fry onions in oil until translucent; season with thyme. Remove from pan. Brush eggplant slices with oil and fry in skillet until both sides are brown and eggplant is soft. Set aside. Brown meat in skillet, add tomato paste and ½ bottle chutney, then season with marjoram, paprika and salt and pepper. Place eggplant slices on bottom and sides of 13 x 9 x 2-inch baking dish. Top with some meat, some onions, and some quince or apple, layering until all are used. Combine eggs, sour cream, and yogurt, and pour over ingredients in baking dish. Sprinkle with Parmesan cheese. Bake at 325° for 40–60 minutes, until custard topping is set.

1 eggplant

2 onions, finely chopped

3 tablespoons olive or vegetable oil

½ teaspoon thyme

1½ pounds ground lamb or beef

1 can tomato paste

1 jar prepared chutney

½ teaspoon marjoram

1 teaspoon paprika

Salt and pepper, to taste

1 quince or cooking apple, peeled, cored and cut into thin slices

3 eggs, beaten

½ pint sour cream

2 cups plain yogurt

½ cup grated Parmesan cheese

S COTTISH BALLERINA Moira Shearer danced her way into movie history in the Academy Award-winning 1948 picture *The Red Shoes,* codirected by Michael Powell and Emeric Pressburger. The role made Shearer a star but practically eclipsed everything else she did. And she did a lot. Unlike the troubled heroine of the film, Victoria Page, Shearer adroitly balanced both career and family. Over the years, she made films (dancing in some and not in others), wrote two books and a newspaper column, and raised four children with her husband, writer Ludovic Kennedy. With all this going on, it's a wonder Shearer found time to make pudding, but she did.

Moira Shearer's apricot pudding

2 cups whole milk

2 tablespoons butter

¼ cup superfine sugar

½ cup bread crumbs

2 egg yolks, beaten

1 jar apricot jam, warmed

2 egg whites

Extra sugar for sprinkling

Melt butter and half the super-fine sugar in milk over low heat and beat together. Add the bread crumbs. Remove from heat and add beaten egg yolks. Pour into a greased baking pan and bake at 375° until set and slightly brown. Remove from oven and spread with warmed apricot jam. Reduce oven temperature to 250°. Whip the egg whites until stiff and then fold in remaining superfine sugar. Top pudding with meringue, sprinkle with sugar, and then bake in the oven at the new lower temperature for about an hour, or until the meringue is crisp and beginning to brown.

after-dinner viewing

a smorgasbord of dance on DVD

To enjoy Gwen Verdon in full Fosse mode, watch the compilation *The Best of Broadway Musicals: Original Cast Performances from The Ed Sullivan Show*, in which Verdon performs "I'm a Brass Band" from *Sweet Charity*. Patrick Swayze shines, of course, in *Dirty Dancing*. Ann Miller taps her way through the soaring musical *On the Town*. The meeting of Juliet Prowse and Kermit the Frog is included on *The Muppet Show: Season One* box set. Then, of course, there's Moira Shearer in *The Red Shoes*, given the deluxe DVD treatment by the folks at the Criterion Collection. It is not considered the most popular film ever made about dance for nothing.

17

Have an egg, Mr. Goldstone

I N ONE OF MY FAVORITE SCENES in *Gypsy*, the Jule Styne, Stephen Sondheim, Arthur Laurents work considered by many to be the pinnacle of the American-musical theatre, Mama Rose, the ultimate stage mother, serves her ragtag brood warmed-over Chinese food for breakfast. It's reheated leftovers beneath the cracked plaster ceiling of a tacky hotel room, and on her daughter Louise's birthday, too! Glamorous, it's not. But those are the breaks when you are trying to catch a break in vaudeville.

Right there, between yesterday's chow and today's mein course, Herbie shows up with good news: their act has been booked on the Orpheum Circuit. Not only that, Herbie has brought the man responsible for that booking with him. Overcome with generosity, Rose does what any showbiz-crazy woman who'd been waiting all her life for that moment would do: she invites Mr. Goldstone to have an eggroll. Actually, she offers him everything from a kumquat to a Coke, with fried rice and spare ribs on the side. Their big fat chance has come. Eat up.

In real life, the story was more complicated, of course, but Louise did become Gypsy Rose Lee, vaudeville segued into burlesque, and the tale remains as wonderful a "musical fable" today as it ever was. Those of us who've seen Broadway productions starring Tyne Daly, Bernadette Peters, and Patti LuPone say it gets better with every passing year. Certainly, the show looms large in the consciousness of those who follow the "neo-burlesque" movement of the last fifteen years. There would be no Dita Von Teese without the pioneers of striptease, and no Bette Midler without the bawdy female comics who got their start in vaudeville and burlesque. The recipes in this chapter prove that the stage wasn't the only place these women sizzled. Have an omelet, Mr. Goldstone.

SOPHie TUCKer 1886–1966

WITH HER "SOPH" JOKES a permanent part of her act, singer/actress Bette Midler has done more to keep the memory of Sophie Tucker alive than anyone. They called Tucker "The Last of the Red-Hot Mamas" and anyone who ever heard her sing "Nobody Loves a Fat Girl, But Oh How a Fat Girl Can Love" or her signature tune "Some of These Days" knows they were right. Tucker came up through vaudeville and burlesque, playing the *Ziegfeld Follies* and various Broadway revues, did radio and played opposite Judy Garland in two films, *Broadway Melody of 1938* and *Thoroughbreds Don't Cry*. She appeared as herself in *Follow the Boys* and *Gay Love*, neither of which is as naughty as their titles would suggest. Perhaps her greatest honor? Paul McCartney liked to say that Sophie Tucker was the Beatles' "favorite American group." He didn't want to hold her hand. His loss.

SOPHie TUCKer's MeaT LoaF

Soak bread in milk and squeeze out excess. Mix with all ingredients except hard-boiled eggs. Grease a loaf pan. Press half the meat in the pan. Layer with sliced hard-boiled eggs. Top with remaining meat, pressing down to form a solid loaf. Cover with foil. Bake at 325° for 45 minutes or until done.

1 slice stale bread

½ cup milk

1 pound ground beef

1 onion, finely chopped

1 egg

½ teaspoon salt

½ teaspoon pepper

2 sliced hard-boiled eggs

Serves 6

GYPSY ROSE LEE 1911–1970

THE WOMAN BORN ROSE LOUISE HOVICK, but better known as Gypsy Rose Lee has been a favorite of mine since I was a toddler. My mother never missed her talk show *Gypsy*, which aired 1965–67. Even as a three-year-old, I found Lee fascinating. I had no idea that she was the "ecdysiast" who had put the tease in striptease back when she was the star of Minsky's Burlesque, or that she'd written two crime novels in the 1940s (one was the basis of the Barbara Stanwyck film *Lady of Burlesque*), or that she was the Gypsy of the musical *Gypsy*. I certainly didn't know she had a son with Otto Preminger (whose Deviled Eggs recipe appears in Chapter 2). Gypsy Rose Lee was just this effervescent woman chatting a mile-a-minute on TV. Lee appeared on such TV staples as *The Hollywood Squares, What's My Line?* and even an episode of *Batman*. She's in the movie *The Trouble with Angels*, too. She cooked the recipe that follows on *The Mike Douglas Show*. It was a pretty squeaky-clean venue for a former stripper, but everyone loved Gypsy. Okay, maybe not her sister June Havoc, but everyone else.

GYPSY ROSE LEE's Linger-Longer omelet

¼ pound Italian link
sausage, sliced ¼-inch
thick

¼ green pepper, cut into
¼-inch strips

2 tablespoons olive oil

½ cup sliced onion, cut
⅛-inch thick

1 small potato, peeled,
sliced ¼-inch thick

½ teaspoon salt

1 slice prosciutto, cut into
½-inch strips

1 tomato, peeled and sliced
¼-inch thick

2 tablespoons chopped
pimento

6 eggs

1 tablespoon chopped
parsley

1 clove garlic

Sauté sausage and pepper in 1 table-spoon oil over low heat, 4–5 minutes or until sausage begins to brown. Add onion, potato, and salt. Cover and continue to cook, stirring gently occasionally, 5–10 minutes or until onions are transparent. Add prosciutto, tomato, and pimento. Cook until tender. Drain excess fat and let cool a bit. Break eggs into mixing bowl. Add parsley. Beat with fork until frothy. Add sausage mixture. In a large omelet pan, heat remaining tablespoon olive oil. Sauté garlic until brown. Discard. Add egg mixture to pan. Move pan back and forth over heat and stir eggs six or eight times. Smooth top of omelet. When edges are done but the center is still creamy, fold omelet in thirds.

Mae West 1893–1980

PLAYWRIGHT, ACTRESS, AND TRUE POP-CULTURE ICON Mae West began working in vaudeville when she was only five years old, and by the time she reached her teens she was known as "The Baby Vamp." Her over-sexed persona only grew from there. She was charged with obscenity and imprisoned in 1926 for her play *Sex*, but found Broadway success a few years later with *Diamond Lil*. Her Hollywood career began when she was almost forty, but even in her first film *Night After Night* she was a sensation. The picture gave her one of her most famous lines. A coat-check girl sees her jewelry and says, "Goodness! What lovely diamonds!" to which Mae responds, "Goodness had nothing to do with it." Among West's best films were *I'm No Angel*, *She Done Him Wrong*, *My Little Chickadee* (with W. C. Fields), and *Klondike Annie*. Two of her most dreadful films—*Myra Breckinridge* and *Sextette*—are among those most beloved, at least by fans of camp cinema. I have a soft spot (although she would have preferred something harder, no doubt) for her appearance opposite a talking horse in a 1964 episode of *Mister Ed*. For a woman who once said, "Too much of a good thing can be wonderful," her fruit compote recipe shows remarkable restraint.

Mae west's Fruit compote

Serves
2

Combine fruits and sprinkle with almonds and raisins. Top with milk and honey.

1 large apple, chopped

1 large pear, chopped

1 large banana, chopped

2–3 almonds, chopped

1 teaspoon raisins

1–2 tablespoons milk

1 teaspoon honey, or to taste

POST Mortem

How mad would Mae West possibly be if you substituted a mix of strawberries, blueberries, and blackberries, or any two of those and some nice ripe peach slices for the apple, pear, and banana in her recipe? Probably not very. Besides, what do you care if she minds? She's dead.

ann corio 1909–1999

ANN CORIO WAS A BURLESQUE QUEEN at Minsky's—part of the "shapely sisterhood" (to quote her *New York Times* obituary) that included Gypsy Rose Lee. Corio proved so popular that she went Hollywood, appearing scantily clad in such low-brow-but-lovable films as *Swamp Woman*, *Jungle Siren, Sarong Girl*, and *Call of the Jungle*. But Corio's greatest accomplishment was on stage, where she kept alive the art of the striptease—what she liked to call "deciduous kinesthetics"—for decades. Her 1965 stage show *This Was Burlesque* played the road for ages and even hit Broadway in the early '80s as competition for *Sugar Babies*, which starred Ann Miller (whose Fettuccine Alfredo recipe appears in Chapter 16). Corio made appearances on various talk shows, including *The Tonight Show*. She was colorful even with her clothes on. Her Chicken Cacciatore is as delicious as she was.

LAST BITES

In 1943, Corio was a volunteer pinup girl for the magazine *Yank,* a U.S. Army publication that was not nearly as dirty as its name would suggest.

ann corio's chicken cacciatore al forno

Preheat oven to 450°. Wash and dry chicken. Season with salt and pepper. Coat a shallow baking dish with oil. Place the chicken in it, skin side down, in one layer. Top with peppers, mushrooms, garlic and bay leaves. Sprinkle with olive oil. Bake 45 minutes, turning chicken once, until it is browned. Combine tomatoes and sugar. Pour over chicken. Reduce heat to 400° and bake ½ hour more. Add wine and bake 10 minutes longer or until chicken is tender.

2 frying chickens, about 2½ pound each, quartered

1 tablespoon salt

1 teaspoon pepper

2 green peppers, cut into ¼-inch strips

½ pound fresh mushrooms, sliced ¼-inch thick

2 cloves garlic, minced

2 bay leaves

½ cup olive oil

2½ cups crushed Italian tomatoes (20-ounce can)

2 tablespoons sugar

¼ cup Italian red wine (optional)

F ANNY BRICE STARTED IN BURLESQUE and found huge success in the *Ziegfeld Follies*, introducing such songs as "Second Hand Rose" and "My Man." She did plenty of Broadway, but Brice was best known for her toddler character Baby Snooks, a devilish role she played for decades. Brice was the funny girl upon which the Broadway musical *Funny Girl*, the subsequent film version, and its less-adored sequel *Funny Lady* are based. Brice herself appears in a handful of movies, including *The Great Ziegfeld*, *Ziegfeld Follies*, and *Everybody Sing*. Her Super Chocolate Cake will become a star in your kitchen.

POST MORTEM

"Super" is a bit of a stretch, but that sounds better than "Fanny Brice's Pretty Darn Good Chocolate Cake." Using semi-sweet rather than bittersweet chocolate makes the cake more kid-friendly. Even Baby Snooks would like it.

Fanny Brice's super chocolate cake

Serves
10

Grease and flour a 13 x 9-inch cake pan. Melt 4 one-ounce squares of chocolate in a double boiler in the cup of hot water. Bring to a boil. Mix the chocolate and butter until melted. Sift the flour, sugar, and salt in a large bowl. Pour the chocolate and butter into the dry ingredients and blend well. Add buttermilk and baking soda and mix again. Then incorporate the eggs and vanilla. Pour batter into pan. Bake in 350° oven for almost 30–40 minutes. Let cool. While the cake is in the oven, prepare the frosting. Melt the remaining 4 squares of bittersweet chocolate in a double boiler. In a medium-size bowl, mix the milk and powdered sugar together and then add the chocolate, 1 tablespoon vanilla, 3 tablespoons melted butter, and salt. Stir until smooth. Frost the cake.

8 one-ounce squares bittersweet chocolate, divided

1 stick butter

1 cup hot water

2 cups flour

2 cups sugar

Pinch of salt

½ cup buttermilk

1¼ teaspoon baking soda

2 eggs, beaten

1 teaspoon plus 1 tablespoon vanilla

7 tablespoons milk

3 cups sifted powdered sugar

3 tablespoons melted butter

Pinch of salt

after-dinner viewing

THIS WAS BURLESQUE (SORT OF . . .)

You can see Natalie Wood play Gypsy Rose Lee in the 1962 film version of *Gypsy* and Barbra Streisand as Fanny Brice in 1968's *Funny Girl* and the 1975 sequel *Funny Lady*. But to see the genuine articles, you can glimpse the real Lee in a cameo role as a lay teacher in the 1966 nun comedy *The Trouble with Angels* and see Brice with such stars as Myrna Loy and William Powell in 1936's *The Great Ziegfeld*. Ann Corio's *Here It Is, Burlesque!* was filmed for posterity but never made the leap from VHS to DVD, and even the tapes are rare. But you can see her opposite Buster Crabbe in the exotic 1942 film *Jungle Siren* available on DVD. Sophie Tucker's turns in *Broadway Melody of 1938* and *Thoroughbreds Don't Cry* keep the old girl alive on DVD. Five of Mae West's best films are available as a box set called *Mae West: The Glamour Collection*. Start with her 1932 film debut *Night After Night* starring George Raft. And don't forget her appearance on *Mister Ed,* which is included on *The Best of Mister Ed: Volume Two* and a fourth-season box set.

18

POOL PARTY ON SUNSET BOULEVARD

POOR DOPE, THAT JOE GILLIS. All he wanted to do was make a living as a screenwriter in Hollywood. Instead, he ended up floating dead in a swimming pool at 10086 Sunset Boulevard, the victim of a crazed actress's jealous rage. But, oh, the decadent fun he (and we) have getting there in Billy Wilder's 1950 drama *Sunset Boulevard*. No wonder the American Film Institute named it the twelfth-best American movie ever. Some of us would rank it even higher.

The classic film, starring William Holden, Gloria Swanson, and Erich von Stroheim, crackles with electricity and bubbles with bile. It's a portrait of Hollywood—complete with a dead monkey—that's etched in acid, faded glamour masking the terrible sadness of a whole lot of obscurity where a wealth of fame used to be. Swanson is astoundingly good as the silent film star Norma Desmond whose career dwindled with the arrival of talkies. When she returns to Paramount Studios after a twenty-year absence and a spotlight is thrown on her again, it's a goose bump–inducing movie moment for the ages. Holden couldn't be better as Joe, the hack-turned-gigolo who falls under Norma's spell. And von Stroheim, as the cuckolded Max, lends pathos to the piece. Every time I watch *Sunset Boulevard*, it gets better.

A screening of such a brilliant motion picture deserves a special evening. Why not invite friends over for a pool party on a gorgeous summer night and show it on the patio? To start the evening off, pass small servings of Gloria Swanson's health tonic of a soup. If anyone tells you that your starters used to be bigger, tell them, "I'm big. It's the portions that got small." Then cook up some of William Holden's exotic burgers for your hungry horde. After the movie, serve Erich von Stroheim's sweet German pastry. It's all fruits and nuts, much like Hollywood. As for cocktails, serve the Joe Gillis. It's just three shots and a splash. Your guests will be ready for their close-ups after a few of those.

erich von stroheim 1885–1957

A CTOR AND DIRECTOR Erich von Stroheim began acting in Hollywood in the teens, working with no less than D. W. Griffith on 1916's *Intolerance* and Jean Renoir on 1937's *Grand Illusion*. Stroheim co-wrote, directed, and starred in such films as *Blind Husbands* in 1919 and *Foolish Wives* in 1922, and he directed ZaSu Pitts in *Greed* in 1924. Stroheim's 1932 film *Queen Kelly*, considered one of his best, starred his future *Sunset Boulevard* cast mate Gloria Swanson. In fact, a clip of that silent classic is shown in *Sunset Boulevard*, a very "meta" move that adds poignancy to the affair. His strudel is sure to add a few extra pounds to yours.

erich von stroheim's strudel

Mix flour, salt, sugar, and baking powder in large bowl. Cut very cold butter into small pieces. Using your fingers, rub the butter into the flour mixture until it has the consistency of coarse crumbs. Add enough milk to make soft dough. Roll out to one-half-inch thick. Cut dough in two pieces. Sprinkle the almonds and raisins over one piece of dough. Cover with other piece of dough and roll together with rolling pin. Cut in four-inch squares. Brush tops with milk, and sprinkle with maple sugar. Bake at 350° for 30 minutes or until lightly brown.

Serves 8

4 cups flour

1 teaspoon salt

1 tablespoon sugar

2 teaspoons baking powder

4 tablespoons butter

Milk, as needed

1 cup chopped almonds

½ pound seedless raisins

½ cup grated maple sugar

GLORIA SWANSON, 1899–1983

L IKE NORMA DESMOND, Gloria Swanson was a queen of the silent screen, appearing in such films as *Sadie Thompson*, *The Love of Sunya*, and *Queen Kelly* in the 1920s and '30s. And like Norma, she hadn't been working in film very much until *Sunset Boulevard* gave her her most enduring role. Playing Norma earned her a Golden Globe, but not an Oscar. None of her three Oscar nominations panned out, in fact. Swanson did television in the 1950s and '60s including, believe it or not, episodes of *The Beverly Hillbillies*, *My Three Sons*, and *The Hollywood Squares*. She played herself in the 1974 disaster movie *Airport 1975*; that's the one with cross-eyed Karen Black flying the plane. Swanson was covered with real bees in the 1974 horror film *Killer Bees*. The old girl looked great right up until the end. Her lifelong obsession with health food paid off. All the more reason to try her unpleasantly named Potassium Broth.

WILLIAM HOLDEN 1918–1981

H OW'S THIS FOR AN IMPRESSIVE ROSTER OF FILMS? *Golden Boy*, *Born Yesterday*, *Stalag 17*, *Sabrina*, *Picnic*, *The Bridge on the River Kwai*, *The Wild Bunch*, *The Towering Inferno*, *Network*, and *S.O.B.* And that's not even counting *Sunset Boulevard*. William Holden showed amazing talent from the 1930s until the year he died, working opposite some of the most beautiful and talented women in movie history: Barbara Stanwyck, Kim Novak, Audrey Hepburn, and Faye Dunaway among them. And, he had an Oscar and an Emmy to show for it. A good sport, Holden took a pie to the face at the Brown Derby restaurant in the famous "Hollywood at Last!" episode of *I Love Lucy*. His recipe for Hamburgers à la Hong Kong isn't nearly as messy as all that.

GLORIA SWANSON'S POTASSIUM BROTH

Serves 8

1 cup string beans, chopped

1 cup celery, chopped

1 cup zucchini, chopped

1 cup Swiss chard, chopped

8 cups spring water

Before chopping, wash all vegetables thoroughly. Pour spring water into a soup pot and add the rest of ingredients. Cover and simmer until celery is tender. Allow the broth to cool to room temperature. Refrigerate in glass jars. Serve hot or cold.

WILLIAM HOLDEN'S HAMBURGERS à LA HONG KONG

Serves 8

2 pounds ground round

1 cup cornflakes

1 large tomato, diced

½ cup barbecue sauce

½ cup soy sauce

Crush cornflakes. Mix with ground round, tomatoes, and barbecue sauce. Form into eight patties. Marinate in soy sauce for 20 minutes, turning to coat both sides. Barbecue or broil to desired doneness.

POST MORTEM

These aren't hamburgers—they're miniature meat loaves—and they're about as exotic as the ethnic foods aisle at the Shop-Rite. But my tasters raved! The smoky flavor of the barbecue sauce mixed into the meat put a Holden their hearts.

aFTer-Dinner Viewing

SHOW Business on Screen

Sunset Boulevard exposes show business and all its broken dreams and unrealized ambitions. Once you've seen it ten or twelve times, you may find yourself hungering for other films that hang the fame game out to dry. John Schlesinger's 1975 *The Day of the Locust* stars Donald Sutherland, Karen Black, and Burgess Meredith (whose Nacho Salad recipe appears in Chapter 2) and paints 1930s Hollywood in a hellish light. The usually sweet Andy Griffith is drunk with power when he goes from hillbilly to media power player in Elia Kazan's 1957 film *A Face in the Crowd*. Patricia Neal costars. With director Sidney Lumet capturing genius performances from Faye Dunaway, Peter Finch, and William Holden (who was still sexy a quarter century after *Sunset Boulevard*), writer Paddy Chayefsky's 1976 satire *Network* reveals an even more knowing take on television today than it did thirty-five years ago. And if Broadway is your bailiwick, a duo of films: 1957's *The Sweet Smell of Success* starring Burt Lancaster and Tony Curtis, and 1950's classic *All About Eve* starring Bette Davis and Anne Baxter are must-sees. If you falsely believe that behind the sequins there are only more sequins, these movies will set you straight.

a Feast OF Funny Fellows

OLD-SCHOOL COMEDIANS LIKE TO COMPLAIN about their wives' cooking. Rodney Dangerfield, for instance, always said dinner at his house was so bad that his family prayed *after* they ate. His wife's meat loaf glowed in the dark! Henny Youngman observed, "My wife dresses to kill. She cooks the same way." But when these funny fellows cooked for themselves, the food didn't turn out any better. Redd Foxx, playing the feisty old junkman Fred Sanford on the classic 1970s sitcom *Sanford and Son*, once mixed a famous "San Francisco treat" with a can of pintos. He called it "Rice-a-Roni-beanie." Fred's mixture of Swiss cheese and guacamole was called "holey moley," of course, which was often his son's reaction to the food his father placed before him. Haute cuisine, it wasn't. Thank heaven these men were better cooks in real life. Dom DeLuise even became a cookbook author. Let's raise a glass of "Champipple" (Fred Sanford's mixture of ginger ale and ripple) to these men, hilarious in every room.

ReDD FOXX 1922–1991

JUNKYARD OWNER FRED SANFORD—that's S-A-N-F-O-R-D period, as he liked to say—was one of the funniest characters ever on television thanks to Redd Foxx. The man could turn finding a pair of glasses in a cluttered drawer into a sidesplitting bit of hilarity, and when he thought he was having a heart attack, forget it. "It's the big one! Elizabeth, I'm coming to join you, honey!" he'd say to his late wife as he looked to the heavens, and audiences would die laughing. Foxx polished his talent as a raunchy stand-up comedian who influenced such modern day comedians as Chris Rock. Jamie Foxx, they say, chose his stage name as a tribute to Redd. Follow-ups to *Sanford and Son* and several films, among them *Cotton Comes to Harlem* and *Norman . . . Is That You?* didn't amount to much. He died making the series *The Royal Family*. It really was the big one that got him in the end. Redd is gone, but the best of his comedy albums are still available. His spaghetti sauce is what you make of it.

ReDD FOXX'S SPAGHeTTi sauce

I meant it when I said this recipe is what you make of it. So use the amount of each ingredient that inspires you, throw everything all in a pot, and simmer until the flavors have blended. Adjust the seasonings until it tastes just right. "It's important that you get an 'ah' reaction," Foxx always said. Serves as many or few as you'd like.

Green peppers, chopped

Fresh garlic, chopped

Onions, chopped

Tomato paste

Tomato sauce

Salt

Pepper

Sugar

1 can water for each can of tomato paste

Seasoning salt

Serves Your Choice

Gary Coleman 1968–2010

BEFORE HE WAS A CHARACTER IN the Broadway musical *Avenue Q*, before his financial troubles and health problems, before he ran for governor of California and finished in eighth place, Gary Coleman was just that cute little kid from *Diff'rent Strokes*. His catchphrase "What'choo talkin' 'bout, Willis?" delivered to his costar, Todd Bridges, became part of the American vernacular. Coleman's big break came after Norman Lear put him into a couple of spots on *Good Times* and *The Jeffersons*. So charming a comedian, Coleman was cast in *Diff'rent Strokes* and soon became a sensation. He made his feature film debut in 1981's *On the Right Track*. Some of comedy's all-time greats, including Lucille Ball, Johnny Carson, and Bob Hope, were said to be huge fans of his. But when *Strokes* ended in 1986, Coleman's fame was quickly replaced by a sour sort of infamy. He did guest roles on such series as *227*, *The Fresh Prince of Bel-Air*, *Married with Children,* and *The Drew Carey Show*, but he ended up as a walking punch line, appearing on series like *The Surreal Life*. Coleman deserved a lot better. When you're feeling down, warm yourself with a bowl of his signature chicken vegetable soup.

Gary Coleman's Chicken Vegetable Soup

Back and ribs of one
  chicken

Salt, to taste

Pepper, to taste

1 bay leaf

1 cup uncooked, long
  grain rice

1 (8-ounce) can tomato
  sauce

1 (10-ounce) box frozen
  mixed vegetables

1 tablespoon sugar

Additional vegetables,
  if desired (leftovers
  work well)

In a stock pot, place chicken in enough cold water to cover. Cook until well done. Remove chicken and bones from stock. Debone chicken and return meat to stock. Discard bones. Add salt, pepper, and bay leaf. Simmer ten minutes. Add remaining ingredients and simmer 1½ hours.

POST MORTEM

Is it rude to suggest a *shortcut* to the diminutive actor's recipe? Too bad, here goes: start with four cans of low-sodium chicken broth, add some chopped leftover chicken and the remaining ingredients, and simmer until the rice is cooked. You'll be back watching *Diff'rent Strokes* in no time.

M AN, COULD BUDDY HACKETT TELL A STORY! The Borscht Belt comedian and comic actor—rubbery faced and endearingly funny-looking—worked blue, as they say, telling dirty jokes to Las Vegas audiences and going about as far as he could go telling them on TV talk shows. I remember one bit of his about a man who achieved "connubial fulfillment" every time he sneezed. "What did he take for that?" the interviewer asked. "Pepper," Hackett replied. For someone so naughty, Hackett found success in such mainstream fare as *The Music Man*, opposite Robert Preston, *It's a Mad, Mad, Mad, Mad World*, and *Muscle Beach Party*. Hackett lent his voice to the role of Scuttle in the Disney animated film *The Little Mermaid*, and received good notices as Lou Costello in a TV movie called *Bud and Lou*. Working up until just a few years before he died, he played Uncle Lonnie in the short-lived comedy *Action*, a satire of modern Hollywood that achieved a cult following. I can't think of Hackett, though, without remembering him shoving an entire frozen yogurt pop in his pie-hole on a TV commercial for those frozen desserts back in the 1970s and '80s. It was obscene and adorable, just like him.

BUDDY HACKETT'S CHINESE CHILI

Sauté the meat with the diced onion, chili powders, oregano, garlic powder, and 1 teaspoon salt. When well cooked, pour off some of the fat then simmer for 20 minutes. Add beef broth and simmer for two hours, stirring frequently. In a separate pan, stir-fry the celery and sliced onion in a small amount of oil. When they're crisp-cooked, add remaining vegetables and salt, and cook for 5 minutes more. Drain the vegetables, add to the chili, and serve.

2 pounds beef cubes, cut small, or ground chuck

1 large onion, diced

1 tablespoon chili powder

2 tablespoons California chili powder

1 pinch oregano

½ teaspoon garlic powder

1 teaspoon salt

1 can (14 ounce) beef broth

3 cups celery, sliced diagonally

1 cup sliced onion

1 can sliced water chestnuts

1 can sliced bamboo shoots

1 cup bean sprouts

½ teaspoon salt

RODNEY DANGERFIELD 1921–2004

F OR A MAN WHO SAID HE GOT NO RESPECT, Rodney Dangerfield was admired by his peers and adored by audiences. It took him a while to find his voice as a stand-up, but when he hit upon the persona of the most downtrodden man in the world, he found comedy gold and mined it for years. He owned his own comedy club in New York, which helped him to launch some of the greatest comedians of the past few decades, and he toured the country telling jokes like "During sex, my wife always wants to talk to me. Just the other night, she called me from a hotel." Dangerfield was pushing sixty when he became a movie star with a string of comedies such as *Caddyshack, Easy Money, Back to School*, and *Meet Wally Sparks*. He recorded a hip-hop single "Rappin' Rodney," gave voice to a canine counterpart called Rover Dangerfield, and even did a dramatic turn in Oliver Stone's *Natural Born Killers*, a performance that earned him plenty of respect from critics. His chicken salad will earn you plenty, too.

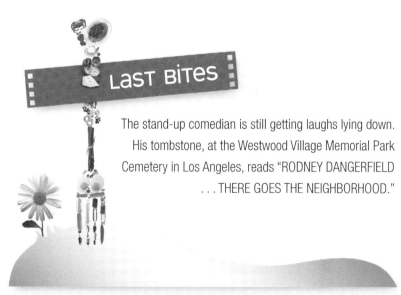

LAST BITES

The stand-up comedian is still getting laughs lying down. His tombstone, at the Westwood Village Memorial Park Cemetery in Los Angeles, reads "RODNEY DANGERFIELD . . . THERE GOES THE NEIGHBORHOOD."

RODNEY DANGERFIELD'S CHICKEN SALAD

Combine chicken, walnuts, celery, grapes, green pepper, and olives. Mix mayonnaise and sour cream, and then add to chicken mixture. Toss to coat. Season with salt and pepper, lemon juice, and curry powder. Serve on a bed of lettuce.

2–3 cups cooked chicken, cut into bite-size chunks

½ cup shelled walnuts

3 stalks celery, chopped

1 cup seedless grapes, halved

1 green pepper, diced

¼ cup stuffed green olives, sliced

½ cup mayonnaise

½ cup sour cream

Salt and pepper, to taste

½ teaspoon lemon juice

1 teaspoon curry powder

BEFORE HE WAS DISHING OUT ZINGERS on *The Hollywood Squares*, Paul Lynde had been a hit on Broadway as the put-upon father Harry MacAfee in *Bye, Bye Birdie*, a role he reprised in the movie version; and he had memorably played prankish Uncle Arthur in about a dozen episodes of *Bewitched*. With that distinctive voice of his, and a cadence that often added syllables to words for maximum comic effect, Lynde made his presence felt in such films as *Send Me No Flowers*, *The Glass Bottom Boat*, and *How Sweet It Is!*. He lent his voice to Templeton the rat in the animated musical version of *Charlotte's Web*. I loved Lynde best as the abusive obstetrician in Joan Rivers's hilariously tasteless 1978 movie *Rabbit Test*. He did guest shots on such 1960's sitcoms as *The Munsters* and *I Dream of Jeannie*, and regularly appeared on such variety programs as *The Dean Martin Comedy Hour* and *Donny and Marie*. His own TV series *The Paul Lynde Show*, in which his catchphrases included "Oh my knees just locked!" and *The New Temperatures Rising Show*, were short-lived efforts in the early '70s. Audiences liked him best as the center square on *The Hollywood Squares*—a gig that landed him on the cover of *People* magazine. "Paul, why do Hell's Angels wear leather?" he was once asked. "Because chiffon wrinkles too easily." Daytime TV was never funnier.

Paul Lynde's Beef Stew

Mix all ingredients well in a large casserole dish. Cover and bake at 250° for 6 to 7 hours.

3 pounds lean stew meat

1 can carrots, drained and diced

1 can small onions, drained

1 can tomatoes, not drained

1 can peas, drained

1 can potatoes, drained

1 can green beans, drained

1 cup beef broth

4 tablespoons instant tapioca

1 tablespoon brown sugar

½ cup prepared bread crumbs

1 bay leaf

½ cup white wine

1½ tablespoons salt

Pepper, to taste

POST MORTEM

The hearty taste of Lynde's stew will take you back to your childhood—in a good way—but unfortunately so will the mushy consistency of the cooked canned vegetables. Unless you're a secret square, you'll want to update the recipe with fresh veggies—you can use frozen peas—for a dish that's a real winner.

Henny Youngman 1906–1998

H E WAS THE KING OF THE ONE-LINERS, and one line in particular —"Take my wife, please"—was enough to get audiences rolling in the aisles. He was, of course, Henny Youngman, the stand-up comedian and violinist. He played a "Stradivaricose," he liked to say, and for sixty years told rapid-fire jokes to any audience that would listen. At the height of his career, he played upwards of 100 gigs a year. When in 1974, the New York Telephone Company created Dial-a-Joke, more than 3 million people called to hear Youngman. He was a hit on radio's *Kate Smith Show*, appeared on *Rowan and Martin's Laugh-In*, and had cameos in Mel Brooks's *Silent Movie* and *History of the World, Part I*. In Martin Scorsese's classic mob film *Goodfellas*, Youngman was seen playing to a room full of gangsters. It wasn't much of a stretch. Youngman said that during his very long career he'd played places so rough, the coat-check girl was named Rocco. Make his recipe, please.

John Ritter 1948–2003

W HEN JOHN RITTER DIED, audiences realized that he wasn't just funny, he was beloved. Although remembered best as Jack Tripper, the not-gay man living with two straight women on the sitcom *Three's Company*, Ritter had numerous other TV hits. He was a recurring character on *The Waltons* and starred in other series, including *Hooperman*, *Hearts Afire*, and *8 Simple Rules*. Born into a show business family—his father was country crooner Tex Ritter—Ritter was particularly adept at physical comedy, but he had chops, too. He appeared in such films as *Sling Blade* and *Bad Santa*, and seems to have passed along his acting genes to look-alike son, Jason Ritter. To the rest of us, he passed along this recipe.

Henny Youngman's Crispy Rice Chicken

Mix crushed cereal with spices. Coat chicken pieces in melted margarine and roll in cereal mixture. Place in a baking pan. Bake at 375° for 1 hour or until done.

6 cups crispy rice cereal, coarsely crushed

½ tablespoon salt

½ tablespoon black pepper

½ tablespoon paprika

2 chickens, cut up

1 cup margarine, melted

John Ritter's Favorite Fudge

Combine sugar and cocoa. Add milk, stirring until smooth. Heat mixture to a boil. Continue cooking at a slow boil, stirring occasionally to scrape mixture from sides of pan. Cook to soft-ball stage (about 238°), Remove from heat and allow to cool 5 minutes. Stir in butter and vanilla. Beat on medium speed until fudge becomes very thick and starts to lose its gloss. Pour into a buttered pan and let cool completely.

2 cups sugar

3–4 heaping tablespoons cocoa

1 cup milk

1½ tablespoons butter

1 teaspoon vanilla

Dom DeLuise 1933–2009

COMIC ACTOR AND COOKBOOK AUTHOR Dom DeLuise first made his name with a bumbling magician character he created called Dominick the Great for whom no trick ever worked. From then on, DeLuise worked plenty on variety shows with his friend Dean Martin, in movies with his buddy Burt Reynolds, and most memorably in collaboration with his pal Mel Brooks. DeLuise appeared in the Brooks films *The Twelve Chairs*, *Blazing Saddles*, *Silent Movie*, *History of the World, Part I*, and *Robin Hood: Men in Tights*. His "French Mistake" dance in *Blazing Saddles* is the nuts, as my mother used to say. Although DeLuise starred in his own sitcom, *Lotsa Luck*, it lasted only one season, but did make it to DVD. One of his best performances is in the underappreciated film *The End,* in which he plays a mental patient who befriends a suicidal Reynolds. Always roly-poly, DeLuise loved to eat and it showed. He believed in the healing power of good comfort food, though, and brought that message to his fans via his cookbook *Eat This . . . It'll Make You Feel Better* and several follow-up volumes. He wrote children's books, too. Any would be perfect reading with a doodlewopper or two, warm from the oven.

Dom DeLuise's Doodlewoppers

Makes about 60

Combine flour, baking soda, and cream of tartar. Add butter, shortening, 1 cup sugar, ginger, eggs, and vanilla, and mix to form dough. In a small bowl, mix remaining ¼ cup sugar and cinnamon. Using a tablespoon of dough at a time, form balls and roll in sugar and cinnamon mixture. Place on an ungreased baking sheet. Gently press a pecan half into the center of each one. Bake at 350° for 10–12 minutes.

3 cups flour

1 teaspoon baking soda

2 teaspoons cream of tartar

½ cup butter, softened

½ cup vegetable shortening

1¼ cup sugar, divided

1 teaspoon ground ginger

4 eggs

1 teaspoon vanilla

2 teaspoons cinnamon

2 cups pecan halves

aFTer-Dinner Viewing

GUYS' NiGHT In

Arnold (Gary Coleman) and Willis (Todd Bridges) form the Jackson Two Brownie Company to sell their new housekeeper's fudge yummies in "Big Business," a season two episode of *Diff'rent Strokes*. When Adelaide Brubaker (Nedra Volz) tells the boys she has too much work to do to make brownies, they decide to make the brownies themselves. All hell breaks loose. "It sounds as if the kitchen is having a nervous breakdown," their father (Conrad Bain) says; and their baked goods flop. "From tycoon to janitor in one day," Arnold observes.

In 1968's *The Love Bug*, the live-action Disney comedy about a Volkswagen bug with a personality all its own, Buddy Hackett's off-the-wall character Tennessee Steinmetz heats up a pot of coffee with a welding iron. "The trick is always remember to have asbestos gloves when you make coffee this way," he says. Don't try it at home, kids.

You can watch any number of Rodney Dangerfield movies and howl, but to see him doing what he did best, watch rare footage of his nightclub act, shot live at the MGM Grand in Las Vegas circa 1995, on the three-DVD set *Rodney Dangerfield No Respect: The Ultimate Collection.*

The best example of Paul Lynde's work to see the laser light of DVD is 1976's *The Paul Lynde Halloween Special.* In the rarely seen show, Lynde confides that when he was young he was "fa-a-a-aaaaat!" and the year he dressed up as the Hindenburg, Halloween was a "dis-as-ter." He wasn't kidding about his girth. Once he lost it, he appeared on the cover of *Weight Watchers* magazine.

In the season-five episode of *Sanford and Son* called "Can You Chop This?," Fred (Redd Foxx) is watching "The Cavorting Connoisseur" (Cesare Danova) when he stumbles upon a get-rich-quick scheme: selling hand-cranked food processors called Whopper Choppers. He uses Lamont's savings as seed money, buys 100 of the cheap devices, but can't unload even one. That is, until he crashes the cooking program and shows the studio audience (and the cameras) just how awful the Whopper Choppers are. The manufacturer agrees to buy them all back on one condition: Fred can never try to sell a Whopper Chopper again.

Believe it or not, Henny Youngman traded his violin strings for g-strings when he appeared in Herschell Gordon Lewis's infamous 1972 exploitation film *The Gore-Gore Girls.* The comedian plays a nightclub owner named Marzdone Mobilie whose go-go girls become the targets of a crazed killer. It was so gory and so outrageous that Youngman denied he was ever in the film until his dying day.

Adorably corpulent Dom DeLuise plays a chronic overeater in *Fatso*, which was written and directed by Anne Bancroft, whose Che-Cha Pasta recipe appears in Chapter Four. DeLuise's character tries to lose weight via a group called Chubby Checkers, but often falls off the wagon. At his lowest point, he starts into a birthday cake he is supposed to pick up and deliver. By the time he gets to the party, it reads "Happy Birthday Anth." "You ate the 'ony'!!!" screams Bancroft, who also stars. It's hilarious and surprisingly poignant.

Aspiring chef Jack Tripper (John Ritter) bakes a pie for the California Technical School's tenth-annual baking contest, but Chrissy (Suzanne Somers) eats it in the season-three *Three's Company* episode "The Bake-Off." Chrissy panics then sends Mrs. Roper (Audra Lindley) off to buy a replacement at the bakery. At the contest, she confesses and, because the show thrived on broad physical comedy, a pie fight ensues. Soon everyone is up to his or her ears in whipped cream and chocolate mousse.

20

Delicious Dames

THERE ARE SOME MEN (Jerry Lewis, most infamously) who maintain that women just aren't funny. To them, I say with all due respect, you're idiots. Women are hilarious, and always have been. We just weren't listening as closely as we are now in this era of *30 Rock* and *Bridesmaids*. Women are funny in as many different ways, if not more, than men. They can drop an acerbic bomb with perfect accuracy, do sidesplitting physical shtick, tickle the funny bone while tugging at the heartstrings, play the ditz who's smarter than anyone, or rock a Vegas mike with cojones as big as those of their male counterparts. Funny women have the added burden of having to be cute, too, while funny men can look barely human. But the gals do it and they're making more people laugh than ever before. They're standing on some pretty big shoulder pads, of course, which is what this chapter is all about. Before audiences adored Tina Fey, Amy Sedaris, Lisa Lampanelli, Kristen Wiig, and Sarah Silverman, they were laughing it up with the women whose recipes appear in this chapter. With dishes as delicious as these dames, no host or hostess could ever go wrong.

TOTIE FIELDS 1927–1978

COMEDIENNE AND ACTRESS Totie Fields got her start on *The Ed Sullivan Show* and always said she was like a dachshund—you only had to see her once to remember what she looked like. Four-ten and zaftig, Fields made fun of her struggle to lose weight. A story she told involved a snooty bathing suit saleswoman who once gave her attitude because of her girth. To muck with her, Fields asked for a size 2, squeezed her ample frame into it, came out of the dressing room and said, "It's perfect, I'll take it." The clerk fainted. A popular Las Vegas stand-up, Fields did a little acting in the 1970s, appearing on *Here's Lucy* and *Medical Center*, and wrote a diet book called *I Think I'll Start on Monday*. Her real forte was being herself on talk shows. Although she was plagued with health problems late in her life, she continued to go for the funny. After losing a leg, brave woman that she was, she incorporated her troubles into her act. In her last year, the American Guild of Variety Artists voted her Entertainer of the Year.

TOTIE FIELDS'S MISH MOSH

Sauté onions in oil. Add ground beef, season with pepper and garlic, and cook until brown. Cook egg noodles according to package directions; drain and mix with beaten eggs. Combine meat and noodle mixtures. Add onion soup mixture and mix well. Bake in a greased casserole at 350° for 1 hour.

Serves 4

3 onions, chopped

3 tablespoons oil

2 pounds ground beef

Pepper and garlic, to taste

8–10 ounces egg noodles

4 eggs, beaten

½ package of onion soup mix, mixed with enough water to make one cup

BeTTY GarreTT 1919–2011

BEFORE HER NAME WAS ETCHED IN pop-culture stone for playing Irene Lorenzo, the liberated woman next door on *All in the Family* from 1973–75, and Edna Babish, the much-married landlady on *Laverne & Shirley* from 1976–81, Betty Garrett was a top-notch MGM hoofer in such films as *Take Me Out to the Ball Game, Neptune's Daughter,* and *On the Town.* She was damn good in *My Sister Eileen,* too. She was almost ruined when her husband, the Oscar-nominated actor Larry Parks, was called before the House Un-American Activities Committee in the 1950s and blacklisted in Hollywood for his ties to the Communist party. Following this indignity, the duo performed together in a nightclub act and in plays. He lived long enough to see her career blossom again with her role on *All in the Family,* but died before she was cast on *Laverne & Shirley.* In what may be the ultimate revenge for a career interrupted, Garrett performed and taught acting right up to the end of her very long life.

LaST BiTes

Garrett appears posthumously in the 2011 film documentary *Carol Channing: Larger than Life.* The two worked together on the so-called Borscht Belt circuit in their early days.

BeTTY GarreTT'S LamB Curry

Brown the meat in the oil in a large skillet. Add remaining ingredients, cover and simmer for 20–30 minutes. Stir frequently. Remove ¼ cup stock and stir in flour. Add this mixture back to pan and stir for two minutes. Serve the curry over cooked rice and garnish with any or all of the following: raisins, chives, nuts, diced tomatoes, coconut, diced cucumber, chopped hard-boiled egg whites, chopped hard-boiled egg yolks, and chutney.

1 pound lamb shoulder, cut into cubes

3 tablespoons oil

1 cup boiling water

½ teaspoon salt

¼ teaspoon pepper

⅔ teaspoon curry powder (or to taste)

1 tablespoon chopped onion

¼ cup chopped celery

1 tablespoon chopped pimento

1 tablespoon chopped parsley

1 tablespoon flour

Cooked rice

Hermione GINGOLD 1897–1987

BRITISH ACTRESS HERMIONE GINGOLD took Sir Thomas Beecham's advice to heart and frequently admitted that she'd tried everything "except incest and folk dancing," which is why her memoir *How to Grow Old Disgracefully* is such a hoot. She was a success on the London stage, made memorable appearances in such frothy films as *The Music Man* and *Munster, Go Home!*, and was a fixture on the best TV couches in America. A frequent guest on *The Tonight Show*, particularly during the years when Jack Paar (whose soup recipe appears in Chapter 1) was at the helm, Gingold could spin a yarn like the best guest at the chicest cocktail party. On Broadway, her performance as the former courtesan Madame Armfeldt in the original cast of Stephen Sondheim's 1973 musical *A Little Night Music* is the stuff of legend. No one has ever sung of a love life well spent with more conviction than she has singing "Liaisons." Too bad the movie version didn't do it justice. Gingold said she wanted to die onstage, preferably to a full house. She almost got her wish. While touring in *Side by Side by Sondheim*, she fell, became bedridden, and died. But she made it as a performer to the ripe old age of eighty-nine and there's nothing disgraceful about that.

Hermione Gingold's Salmon Pie

Sauté onion in butter for several minutes. Stir in parsley and then salmon. Remove from heat and allow to cool. Beat eggs with milk and then stir in sour cream. Season with salt and pepper. Add salmon mixture and combine well. Make pastry crust by combining flour, baking powder, salt, shortening, egg, and ice water, and mixing well. Divide dough in half. Roll out to ⅛-inch thickness on floured board. Line a pie plate with dough. Fill with salmon mixture. Roll out remaining dough. Cover pie with top crust. Pinch edges together and trim neatly. Cut a few steam vents in top crust. Bake 15 minutes in a preheated 400° oven. Reduce heat to 350° and bake another 25 minutes.

Filling:

1 onion, minced

2 tablespoons butter

1 tablespoon chopped parsley

1 (1-pound) can red salmon, flaked

2 eggs

½ cup milk

½ cup sour cream

½ teaspoon salt

⅛ teaspoon black pepper

Pastry Crust:

2½ cups flour

1 teaspoon baking powder

¾ teaspoon salt

⅔ cup shortening

1 egg

3 tablespoons ice water

Imogene Coca 1908–2001

I F SID CAESAR WERE FRED ASTAIRE, Imogene Coca would be remembered as his Ginger Rogers. As the comic master's frequent partner on *Your Show of Shows*, Coca performed live sketch comedy as well as anyone ever has. Their spoof of *From Here to Eternity*, which they renamed "From Here to Obscurity," is a classic bit of waterlogged funny business. Coca won an Emmy for her work with Caesar and continued to appear on television. She played a cave woman in the infamous (and mercifully short-lived) time-travel sitcom *It's About Time*, opposite Joe E. Ross. Baby boomers know her as the eccentric Aunt Jenny whose looks horrified Jan on a memorable episode of *The Brady Bunch*. And, at eighty, she guest starred on *Moonlighting* and received her fifth Emmy nomination. Coca appeared on Broadway in shows from the 1930s to the late 1950s. After a twenty-year absence, she again delighted Broadway audiences as the nutty Letitia Primrose in the Cy Coleman musical *On the Twentieth Century* in 1978 and was nominated for a Tony Award. Mrs. Primrose urged everyone aboard the train to repent for their sins . . . after they'd tried everything. This recipe, included.

imogene coca's beef quixote

Soak beef slices in lemon juice and garlic overnight. Then drain in a colander. Cut into large bite-sized pieces and fry in olive oil. Serve over cooked rice accompanied by plantains, which have been peeled, sliced on a diagonal to create oval pieces, and fried in olive oil in a separate skillet.

Serves 2

1 pound thinly sliced beef, pounded thin

½ cup lemon juice

1 clove garlic, minced

4 tablespoons olive oil or more as needed

Plantains, as side dish

2 cups cooked rice

POST Mortem

It's no "impossible dream" to turn this Beef Quixote recipe into a tasty stir-fry. Add some sliced scallions and a couple of chopped peppers to the sauté and you'll be able to invite your own Sancho or Aldonza over for dinner!

vivian vance 1909–1979

ONLY ONE PERSON EVER HAD THE physical comedy chops to stand side-by-side with Lucille Ball, and it wasn't her husband or her children. It was Vivian Vance, who won an Emmy playing Ethel Mertz on *I Love Lucy* and then went on to play similar sidekicks on *The Lucy-Desi Comedy Hour*, *The Lucy Show*, and *Here's Lucy*. Vance had done Broadway, appearing in such shows as *Anything Goes*, before becoming immortalized on television. While she did do some films, most notably Blake Edwards's *The Great Race*, television was her medium. When she appeared on an episode of *Rhoda*, it was like one generation of TV royalty passing a crown along to another. An interesting note: William Frawley, who played Ethel's husband, Fred Mertz, on *I Love Lucy*, and Vance hated each other. Vance reportedly said, "Champagne for everyone!" upon hearing of his death.

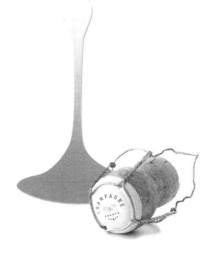

THE DEAD CELEBRITY COOKBOOK

vivian vance's chicken kiev

Cut each chicken breast in half and pound until thin. Lay a frozen pat of butter in the middle of each breast piece. Sprinkle each with ½ teaspoon garlic powder, ½ teaspoon onion powder, salt, pepper, and tarragon. Roll up tightly, tucking in the ends to contain the butter when it melts. Use toothpicks to secure ends. Dredge each roll in flour. Mix sour cream with egg and beat well. Dip roll in this mixture, then coat heavily with bread or cornflake crumbs. Wrap individually in freezer paper and place in freezer until thoroughly chilled, one hour or more. Heat oil in deep skillet to 370°, and fry the rolls until golden, turning only once. Drain on paper towel and serve hot, with dab of sour cream and sprinkles of parsley or chives.

4 boneless, skinless chicken breasts

¼ pound butter, cut into 8 pats and frozen

4 teaspoons garlic powder

4 teaspoons onion powder

Salt and pepper, to taste

1 teaspoon tarragon

Flour for dredging

1 egg

1 tablespoon sour cream plus more for garnish

2 cups finely ground bread crumbs or cornflake crumbs

Vegetable oil for deep-frying

Parsley or chive for garnish

C OMIC ACTRESS ALICE GHOSTLEY has been called "the female Paul Lynde," but maybe it was the other way around. For sure, the two shared impeccable comic timing and a similar delivery and both had recurring roles on *Bewitched*. Ghostley played Esmeralda, who vanished (at least partially) when she got upset. She appeared over the years on numerous TV shows from *Car 54, Where are You?* to *Punky Brewster*, and did a few movies, most notably *To Kill a Mockingbird* and *The Graduate*. But she is best remembered for her hilarious stint as the dotty Bernice Clifton on *Designing Women*. Singing "Black man, black man, where have you gone to?" or wearing a Christmas tree skirt that was intended for a Douglas fir, she was one hot hilarious mess. "It's a gift!" she'd say of her talents, and I have to agree. Her performance as an evil stepsister (opposite Kaye Ballard) in the 1957 TV version of Rodgers & Hammerstein's *Cinderella* (with Julie Andrews) is brilliant, too.

aLice GHOSTLeY's German chocoLaTe cake

Have all the cake ingredients at room temperature. Melt chocolate in pan set in boiling water, set aside to cool. Cream butter and sugar until fluffy. Add egg yolks one at a time, beating well after each addition. Blend in vanilla and cooled chocolate mixture. In a separate bowl sift the flour, baking soda, and salt, and add to chocolate mixture alternately with the buttermilk. Fold in the beaten egg whites. Pour into 3 greased and floured 8- or 9-inch round cake pans. Bake for 30–40 minutes at 350°. Test with a toothpick for doneness. Set aside to cool.

While the cake cools, make the frosting. In a saucepan over medium heat, heat milk, sugar, egg yolks, butter and vanilla, stirring constantly until thick, about 12 minutes. Stir in coconut and pecans. Cool slightly before frosting the tops of each layer. Leave sides unfrosted.

Cake:

4 (1-ounce) squares Baker's German Sweet Chocolate

½ cup boiling water

1 cup butter, softened

2 cups sugar

4 egg yolks

1 teaspoon vanilla

2½ cups sifted cake flour

1 teaspoon baking soda

½ teaspoon salt

1 cup buttermilk

4 egg whites, stiffly beaten

Frosting:

1 cup evaporated milk

1 cup sugar

3 egg yolks, slightly beaten

½ cup butter

1 teaspoon vanilla

1¾ cups coconut

1½ cups chopped pecans

MADELINE KAHN 1942–1999

MADELINE KAHN WOULD HAVE BEEN FUNNY reading the phone book, which was a problem for her because she wanted to be a dramatic actress. But drama's loss is the world's gain. Her performances as the sexually charged Lili Von Shtupp in *Blazing Saddles*, the stripper (with a bladder the size of a peanut) Trixie Delight in *Paper Moon*, and the murder suspect Mrs. White in *Clue* are side-splitting. Mel Brooks, who directed her in *Blazing Saddles*, was her best collaborator and cast Kahn in *Young Frankenstein, High Anxiety*, and *History of the World, Part I*. Various attempts at television including *Oh Madeline* and *Mr. President* didn't work, but she found a sitcom home on *Cosby* from 1996 until her passing. She did Broadway in such vehicles as *On the Twentieth Century* with Imogene Coca, the 1989 revival of *Born Yesterday*, and as Dr. Gorgeous in Wendy Wasserstein's *The Sisters Rosensweig*, which earned Kahn a Tony. Her performance of "Getting Married Today" from *Company* is captured on the DVD of *Sondheim: A Celebration at Carnegie Hall* from 1992.

Madeline Kahn's Foot Cookies

Cream butter and sugar. Then add milk, beaten eggs, and vanilla. Sift together flour and baking powder and add to butter and egg mixture until well blended. Chill for an hour or overnight. Roll out dough on floured board and cut with a foot-shaped cookie cutter. If you can't find a foot-shaped cookie cutter, draw a foot on a piece of parchment paper, cut it out and use it as a template while cutting dough with a sharp knife. Bake the feet on a greased cookie sheet at 350° for 10 minutes, or until lightly brown.

Makes about 24

½ cup butter, softened

1 cup sugar

1 tablespoon milk

2 beaten eggs

1 teaspoon vanilla

2½ cups flour

3 tablespoons baking powder

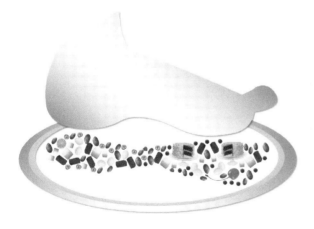

GiLDa RaDNer 1946–1989

ARGUABLY THE MOST BELOVED MEMBER of the Not Ready For Prime Time Players (as the original cast of *Saturday Night Live* was known), Gilda Radner created some of the most memorable characters that show has ever produced. Among them were Emily Litella, a little old lady who never quite heard things correctly, Roseanne Roseannadanna, a newswoman prone to gross-out stories, and Baba Wawa, a severely speech-impaired version of Barbara Walters. Radner did hilarious impressions of Lucille Ball, Patti Smith, and Nadia Comăneci, too! The gig earned her an Emmy. Working with Gene Wilder, who would become her husband, Radner appeared in *Hanky Panky*, *The Woman in Red*, and *Haunted Honeymoon*, which featured Dom DeLuise (See Chapter 19) in drag. Her book *It's Always Something* will make you cry. But a piece of Radner's Dutch Apple Cake is sure to cheer you up.

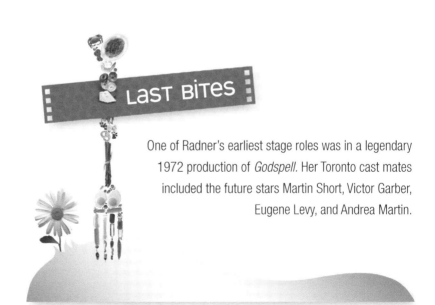

LaST BiTeS

One of Radner's earliest stage roles was in a legendary 1972 production of *Godspell.* Her Toronto cast mates included the future stars Martin Short, Victor Garber, Eugene Levy, and Andrea Martin.

Gilda Radner's Dutch Apple Cake

Mix flour, sugar, baking powder, and salt in a bowl and set aside. In another bowl, cream the one cup of room temperature butter, then beat in vanilla, egg, and milk. Add wet ingredients to dry ingredients and combine to make stiff dough. Spread in a greased 9-inch square baking pan. Press thin edge of apple slices into dough very tightly together. Sprinkle with brown sugar, butter pieces, and then cinnamon. Bake 45 minutes to 1 hour at 375°.

1 cup flour

¼ cup sugar

2 teaspoons baking powder

Pinch of salt

1 cup butter at room temperature, plus ½ stick cold butter cut into small pieces

1 teaspoon vanilla

1 egg

¼ cup milk

6 apples, peeled, cored, and sliced into eighths

½ cup brown sugar

Cinnamon

DODY GOODMAN 1914–2008

ONE COULD LOVE DODY GOODMAN on the basis of two performances alone: as Martha Shumway, the mother of Mary Hartman on *Mary Hartman, Mary Hartman,* and as the principal's assistant Blanche in *Grease* and *Grease 2* opposite Eve Arden. Whatever the role, her persona was that of a deluxe ditz, that is, someone cheerful to the point of mental illness. This made her perfect for talk shows. Goodman first made a splash on television on the *The Tonight Show,* but, as the story goes, she was dropped for upstaging host Jack Paar. Other chat programs were happy to have her. Among her TV credits were recurring roles on *Diff'rent Strokes, St. Elsewhere,* and *Alvin and the Chipmunks.* Her resume included the Broadway musicals *High Button Shoes, Wonderful Town,* and *Lorelei.* Goodman's comedic talents came naturally. "I just opened my mouth and people laughed," she once said. You'll smile when you open your mouth to taste her zabaglione.

DODY GOODMAN'S ZABAGLIONE

Beat egg yolks lightly in a bowl with the sugar. Pour into a double boiler over, not in, boiling water and beat the custard constantly with a wire whisk. When foamy, gradually add the wine. Continue to beat until double in bulk. Remove from heat. Whip the egg whites until stiff but not dry and fold into the custard. Pour into 6–8 glasses and serve immediately while warm, topping each with a strawberry.

Serves 6–8

8 egg yolks

3–4 tablespoons sugar

½ cup dry sauterne, Marsala, or Madeira

8 egg whites

Strawberry to top each serving

AFTer-DInner VIEWING

Dames on DISC

Betty Garrett shines as an aspiring writer who moves from Ohio to Manhattan with her gorgeous sister (Janet Leigh) in 1955's *My Sister Eileen*. In the film version of the Lerner and Loewe musical *Gigi*, Hermione Gingold sings the duet "I Remember It Well" with Maurice Chevalier. A 1977 Las Vegas comeback performance by Totie Fields, released on DVD as *On Location With: Totie Fields*, preserves her irresistible wit. In the 1983 comedy *National Lampoon's Vacation*, Imogene Coca plays the fruitcake-hating Aunt Edna. "Do you enjoy throwing up every five minutes, Claude?" she asks. Once you've committed *I Love Lucy* to memory, watch Vivian Vance as Vivian Bagley, a divorced version of Ethel Mertz, on *The Lucy Show*. The revue that launched Alice Ghostley's career— *New Faces of 1952*—was made into a movie two years later. Dody Goodman is hilarious in *Grease*. "Xylophone" is the word in her case. In her big-screen debut in the 1972 comedy *What's Up, Doc?*,

Madeline Kahn plays Eunice Burns, Ryan O'Neal's fiancée. You only have to hear her say, "You have Howard Bannister's rocks" to love her. Gilda Radner's five seasons on *Saturday Night Live* have been released on DVD; but for an all-Gilda treat, watch her Broadway concert film *Gilda Live!* released as part of the Warner archive collection of semi-obscure titles.

21

HUNGRY Men Dinners

I'T'S EASY TO IMAGINE HOLLYWOOD'S leading-est men killing some-thing to eat, but not so easy picturing them cooking and serving it. It's a safe bet that no one ever called John Wayne "Connie Casserole" despite the fact that a very cheesy one was his favorite at-home meal. If you look at their best-known movies, even sharing fruit was a problem for tough guys. Look what James Cagney did to poor Mae Clarke with that grapefruit in *The Public Enemy*. Can you say "citrus facial"? But in real life, some of these fellows did cook—hearty main dishes and superior desserts, if you go by the recipes these cats left behind. They answer the age-old question, how do you handle a hungry man? Those vintage Campbell's Soup commercials said serve him a "man-handler." These leading men can certainly handle themselves in the kitchen.

GreGOrY PeCK 1916–2003

H E WAS THE MAN (Tom Rath) in *The Man in the Grey Flannel Suit*, Atticus Finch in *To Kill a Mockingbird*, Dr. Josef Mengele in *The Boys from Brazil*, and Damien's father in *The Omen*. From the mid-forties when he starred in Hitchcock's *Spellbound* to the 1990s when he appeared in Martin Scorsese's remake of *Cape Fear*, Peck made an indelible impression on audiences. (It didn't hurt that he was stunning looking.) Peck won the Oscar for *To Kill a Mockingbird* and he was nominated four other times; but he was celebrated for his work in *The Yearling*, *The Guns of Navarone*, *Roman Holiday*, and the original *Cape Fear*, among many others. In 2011, Peck received the honor of appearing on a stamp as part of the U.S. Postal Service's "Legends of Hollywood" series. Fans couldn't lick the back of Peck's head, alas, stamps are self-stick now, but you might want to taste his ratatouille.

GreGOrY PeCK'S RaTaTOUiLLe

Heat olive oil in a casserole. Add onions and cook, stirring frequently, until they are soft but not brown. Julienne-slice peppers, and peel and chop remaining vegetables. Add all vegetables to casserole. Season with salt and pepper and cook uncovered over low heat for about 30 minutes, stirring occasionally. When vegetables are tender, allow to cool. Transfer to a serving dish and sprinkle with a mixture of such herbs as celery seed, chervil, tarragon, fennel seed, parsley, basil, rosemary, thyme, and bay leaf.

Serves 6

4 tablespoons olive oil

2 large onions, chopped

4 sweet peppers

4 tomatoes

1 pound zucchini

1 medium eggplant

Salt and pepper, to taste

¼ cup fines herbes

BEFORE HE WAS THE STAR of *The Rifleman*, the role for which he'll always be remembered, Chuck Connors was a Boston Celtic, a Brooklyn Dodger, and a Chicago Cub. Talk about a he-man! Both a professional basketball and professional baseball player, Connors switched to acting because he was even better at that, making his debut in the Tracy and Hepburn favorite *Pat and Mike* in 1952. Other early films include *South Sea Woman*, *Old Yeller*, *Flipper*, and *Move Over, Darling*.

Playing the widowed cowboy Lucas McCain on *The Rifleman* made Connors the go-to guy for westerns in the decades that followed. He starred in such ranch-flavored series as *Branded*, *Cowboy in Africa*, and *The Yellow Rose*. More interesting is that he appeared in the landmark series *Roots*, and in k. d. lang's 1991 feature film debut *Salmonberries*. His chowder doesn't call for any of those.

CHUCK CONNORS'S CLAM CHOWDER

Combine all ingredients in a stock-pot. Simmer 3–4 hours. Remove bay leaf. Serve hot.

2 (12-ounce) cans chopped clams

¾ cup clam juice

2 (28-ounce) cans crushed tomatoes

1 (12-ounce) can tomato paste

4 large potatoes, peeled and diced

4 stalks celery, sliced

2 large onions, diced

2 cloves garlic, minced

6 large carrots, sliced

1 teaspoon oregano

1 bay leaf

1 cup chopped fresh parsley

16 cups water

Black pepper, to taste

½ cup olive oil

POST MORTEM

A loaf of warm, crusty bread and a simple green salad turns this seaworthy soup into a hearty supper. If you think they'll get along, invite Klaus Nomi's Lime Tart (See Chapter 11) over for dessert.

J AMES CAGNEY STARTED AS A HOOFER and comedian in vaudeville, skills that would serve him in his Academy Award–winning performance in *Yankee Doodle Dandy*. But it is his performances as pugnacious little hood-lums like Tom Powers in *The Public Enemy*, in which he famously smashed a grapefruit in Mae Clark's face, Cody Jarrett in *White Heat*, and Rocky Sullivan in *Angels with Dirty Faces* that Cagney is best remembered. He kept impressionists of the "you dirty rat!" variety employed for decades. Among his other celebrated films were *Mister Roberts*, *Man of a Thousand Faces*, and his final feature film, *Ragtime*. It is no wonder he ranks eighth on the American Film Institute's list of Greatest Male Stars of All Time. His beans and burgers will be right up there on your list, too.

Last Bites

Cagney's *New York Times* obituary includes this tidbit: The tough guy's first role was as a chorus girl in a female-impersonation act.

THE DEAD CELEBRITY COOKBOOK

James Cagney's Beans and Burgers

Combine ground chuck, onions, steak sauce, parsley, oregano, rosemary, paprika, salt, and pepper. Form into meatballs. Roll meatballs in bread crumbs to coat. Brown meatballs in oil in skillet. Combine remaining ingredients (except beans) and add to meat. Add beans and simmer until meatballs are cooked through and beans are hot.

1½ pounds ground chuck

1 small onion, chopped

1 tablespoon steak sauce

1 tablespoon parsley, minced

½ teaspoon dried oregano

½ teaspoon dried rosemary

Dash of paprika

1½ teaspoons salt

¼ teaspoon pepper

¼ cup dried bread crumbs

2 tablespoons oil

1 (8-ounce) can tomato sauce

⅓ cup ketchup

½ cup sour cream

¾ teaspoon salt

1 (15-ounce) can red kidney beans, rinsed and drained

I S IT WRONG TO REMEMBER JOHN WAYNE, first and foremost, for his appearances on *I Love Lucy* in 1955 and *Maude* in 1974 when he made almost 250 films? Probably. But the Duke, as he was known, did do guest shots on both TV shows, each playing off his hyper-masculine movie persona. He was awfully butch for a man born Marion Morrison. Wayne made some of his greatest screen appearances in John Ford films, including *Stagecoach*, *The Searchers*, and *The Man Who Shot Liberty Valance*. His other celebrated films include *Rio Bravo*, *The Green Berets*, *The Quiet Man*, and, of course, *True Grit*, for which he won the Best Actor Oscar. He made no bones about being a conservative Republican, but he was such a formidable on-screen presence that those who disagreed with his politics—even Maude—couldn't help but admire him. You'll admire his cheese casserole.

JOHN WAYNE'S FAVORITE CASSEROLE

Combine chilies with cheese in a large bowl and turn into a well-buttered shallow 2-quart casserole dish. Beat the egg whites until peaks form. Mix egg yolks, milk, flour, salt and pepper in a small bowl. Fold the egg yolk mixture into the eggs whites. Pour over the cheese and chili mixture. Comb through with a knife and fork gently until combined. Bake for 30 minutes. Arrange tomatoes on top and bake another 30 minutes. Garnish with extra chilies, if desired. Let sit 15 minutes before serving.

2 (4-ounce) cans diced mild green chilies

1 pound Monterey Jack cheese, grated

1 pound cheddar cheese, grated

4 egg whites

4 egg yolks

$\frac{2}{3}$ cup evaporated milk

1 tablespoon flour

$\frac{1}{8}$ teaspoon pepper

$\frac{1}{2}$ teaspoon salt

2 medium tomatoes, sliced

POST MORTEM

This isn't so much a casserole as it is a macho cheese soufflé. It's so cheesy, in fact, that I was tempted to griddle the leftovers between slices of bread. But, if you like your cheese with more cheese on top, then the Duke's favorite casserole may be your favorite, too.

Humphrey Bogart 1899–1957

THE AMERICAN FILM INSTITUTE ranked Humphrey Bogart as the greatest male movie star in history. Who could argue? Bogart starred in such classics as *The Maltese Falcon, Casablanca, High Sierra, Sabrina, The Caine Mutiny, The Treasure of the Sierra Madre,* and *The African Queen,* for which he won the Oscar. He was also half of the greatest May-December romance Hollywood ever produced: Bogie and Bacall, as he and Lauren Bacall will always be known. She was more than twenty-five years his junior, but the pair made magic on screen in such films as *To Have and Have Not* and *The Big Sleep* and offscreen as husband and wife. Few have uttered as many memorable lines as Bogie did in his films. Try his Coconut Spanish Cream and your guests may like it so much they'll come back for more. You'll hear them clamor, "Make it again, Sam."

Last Bites

Bogart topped a 1997 *Entertainment Weekly* ranking of movie legends and that same year his likeness was featured on a U.S. postage stamp. Mail it again, Sam.

HUMPHreY BoGarT's COCONUT Spanish cream

Soften gelatin in ¼ cup milk. Stir beaten yolks, salt, and sugar in the top of a double boiler over hot water. Add gelatin. Add scalded milk gradually, stirring until the mixture coats the back of a spoon. Cool. When completely cool, stir in coconut. Fold beaten egg whites and extract into custard. Pour into mold and refrigerate until firm. Unmold and serve garnished with coconut and orange sections.

1 tablespoon unflavored gelatin

¼ cup milk

4 egg yolks, beaten

¼ teaspoon salt

½ cup sugar

2 cups scalded milk

1 cup shredded coconut, plus additional for garnish

2 egg whites, beaten stiff

½ teaspoon orange extract

Orange segments, for garnish

ROCK HUDSON 1925–1985

I F ROCK HUDSON HAD BEEN ANY MORE HANDSOME, you'd go blind looking at him. He was six-foot-five and so gorgeous that even Doris Day, the original 40-year-old virgin, wanted him . . . bad. He starred with Day in such delicious romantic comedies as *Pillow Talk*, *Lover Come Back*, and *Send Me No Flowers*. He did his best work, though, for director Douglas Sirk in the 1950s, appearing in *Magnificent Obsession*, *Written on the Wind*, *All That Heaven Allows*, *Battle Hymn*, and *The Tarnished Angels*. Hudson also made a splash when he starred with Elizabeth Taylor (See Chapter 4) and James Dean in the oil epic *Giant*. For much of the 1970s, the aging dreamboat was known as half of the mystery series *McMillan & Wife* on television. After its long run ended, Hudson joined the cast of *Dynasty*, but by then AIDS was taking its toll on his health. A physically ravaged Hudson became the public face of that dreaded disease at a time when almost nothing was known about it. His most famous leading ladies—Day and Taylor—rallied to his side. Because of Hudson, the original gay BFF, no one could say they didn't know someone with AIDS, and the fight against the pandemic began.

ROCK HUDSON'S cannoli

Using an electric mixer, beat the ricotta in a large bowl for 1 minute. Add confectioner's sugar and beat until light and creamy, about 5 minutes. Add cinnamon, chopped citron, and chocolate chips and mix until well blended. Refrigerate until ready to use. To make cannoli shells, sift flour, sugar, and cinnamon together into a large bowl. Make a well and pour wine into it and mix until incorporated. On a floured cutting board, knead dough until smooth and stiff, about 15 minutes. If dough is too moist or sticky, add some flour. If it's too dry, add more wine. Cover dough and let it rest two hours in a cool place. Then roll paper-thin on a lightly floured board. Cut into 5-inch circles. Wrap each circle around a cannoli tube loosely, overlapping ¼ inch of dough. Seal dough by brushing with slightly beaten egg yolk. With the tube in place, deep fry 2 cannoli at a time in hot oil for 1 minute until light brown. Lift gently with slotted spoon or tongs, drain on paper towel and cool. Remove tubes gently and fill.

Filling:

3 pounds ricotta

1¾ cups confectioner's sugar

½ teaspoon cinnamon

2 tablespoons chopped citron

¼ cup semi-sweet chocolate chips

Pastry Shells:

4 cups flour

1 tablespoon sugar

¼ teaspoon cinnamon

¾ cup Italian red wine

George Reeves 1914–1959

I N THE 1950S, SUPERHERO LOVERS had one rallying cry: "It's a bird, it's a plane, it's Superman!" That super man, of course, was George Reeves who made more than 100 episodes of *The Adventures of Superman* between 1952 and 1958. Earlier in his career, Reeves appeared in *So Proudly We Hail!* with a trio of stunning women, Claudette Colbert, Paulette Goddard, and Veronica Lake, but that didn't make him the star everyone had expected it would. Reeves had a blink-and-you'll-miss-him role in *From Here to Eternity* and a small part in the Fritz Lang–directed *Rancho Notorious*. *Superman* both immortalized Reeves and ruined his career. His death was ruled a suicide by gunshot, but enough mystery surrounds his tragic end that it was made into the 2006 film *Hollywoodland* starring Ben Affleck.

George Reeves's super cookies

Cream butter and sugar together. Blend in beaten egg. Add flour, half a cup at a time. Add soda dissolved in a tablespoon of hot water. Add chocolate and corn flakes. Drop by rounded teaspoonfuls onto parchment paper. Bake at 375° for 10–12 minutes. Cool on a cake rack.

Makes about 24

¼ pound butter, softened

½ cup sugar

½ cup light brown sugar

1 large egg, beaten

1½ cups flour

¼ teaspoon baking soda

½ cup coarsely grated chocolate

1 cup corn flakes

aFTer-Dinner viewing

men on FiLm

Chuck Connors plays a murderous bodyguard in Richard Fleischer's grim futuristic shocker *Soylent Green,* which is the name of a foodstuff being fed to an overpopulated earth. Stick with the clam chowder. Gregory Peck stars in the 1959 war epic *Pork Chop Hill,* which has everything to do with the Korean War and nothing to do with Korean Barbecue. James Cagney hoofs his way through the 1942 musical *Yankee Doodle Dandy* playing George M. Cohan. Serve Yankee Doodle snack cakes during this one. If you find yourself without reservations some night, stay in and enjoy Mervyn LeRoy's 1946 romantic comedy *Without Reservations* starring John Wayne. Humphrey Bogart plays a racketeer named Turkey Morgan in the 1937 fight film *Kid Galahad.* The best reason to view the delightful romantic comedy *Pillow Talk* is to watch Rock Hudson discuss just how much he likes collecting recipes. It's hilarious and oh-so-ironic. George Reeves was never more handsome than as Stuart Tarleton, one of Scarlett's many beaus, in *Gone with the Wind*. It's a long movie, so make a lot of his cookies, and, as God as my witness, you'll never go hungry.

22

MONKEYING AROUND IN THE KITCHEN

T HERE IS A SCENE IN 1971'S *Escape from the Planet of the Apes*, the third movie in the popular Planet of the Apes series, in which the chimpanzee Zira (Kim Hunter) refuses to take a banana from her human captor. He has no idea she can talk, let alone that she's a highly trained scientist from the future. Why, he keeps wondering aloud, won't she take the fruit monkeys are supposed to adore? Having had enough of his goading—Zira didn't travel through time and space to have some twerp in a lab coat treat her like a baboon—she finally blurts out, "Because I loathe bananas." Ok, it's not *Babette's Feast*, but it's a really good food-in-the-movies moment.

With that admission, of course, Zira's cover is blown, ditto her husband Cornelius's (Roddy McDowall). Here's what happens: after being wined and dined by the media and the American government, during which time Zira develops a fondness for what she's told is "grape juice plus," she's discovered to be pregnant and all sorts of hell breaks loose.

Things don't end happily for the monkey couple; it's not all coconuts and moonbeams, but they are aided by a kindly circus owner named Armando (played by Ricardo Montalban, whose recipe for Carne Asada appears in Chapter 23). He rescues their baby Milo, switching him for a more ordinary newborn chimp, and raises Milo so that when he's grown, he can change his name to Caesar, and Roddy can play him in two more sequels.

The truly amazing thing about the Planet of the Apes movies is how good the acting is. McDowall and Hunter were award winners; he had an Emmy, she'd won an Oscar. Even under all those prosthetics, their performances are nothing short of brilliant. Acting only with their eyes, really, they're able to impart such a range of emotions, even when acting opposite a banana. Charlton Heston, however, is another story. Let's face it. We all loved Chuck. But his acting was as deliciously cheesy as the recipe of his that follows.

CHARLTON HESTON 1923–2008

NORTHWESTERN UNIVERSITY ALUM Charlton Heston played Moses in *The Ten Commandments*, Michelangelo in *The Agony and the Ecstasy*, and a Mexican in *Touch of Evil*. Talk about range! But it is for his turn as the time-traveling astronaut Taylor in the 1968 film *Planet of the Apes* that so many baby boomers remember him. For a really bad actor, he was really good in it. No one could have spat out the line, "Get your hands off me, you damn dirty ape" with more righteous venom than he did. Now get your hands on his recipe for a glorified tuna melt, but wash them first, okay?

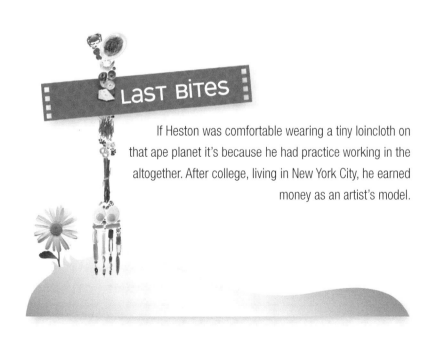

LAST BITES

If Heston was comfortable wearing a tiny loincloth on that ape planet it's because he had practice working in the altogether. After college, living in New York City, he earned money as an artist's model.

CHARLTON HESTON'S CHEESE TUNA PUFF

1 tablespoon butter

3 tablespoons flour

1 (14½-ounce) can evaporated milk

1¾ cups grated cheddar cheese, divided

2 (6½-ounce) cans tuna

½ cup chopped celery

2 tablespoons chopped green pepper

½ teaspoon Worcestershire sauce

Salt and pepper, to taste

1 9-inch frozen pie shell

2 eggs, separated

Melt butter over low heat, blend in flour. Gradually add evaporated milk, stirring constantly. Cook until thickened. Add 1½ cups cheddar cheese and stir until melted. Combine tuna, celery, pepper, Worcestershire sauce, and salt and pepper. Reserve 1 cup cheese sauce for topping. Combine remaining sauce with tuna mixture and blend well. Spoon into pie shell. Bake at 425° for 15 minutes. Meanwhile, make topping. Beat egg whites until stiff but not dry. Beat egg yolks and combine with remaining cup of cheese sauce, and then fold in egg whites. Remove pie from oven and cover with cheese puff topping. Decrease heat to 375° and bake 20 more minutes or so. Sprinkle with remaining ¼ cup grated cheddar and serve.

R ODDY MCDOWALL THREW DINNER PARTIES better than anyone. These legendary affairs were as well known in Hollywood as the star of such films as *How Green Was My Valley, My Friend Flicka*, and all five of the Planet of the Apes movies, plus the TV series. If you were lucky enough to be invited, you went, because you never knew who might be seated near you. It could be a goddess of the silent screen on her last legs, or a gorgeous young thing who'd just blown into town; maybe Mae West, perhaps Pee-wee Herman. Repeat guests had one unspoken rule, however: eat first, and then show up. Roddy was a brilliant actor—his villainous Bookworm on *Batman* was all prissy petulance—and a terrific photographer, the consummate host, and, to hear friends tell it, a dignified presence in a tawdry town. But he apparently wasn't much of a cook. You can decide for yourself.

RODDY MCDOWALL'S RED CABBAGE

Shred cabbage. Wash and drain well. Melt butter in a Dutch oven. Add onions. Cook until translucent. Add cabbage, cover and cook for 10 minutes. Add remaining ingredients. Cover and cook over low heat for 20 minutes, or until cabbage is tender.

1 medium head red cabbage

3 tablespoons butter or bacon drippings

2 tablespoons finely chopped onion

¼ teaspoon salt

¼ teaspoon black pepper

2 tablespoons vinegar

1 tablespoon sugar

½ cup raisins

1 apple, cored and thinly sliced

POST MORTEM

For a man reputed to be a lousy cook, his red cabbage is quite tasty. This Germanic side dish could use a little more sugar—brown would be great—and a hint of allspice, cloves, and cinnamon would spice up the proceedings nicely.

Kim Hunter 1922–2002

A CADEMY AWARD-WINNING ACTRESS Kim Hunter, who studied at the prestigious Actors Studio, made her Broadway debut as Stella in *A Streetcar Named Desire* in 1947. Four years and two screen tests later, she reprised the role on film and won the Oscar. She acted for the next half century, mostly on television, appearing on everything from *Mannix* to *Mad About You*. She even did a stint on the soap *The Edge of Night*. But it is as Dr. Zira, the brilliant chimpanzee scientist in the first three Planet of the Apes movies for which she will best be remembered. Her interspecies kiss with Charlton Heston is a sweetly funny bit for the cinema ages. On stage or on screen—and particularly in the kitchen—Hunter didn't monkey around. You'll go bananas for her way with a bird.

Last Bites

Preparing for her role as Dr. Zira in *Planet of the Apes,* Hunter spent hours studying primate behavior at the Bronx Zoo in New York. The real challenge of playing a chimpanzee, however, was the makeup. "The only part of me uncovered was my eyeballs," she said.

kim Hunter's cape scott chicken

1 chicken, about three
  pound, cut into 8–10
  pieces

Garlic salt

Fresh ground black pepper

Paprika

3 cups chicken stock

1 teaspoon salt

½ teaspoon saffron

1 cup brown rice

1 pound carrots, peeled
  and cut into 1-inch slices

2 or 3 medium onions,
  peeled and cut into
  8 wedges each

2 tablespoons finely
  chopped parsley

3 tablespoons raisins

½ pound fresh green peas

Preheat oven to 550°. Wash and dry chicken pieces. Sprinkle with garlic salt, pepper, and paprika. Place the chicken pieces, skin side up, in a shallow baking pan large enough for them to fit in one layer without touching. Bake 10–15 minutes at 550°or until the chicken is brown and crispy and well-rendered of fat. Then remove to paper towel to drain. Reduce oven temperature to 325°.

Bring the chicken stock to a boil in a Dutch oven. Add the salt, a bit more pepper, saffron, and rice. Stir well. Mix in the carrots, onions, parsley, and raisins. Place the chicken on top, skin side up. Do not overlap. Cover the pot and bake in the oven for one hour. Remove pot from oven. Lift the chicken out. Scatter the peas over the vegetables. Put the chicken back on top, cover the dish and continue to bake for ½ hour.

after-dinner viewing

escape from the planet of the apes

A social satire as much as a science fiction adventure, the third installment in the Planet of the Apes series is the best of the sequels. It says so much about the 1970s, touching on the issues of the day, but watching as Dr. Zira discovers fashion, wine, and the bubble bath are the biggest delights for me. *Escape* also marked Sal Mineo's last film appearance. He plays a fellow chimp traveler named Milo who's killed in the film, strangled ironically by a grunting gorilla, and becomes the namesake of Zira and Cornelius's baby. The monkey makeup was said to have bothered Mineo so much that he was happy to get offed. You'll get off on the film, particularly if you open a bottle of "grape juice plus."

a SOUTH-OF-THE-BORDER BUFFET

H ISPANIC STARS OF EARLY HOLLYWOOD WERE pioneers who opened the doors for generations of Latino actors to follow. Yes, some of the roles they played, the ruthless bandito, the fiery sex bomb, were stereotypical. But these trailblazers were as essential to the motion picture industry of the silent film era as their modern day counterparts are to the Hollywood of today's blockbuster era. Ramon Novarro's box-office appeal in the epic *Ben Hur: A Tale of the Christ*, for instance, is credited with keeping MGM afloat in the mid-twenties. And Dolores del Rio made plenty of money for studio moguls in her day. Some of these stars, like the closeted Novarro, met with sorry ends. But when you're charting new territory, those very often are the breaks. Some chose to be more than actors: they chose to be activists. More than forty years ago, Ricardo Montalban founded a group called Nosotros dedicated to the inclusion and accurate depiction of Hispanics in the arts. The legacy he and his compatriots left on film and television is certainly one worth exploring. Their culinary triumphs pale in comparison to their cultural impact, but we shouldn't forget that they were pretty darn good in the kitchen, too.

DOLOres DeL RiO 1905–1983

MEXICAN ACTRESS Dolores del Rio became an international sex symbol, which was a huge deal for a Latina actress in the 1920s and '30s. She's best known in America for her starring role in *Flying Down to Rio*, the 1933 musical that first paired Fred Astaire and Ginger Rogers. But she had a big career in Spanish language films in her native country. Del Rio, who was a cousin of Ramon Novarro, returned to Hollywood in the 1960s to appear in such movies as *Flaming Star*, the Elvis Presley picture, and *Cheyenne Autumn*, the John Ford film starring Richard Widmark. A little TV work followed. One of her last roles was on an episode of *Marcus Welby M.D.*

DOLOres DeL RiO'S enCHiLaDaS

Blanch tomatoes, peel and chop. In a large sauté pan on medium heat, cook onions in lard or vegetable oil, then add tomatoes and chilies. Season with salt and add cheese, cooking until cheese begins to melt. In a separate, lightly greased pan over medium heat, warm tortillas one by one until soft. Put some of mixture in the middle of each tortilla, roll and cover with sour cream. Serve immediately.

Serves 6

- 1 pound fresh tomatoes
- 1 onion, finely chopped
- 3 tablespoons lard or vegetable oil
- 2 small cans green chilies, chopped fine
- 2 pounds Queso Oaxaca, shredded
- 1 dozen tortillas
- 1 pint sour cream

I N THE SILENT MOVIE ERA, Mexican actor Ramon Novarro was a lead-ing contender to become the "New Valentino," but that didn't quite hap-pen. In the 1920s, he appeared in such films as *Scaramouche*, *The Student Prince in Old Heidelberg*, with Norma Shearer, and *Across to Singapore*, with Joan Crawford. His best-known performances were as Ben Hur in the 1925 version of *Ben Hur: A Tale of the Christ* and in the 1931 Greta Garbo pic-ture *Mata Hari*. He worked throughout the 1930s, '40s, and '50s. Late in his life, Novarro did a string of TV appearances on such series as *Dr. Kildare*, *Combat!*, *Bonanza*, and *The Wild Wild West*. He met a sad end when he was murdered in his own home by two hustlers. As the story goes, they thought Novarro had money in the house, but he didn't. That year, the actor appeared in his final role on the Western series *The High Chaparral*.

Ramon Novarro's Guacamole

Peel and mash avocados. Drain green chilies, mash, and add to avocados. Season with salt, vinegar, and olive oil. Wash pomegranate seeds and add to avocado mixture. Serve with tortilla chips.

Serves
4

2 ripe avocados

½ can green chilies

Salt, to taste

Olive oil, to taste

Vinegar, to taste

Pomegranate seeds, in the
amount you favor

POST Mortem

The pomegranate seeds, available in ready-to-eat packages in the produce department, add a sweet crunch, making for some of the best "guac" you've ever tasted. You may *Novarro* make it any other way.

Fernando Lamas 1915–1982

BEFORE ARGENTINE ACTOR Fernando Lamas was thought of as Lorenzo Lamas's father and Esther Williams's husband, he was a star in his own right. He appeared in such films as *The Merry Widow,* with Lana Turner, *Dangerous When Wet,* with his future wife Williams, and the 1960 Irwin Allen adventure *The Lost World.* Lamas directed and starred in two films, 1963's *Magic Fountain,* and 1967's *The Violent Ones.* In the '60s and '70s, he did guest shots on such series as *The Girl from U.N.C.L.E., Mission: Impossible, Mod Squad, Charlie's Angels,* and *Police Woman.* Lamas is best known, though, as the inspiration for the Billy Crystal character Fernando, who always said "It is better to look good than to feel good." Lamas may or may not have said that in real life. But right up until the end, he looked "mah-velous!"

Last Bites

When Lamas dropped out of what would have been his last role, playing a South American bon vivant on the short-lived series *Gavilan,* he was replaced by Patrick MacNee, the British star of *The Avengers.* Talk about going in a different direction!

Fernando Lamas's empanadas

To make pastry, mix dry ingredients. Make a well in the center and add egg, sherry, and melted butter. Mix quickly with a spatula to form smooth dough. Knead lightly on a floured board. Cover and refrigerate one hour. For the filling, sauté garlic, beef, and onion in olive oil until meat is browned. Add green pepper, tomato, seasonings, and herbs, and cook over low heat for a few minutes, stirring frequently. Add chopped eggs and raisins and heat through. Skim off and discard any fat that forms on top. Mixture should be dry. Cool and refrigerate one hour.

Roll out dough to ¼-inch thickness on a floured board. Using a coffee can for a cutter, cut out rounds and lay them on wax paper. Cover to prevent drying. Lightly brush circles with egg white. Place a spoonful of cold filling in the center of each circle. Fold over to form a crescent. With wet fingers, press and seal edges. Heat oil to 375°. Carefully add empanadas. Do not crowd pan. Cook three minutes or until golden brown and puffy. Turn them over and cook until brown on all sides. Remove carefully with slotted spoon and drain on absorbent paper.

Pastry:

1 scant cup flour

½ teaspoon baking powder

1½ teaspoons sugar

½ teaspoon salt

1 egg

¼ cup sherry

3 tablespoons butter, melted

Filling:

1 small clove garlic, mashed

1 pound ground beef

1 medium onion, finely chopped

2 tablespoons olive oil

1 medium green pepper, finely chopped

1 medium tomato, finely chopped

Salt and pepper, to taste

Pinch of oregano

Pinch of basil

2 hard-boiled eggs, finely chopped

½ cup raisins

1 egg white

Safflower oil, for deep-frying

I F HE'D ONLY DONE ONE ROLE—the ruthless title character of *Star Trek II: The Wrath of Khan*—Ricardo Montalban would have been enshrined in pop culture history. But he did so much more than that. Besides playing Khan twice—he originated the role on the 1960s TV series—Montalban appeared on Broadway, did radio, and juggled both film and television roles. He was the mysterious Mr. Roarke on *Fantasy Island*, the kindly circus owner Armando in *Escape from the Planet of the Apes* and *Conquest of the Planet of the Apes*, and the White King in the 1966 TV version of *Alice Through the Looking Glass*, with Jack Palance as the Jabberwock, the Smothers Brothers as Tweedledee and Tweedledum, and costumes by Bob Mackie. And no one ever sold "smooth Corinthian leather" better than he did on a series of Chrysler commercials. In his eighties, Montalban continued to do voice work on such series as *Family Guy, Kim Possible* (on which he portrayed Señor Senior Sr.), and *Dora the Explorer*. He also appeared in a couple of the Spy Kids movies, letting yet another generation fall in love with him. You'll fall for his Carne Asada.

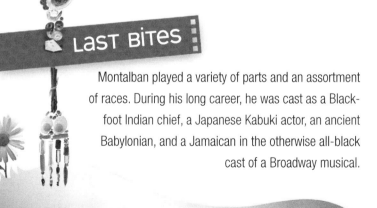

Last Bites

Montalban played a variety of parts and an assortment of races. During his long career, he was cast as a Blackfoot Indian chief, a Japanese Kabuki actor, an ancient Babylonian, and a Jamaican in the otherwise all-black cast of a Broadway musical.

Ricardo Montalban's carne asada

Serves
6

Place onions, tomatoes, chilies, guacamole, and salsa in individual bowls and
refrigerate until ready to serve. Place
tortillas in two stacks of 9 tortillas, wrap
in foil and bake in a 425° oven for 15
minutes. Remove from oven and wrap
in cloth napkins to keep warm. Season
meat with salt and pepper. Melt butter or
heat oil in skillet and sauté meat slices
until brown on the outside, pink on the
inside. Serve meat with tortillas and top-
pings. Roll up and eat.

2 onions, chopped

3–4 tomatoes, chopped

1 can green chilies,
   chopped

1 cup guacamole
   (see Ramon Novarro's
   recipe)

1 cup salsa

18 corn or flour tortillas

3 pounds beef fillet, sliced
   very thin

Salt and pepper, to taste

4 tablespoons butter or oil,
   use more if needed

aFTer-Dinner Viewing

Las Películas

Heller in Pink Tights, starring Sophia Loren and Anthony Quinn, was Ramon Novarro's last feature film. George Cukor directs this tale of an acting troupe in the Old West.

If you've ever confused Ricardo Montalban and Fernando Lamas, this isn't going to help. In the 1949 comedy *Neptune's Daughter*, Montalban plays the captain of a South American polo team who falls for a swimwear designer played by Esther Williams. In real life, Williams did become a swimwear designer but was married to Lamas. To see Lamas fall for Williams, you have to watch the 1953 musical *Dangerous When Wet*.

Dolores del Rio's nude swim in the pre-Hays Code 1932 film *Bird of Paradise* is the stuff of legend. And, oh, to watch her eat fruit!

24

WATCHING THE DETECTIVES (COOK)

T HE HARD-BOILED DETECTIVES OF 1970s television were some of the baddest cats ever to fight crime. They drove cool cars, wore funky threads, and each had his own groovy gimmick. Theo Kojak (Telly Savalas), for instance, was bald. Thomas Banacek (George Peppard) was Polish. Frank Cannon (William Conrad) was fat. But as much as they tried to distinguish themselves, the titular detectives had one thing in common. Besides their ability to solve mysteries in just about an hour, they knew their way around a pantry. These guys liked prepping a day's catch as much as catching a day's perp, and they usually did it all with very little beating or whipping.

Kojak was rarely seen without a lollipop in his mouth. The tough-talking, chrome-domed detective was forever on the suck because he was trying to quit smoking while ridding the streets of criminal scum back in the days when New York was called "Fun City," for all the wrong reasons. The Tootsie Pop–like candies were as connected to the character as the slogan "Who loves ya, baby?" so much so that Savalas bought a racehorse and named it, "Telly-pop." He loved that horse.

A wealthy insurance investigator turned private eye, Banacek would, in each episode, recite a cockamamie proverb from his ancestral homeland, and very often it was food-related. "When a wolf is chasing your sleigh," he once said, "throw him a raisin cookie, but don't stop to bake a cake." Huh? Of course, with his salt-and-pepper Caesar haircut and mod turtleneck, Peppard was so ridiculously handsome it didn't matter that he made no sense. "Is a duck with three wings and a loaf of bread really brother to the turkey?" Who cares? The man looked fabulous saying it.

Cannon wasn't half as cute—in fact, Ironside (Raymond Burr) was considered hot in comparison—but boy could he cook. Cannon was a gourmet with a gun. When he wasn't catching a crook, he was whipping up something exotic. And obviously, he was a good eater. Kojak may have had his all-day suckers, but Cannon had everything else in the larder. His girth was the subject of many cruel jokes over the years. (You should see him run! Hilarious!) And the double-slabs of ribbing continued even after the show's cancellation. TV Land touted reruns of the series with an ad for a fake Frank Cannon diet that was a montage of Conrad shoving everything from burgers to bon bons into his bagel slot. In it, a young smart-aleck asks him, "How'd you get that fat?" Certainly, it wasn't from eating gazpacho alone.

Here from the private files of TV's best private dicks are some criminally good recipes. With them, you too can be a "Law & Short Order" cook.

W ILLIAM CONRAD LENT HIS DEEP VOICE to the role of Marshall Matt Dillon on the radio version of *Gunsmoke* in the 1950s. (CBS cast James Arness instead of Conrad when the series went to television, well, because he could see his boots.) Conrad found voice work on TV, though, narrating both *The Fugitive* and *Rocky and Bullwinkle* in the 1960s. But it wasn't until he was past the age of fifty that his corporeal frame became a fixture on the small screen. Conrad played not only Frank Cannon for five seasons on *Cannon* and couple of crossover episodes of *Barnaby Jones,* but also the title character in *Nero Wolfe* in 1981, and from 1987 to 1992 Jason Lochinvar "Fatman" McCabe in *Jake and the Fatman* opposite the eye candy known as Joe Penny. Is Conrad's soup good? Well, if you can't trust someone who was three-fourths of *Jake and the Fatman* to make good gazpacho, who can you trust?

WiLLiam ConraD's GaZPaCHo VaLenciana

Mix garlic with salt and cumin, and then beat in olive oil. Combine with tomato purée and vinegar, and blend briefly in blender. Soup should not be completely smooth. Chill thoroughly 3 or 4 hours. Prepare croutons by frying bread cubes in more olive oil until crispy and golden. Drain on paper towels. Pour chilled tomato mixture into soup dishes. Add a small amount of club soda to each bowl and stir. Garnish with croutons and diced vegetables.

2 cloves garlic, crushed

1 teaspoon salt

¼ teaspoon cumin

¼ cup olive oil, plus more for frying bread

2 cups canned tomato purée

1 tablespoon vinegar

1 cup bread cubes

1 bottle club soda, chilled

½ large cucumber, peeled and coarsely chopped

1 sweet red or green pepper, coarsely chopped

2 scallions, chopped

1 dozen small radishes, thinly sliced

ROBERT URICH 1946–2002

E'D BEEN ON *S.W.A.T.*, but it was as tennis pro and gigolo Peter Campbell on *Soap* that TV audiences noticed Robert Urich, got the vapors, and asked, "Who is that!?!" The handsome actor went on to star as a private investigator in two TV series. He was Dan Tanna on *VEGA$* from 1978 to 1981 and Spenser on *Spenser: For Hire* from 1985 to 1988. Here, he cooks up a rich soup that speaks of his heritage.

Last Bites

The year he died, Urich donated his winnings of $125,000 from a celebrity version of the game show *Who Wants to Be a Millionaire* to cancer research.

ROBERT URICH'S CZECHOSLOVAKIAN SOUP

Soak the leeks in water and rinse thoroughly to remove all sand. Slice them, using only some of the green part. In a Dutch oven, sauté the leeks in a stick of butter. Make a roux with 3–4 tablespoons butter and some flour and stir into the leeks. Stir in chicken broth, beans, and mushrooms. Add the can of tomatoes and simmer covered for 10–12 minutes. Add the wine, potatoes, salt, and pepper, and continue simmering for 5 minutes. Stir in cream and return to heat to simmer and cook five minutes more. Pour into individual soup bowls, decorate with freshly chopped parsley.

Serves 8

8 medium leeks

¼ pound butter

Some flour

3 to 4 tablespoons butter

4 cans chicken broth

½ pound raw green beans, cut in half

¾ pound raw fresh mushrooms, sliced

1 (19-ounce) can whole, peeled tomatoes, seeded and chopped

¼ cup white wine

2 large raw potatoes, finely diced

Salt and pepper, to taste

1 cup heavy cream

Fresh chopped parsley

RAYMOND BURR 1917–1993

R AYMOND BURR MADE HIS MARK ON TELEVISION as defense attorney Perry Mason, a role he played on and off from 1957 until his death. He also played the title role of Robert Ironside, in *Ironside*, in which his character was confined to a wheelchair following a failed assassination attempt. In the movies, there are those who love him in *Godzilla*, but his best film role was as the creepy murder suspect in Alfred Hitchcock's *Rear Window*. (Hitch's quiche recipe appears in Chapter 12.) Burr, a gay host at dinner parties, was said to be as good a gourmet cook as he was an actor, which means his Chicken Lolo will knock your socks off. Your own Della Street will love it.

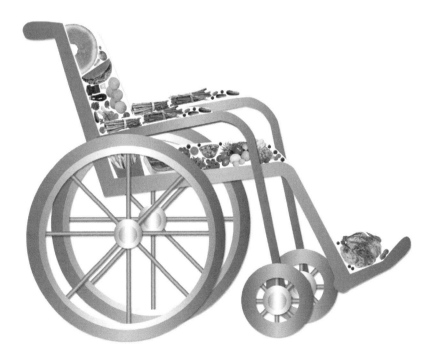

RAYMOND BURR'S CHICKEN LOLO

1 cup fresh coconut, grated

1 cup water

1 lemon, peeled and sliced

½ cup chopped onion

2 tablespoons butter

6 chicken breasts, boned, skinned and cut into chunks

½ teaspoon ground ginger

1 teaspoon salt

1 canned green chili pepper, sliced

1 tablespoon flour

In a saucepan, combine coconut, water, lemon, and onion. Bring to boil. Remove from heat and strain. Melt butter in a large skillet and add chicken breasts. Cook until meat is no longer pink. Add ginger, salt, and chili pepper. Pour in strained coconut mixture, cover and simmer 10 minutes. Mix flour with a small amount of cold water to make a paste. Stir that into the sauce, bring it to a boil, simmer two minutes, and serve.

Jerry Orbach 1935–2004

JERRY ORBACH PLAYED HOMICIDE DETECTIVE Lennie Briscoe for twelve seasons on *Law & Order* and then died and donated his eyes so others could see. (I learned that on a subway poster.) Whoever has those eyes today can, like the rest of us, watch Orbach on an episode of that long-running crime drama at virtually any hour of the day or night. It's on constantly. But to those who love Broadway, Orbach was a musical-comedy god first and foremost. He won the 1969 Tony for playing the basketball-loving romantic Chuck Baxter in *Promises, Promises*, and followed it up with two very memorable performances: the razzle-dazzling lawyer Billy Flynn in the original 1975 production of *Chicago*, and the hotshot producer Julian Marsh in the 1980 hit *42ⁿᵈ Street*. Orbach also played Lumière, the singing, dancing candelabra in the 1991 Disney animated classic *Beauty and the Beast*. Be our guest and try his Pan-Fried Steak.

Jerry Orbach's Pan-Fried Steak

Serves 4

Stir together cumin, coriander, ½ teaspoon salt, and pepper, and rub over the steaks. Heat oil in skillet over medium-high heat. Add the steaks and cook 3–4 minutes per side for medium-rare. Transfer to a large platter. Add the onion and garlic to pan and cook, stirring often, until lightly browned. Add the rosemary and stir. Add vinegar, sugar, and remaining ¼ teaspoon salt, and bring to a boil. Cook until slightly reduced, about 2 minutes. Swirl in butter. Spoon sauce over the steaks and serve.

1 teaspoon cumin

1 teaspoon coriander

¾ teaspoon salt

½ teaspoon freshly ground pepper

4 (1-inch-thick) boneless sirloin steaks (about 2 pounds)

1 tablespoon olive oil

1 small red onion, finely chopped

1 clove garlic, minced

1 teaspoon finely chopped fresh rosemary

⅓ cup balsamic vinegar

1 teaspoon brown sugar

1 tablespoon cold unsalted butter

THE ICONIC POSTER, A SWIMSUIT SHOT that launched 8 million puberties and just as many lookalike hairdos, clinched what keen-eyed observers already knew about Farrah Fawcett. Those who'd seen her in *Myra Breckinridge*, on *Harry O*, and doing commercials knew she wasn't just gorgeous, she was a star destined for bigger things. Her TV moment came when Aaron Spelling cast her as Jill Munroe, one of three recent police academy graduates who'd been assigned the most "hazardous" (that is, mundane) of duties. *Charlie's Angels* took Fawcett away from all the bit parts and launched her into the stratosphere. Tabloids followed her marriage to (and divorce from) *Six Million Dollar Man* Lee Majors and then the ups and downs of her long relationship with actor Ryan O'Neal. Critics took note when she took on a pair of dramatic roles in *The Burning Bed* and *Extremities*, two battered-women tales. Late in her career, the press reveled in Fawcett's bizarre antics: naked painting videos, incoherent talk show appearances, and the like. But fans never stopped loving her. When she appeared with her fellow "Angels," Kate Jackson and Jaclyn Smith, in an emotional 2006 Emmy tribute to Spelling, the audience was floored. The trio, who'd rarely been seen together since their glory days, still looked as fabulous as ever. Time stood still, if only for a little while. Whether Farrah Fawcett's recipe lives up to its name, you'll have to decide. Certainly, though, she was supreme.

Farrah Fawcett's Sausage and Peppers Supreme

3 green bell peppers

3 tablespoons olive oil

Salt and freshly ground
black pepper, to taste

1 pound hot Italian pork
sausages

¾ cup dry red wine

Preheat oven to 350°. Wash peppers, remove stems and seeds, and cut into chunks. In a covered ovenproof pan, sauté peppers in olive oil until they start to soften. Season with salt and pepper. Remove and reserve. Brown sausages in the same pan. Add wine, cover and bake 40 minutes. Uncover, add sautéed peppers, bake about 30 minutes longer, and serve.

POST MORTEM

Who knew Charlie's most glamorous Angel knew her way around an Italian kitchen? As it turns out, her sausage and peppers are heavenly. Some chopped onion sautéed with the peppers would be a welcome addition.

Peter Falk 1927–2011

HE WAS ONE OF THE GREAT ONES—appearing in films as disparate as *The Princess Bride* and *Wings of Desire* in the same year, 1987. But no matter what Peter Falk did (and he did a lot), he will always be remembered as the police detective in the rumpled raincoat on the mystery series *Columbo*. The character, one he played for more than thirty years beginning in 1971, is one of TV's most indelible portraits. Among Falk's most beloved films were the cult hit *The In-Laws*, the one-two Neil Simon punch of *Murder by Death* and *The Cheap Detective,* and six pictures with his buddy, the director/actor John Cassavetes, including the 1974 classic *A Woman Under the Influence.* The Emmy- and Oscar-nominated actor published his memoir *Just One More Thing* in 2006, and it wasn't a moment too soon. Falk was diagnosed with dementia two years later. Just one more thing: his pork chops are as toothsome as he was.

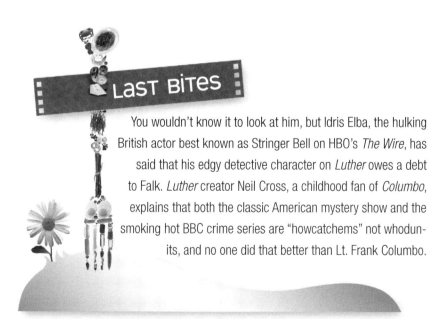

Last Bites

You wouldn't know it to look at him, but Idris Elba, the hulking British actor best known as Stringer Bell on HBO's *The Wire*, has said that his edgy detective character on *Luther* owes a debt to Falk. *Luther* creator Neil Cross, a childhood fan of *Columbo*, explains that both the classic American mystery show and the smoking hot BBC crime series are "howcatchems" not whodunits, and no one did that better than Lt. Frank Columbo.

PeTer FaLK's PorK CHOPS

Serves
8

Preheat oven to 350°. Brown pork chops in olive oil in a heavy frying pan and remove to a casserole. Cook onions until translucent in same oil and add to casserole. Deglaze pan by adding white vinegar and stirring up all brown bits. Add to casserole along with all remaining ingredients except vinegar peppers. Bake for 1½ hours. Add vinegar peppers and cook 15 minutes more. Remove pork chops and peppers to a warm serving plate. Add 2 teaspoons corn starch to pan drippings to make gravy. Pour over pork chops and peppers and serve.

6 pork chops

1 medium onion, finely chopped

¼ cup olive oil

¼ cup white vinegar

Salt and pepper, to taste

1 teaspoon thyme

1 cup water

½ cup liquid from jarred vinegar peppers

1 cup (or more) vinegar peppers

2 tablespoons cornstarch

Dennis weaver 1924–2006

ENNIS WEAVER TRAINED AT The Actors Studio and won an Emmy in 1959 for playing Chester Goode on *Gunsmoke*. He came up with the idea to give his character a bum leg and then regretted it: he had to hobble around like that for nine years! After that landmark show, Weaver starred opposite a bear in *Gentle Ben* in the late 1960s. I loved that program! He then parlayed his homespun charm into a bigger hit with *McCloud*, playing Sam McCloud, a cowboy transplanted to the mean streets of New York City. He also appeared in a great TV movie called *Duel*, a suspense thriller about a killer truck-driver, which was one of Steven Spielberg's first directing jobs. In real life, Weaver was a vegetarian and he practiced yoga long before it was fashionable. The man was "green" from the get-go. His recipe for Eggplant Parmigiana would make my Italian grandmother weep. Cheddar cheese? But it's healthier than the traditional version and Nana's dead. As McCloud would say, "There ya go!"

Last Bites

Hollywood didn't welcome the young Weaver with open arms. Before being cast on *Gunsmoke* at age thirty, Weaver sold pantyhose and delivered flowers to pay the bills.

Dennis Weaver's Eggplant Parmigiana

Serves 6

2 large eggplant

1 egg, beaten

1 cup cornflake crumbs

¼ cup safflower oil

1 pound cheddar cheese slices

1 red or green pepper, chopped

2 cups tomato sauce

½ cup Parmesan or Romano cheese

¼ cup bread crumbs

Slice eggplant into ½-inch slices. Wash and pat dry. Salt and put under a plate for about an hour or until the juice drains out. Dip eggplant slices in egg and bread using cornflake crumbs. Fry in safflower oil. Drain excess oil off with paper towels. Alternate layers of eggplant, cheddar cheese slices, peppers, and tomato sauce in a 2-quart pan. Sprinkle top with Parmesan or Romano cheese and bread crumbs. Bake in 350° oven for about 45 minutes or until top is slightly brown.

TeLLY SaVaLaS 1922–1994

BEFORE LANDING THE ICONIC TITLE ROLE in *Kojak*, Telly Savalas appeared in such films as *Birdman of Alcatraz*, for which he was nominated for an Oscar, *The Dirty Dozen*, and *On Her Majesty's Secret Service*, in which he played the villain Ernst Stavro Blofeld. Much to most people's surprise, he wasn't always rocking Mr. Clean's look. Savalas didn't shave his head until 1965 when he played Pontius Pilate in *The Greatest Story Ever Told*. But when he saw himself clean shaven, he knew he was on to something, and kept the look for the rest of his life. With all due respect to Yul Brynner, Savalas remains the sexiest cue ball of all time. "Who loves ya, baby?" We all do. Now gimme a cookie.

GeORGe PePPaRD 1928–1994

YOU CAN ADORE GEORGE PEPPARD for so many reasons: for playing Holly Golightly's neighbor-turned-love-interest in *Breakfast at Tiffany's* opposite Audrey Hepburn, for his turn as the Polish proverb–spouting insurance investigator Thomas Banecek on *Banacek*, or for the way he smoked a cigar as Hannibal on *The A-Team*. If Paul Newman hadn't been Paul Newman, Peppard would have been. A Method actor, Peppard was born in Detroit, which does nothing to explain why he left behind a dessert recipe with a Louisiana pedigree. Then again, would anyone eat Detroit Pecan Pie?

Telly Savalas's Butter Cookies

Melt butter. Let it settle, and discard milky white residue that forms in the bottom of pan. Put cooled butter in mixing bowl with vegetable oil. Add egg and sugar. Beat until light and fluffy. Sift together flour, baking powder, and cinnamon. Add to egg mixture, mixing well. Add ground almonds, mix well. Roll out with rolling pin on lightly floured board. Cut into shapes with cookie cutters. Place on an ungreased baking sheet. Bake at 350° for about 10 minutes or until lightly browned. Remove from oven and sprinkle with confectioners' sugar while still warm.

Makes about 48

1 pound butter, softened

½ cup vegetable oil

1 egg

½ cup sugar

4½ cups all-purpose flour

1 teaspoon baking powder

Pinch of ground cinnamon or cloves

1 cup blanched almonds, ground

Confectioners' sugar

George Peppard's Louisiana Pecan Pie

In a mixing bowl, cream butter and sugar until fluffy. Add molasses and beat well. Add eggs, one at a time, beating well after each addition. Stir in vanilla, salt, and pecans. Pour filling into pie shell. Bake pie on bottom rack at 375° for 40–45 minutes, or until just set. Cool on rack. Serve with sweetened whipped cream.

Serves 8

⅓ cup butter

1¼ cups sugar

½ cup light molasses

3 eggs

1 teaspoon vanilla

¼ teaspoon salt

1 cup coarsely chopped pecans

1 (9-inch) unbaked pie shell

aFTer-Dinner Viewing

Banacek

You can watch any of these detectives on DVD: almost every series mentioned above has released at least one season. But I say spring for *Banacek: The Complete Series* box set while it's still available. The show specialized in "locked room mysteries," which meant that in each installment, a seemingly impossible heist took place right under the victims' noses. Although others would try to crack the case, only the well-heeled ladies' man Banecek, a self-described "smug Boston dandy," was smart enough to recover the goods and collect 10 percent of their value as his fee. The form is as old as Edgar Allan Poe's *The Murders in the Rue Morgue*, but it was relatively novel on television in the '70s, and Poe wasn't writing for guest stars like Stella Stevens or Jessica Walter. Besides, it's a chance to see Broderick Crawford alive and Brenda Vaccaro thin, and hear Peppard purr to one of his many transposable female play-things, "I assure you my intentions are purely immoral."

25

THANK YOU FOR FEEDING a FRIEND

I T WAS A TV SHOW ABOUT THE FRIENDSHIP of four seniors living out their twilight years together in Miami. But really, *The Golden Girls* was a show about cheesecake. When a hot date didn't show up or a "yutz" of an ex-husband did, as often happened during the series' seven seasons, all Dorothy (Bea Arthur), Blanche (Rue McClanahan), Rose (Betty White), and Sophia (Estelle Getty) had to do was open the fridge and, voila, their problems would fade into a ricotta-and-graham-cracker haze. No dessert has more late-night healing power than a good cold one: that was the show's biggest life lesson. Food was always good for a giggle on *The Golden Girls*, too. Sophia could turn the word *cannoli* into a sexual double-entendre, and Rose's Scandinavian recipes, her *geneukenfleuken* cake, for instance, were always played for laughs. But it was that cheesecake that kept them— and us—coming back for more. The women in this chapter may have gone to the Great Lanai in the Sky, but their recipes still bask in the Florida sun. Share these dishes with your friends. The girls wouldn't want you to eat alone.

THANK YOU FOR FEEDING A FRIEND

Bea arTHur 1922–2009

S HE WAS MAUDE FINDLAY, the liberal feminist, of the groundbreaking TV series *Maude*, and Vera Charles, the boozy bosom buddy of both the Broadway and film versions of the musical *Mame*. But to generations of TV watchers, Bea Arthur will always be, first and foremost, Dorothy Petrillo Zbornak Hollingsworth, the school teacher with the acid wit on *The Golden Girls*. Arthur has been a part of the TV landscape since making a splash as a guest star on *All in the Family* in 1971. The woman not only appeared on the infamous *Star Wars Holiday Special* in 1978, she played Larry David's mother on *Curb Your Enthusiasm* in 2005. In between, she did a short-lived Americanization of the Brit hit *Fawlty Towers* called *Amanda's*, nabbed two Emmy Awards, became a vegetarian and an animal rights activist, and guest-starred as an elderly babysitter on *Malcolm in the Middle* in one of the most charming episodes of a sitcom ever. Her most famous stage roles were Lucy Brown in *The Threepenny Opera* and Yente the matchmaker in *Fiddler on the Roof.* Arthur had a nice part in the 1970 film comedy *Lovers and Other Strangers*. For an extra thrill, check out YouTube clips from her 1980 variety program, *The Beatrice Arthur Special.* She and Rock Hudson (whose cannoli recipe appears in Chapter 21) sing "Everybody Today Is Turning On." With this recipe, she may turn you on to vegetarianism.

Bea Arthur's Vegetarian Breakfast

1 tablespoon margarine

2 medium tomatoes, sliced

¾ cup chopped fresh mushrooms

Salt and pepper, to taste

4 slices bread, toasted

Preheat oven to 250°. Melt the margarine in a small sauté pan over medium heat. Add the tomatoes and mushrooms, and sauté until soft, about 4 minutes. Season to taste with salt and pepper. Put some tomato-mushroom mixture on each piece of toast. Heat in the oven for 2 minutes before serving.

POST MORTEM

Toast slices of sturdy seven-grain bread for this recipe and melt a slice of soy cheese over the top for added flavor. You can use dairy cheese, of course, but be forewarned: somewhere Bea will be saying, "God'll get you for that!"

ESTELLE GETTY 1923–2008

FOR SOMEONE WHO WAS UNDER FIVE FEET TALL and a year younger than the actress playing her TV daughter, Estelle Getty packed a huge punch as little old lady Sophia Petrillo on *The Golden Girls* and its follow-up series, *The Golden Palace*. She also played the role on *Empty Nest*, *Nurses*, and *Blossom*, if you're keeping track. Her straw handbag became an iconic TV prop. Getty worked for decades in theater before becoming a TV star. It was her work on Broadway as the mother to Harvey Fierstein's drag queen character in *Torch Song Trilogy* that set her on her way to fame and fortune in her sixties. Getty also had a role in the Cher film *Mask* and starred with Sylvester Stallone in the action comedy *Stop! Or My Mom Will Shoot*. She found her most ardent fan base among gay men. When Getty went out, she always said, her entourage had a "five-gay minimum." Her chicken fingers, though, might be just enough to keep them home.

LAST BITES

Before striking it rich with *The Golden Girls,* Getty worked as a secretary and would secretly audition for roles during meal breaks. Asking for a 10 AM lunch hour one day and a 2:30 PM lunch hour the next, she raised the suspicions of the office manager at her last day job. He told her, "You have the strangest eating habits of any secretary we've ever had."

estelle getty's baked chicken fingers

Preheat oven to 450°. Spray two cookie sheets or jelly roll pans with olive oil cooking spray. Combine the pecan meal, bread crumbs, salt, and Cajun seasoning in a large bowl and mix well. Dip chicken fingers in beaten eggs and dredge in crumb mixture. Place chicken on pans without crowding. Spray chicken fingers with olive oil spray. Bake for 20 minutes. Switch pans on baking racks for even cooking, and bake for 15–20 minutes more, or until golden brown and juices run clear.

Serves 6

- 3½ cups pecan meal
- 2 cups dry bread crumbs
- 1 tablespoon salt
- 1 tablespoon Cajun seasoning
- 2½ pounds boneless, skinless chicken breast, cut into fingers
- 2 large eggs, beaten

Rue McClanahan 1934–2010

FANS OF *The Golden Girls* weren't prepared for the death of Rue McClanahan, who played the saucy, oversexed Southern belle Blanche Devereaux on the show. She was the youngest cast member and the most vivacious. She was married six times! And her passing caught everyone by surprise. What she left behind, though, was a body of work as delicious as she was. Along with *The Golden Girls*, McClanahan was a regular on *Maude*, as the title character's best friend; on *Mama's Family* as Aunt Fran; and late in her life on the TV comedy *Sordid Lives: The Series*, as Peggy, a church lady having an affair with a younger man, who happened to be missing a leg. She had an impressive stage career, capped off by her turn as Madame Morrible in *Wicked*. For something extra juicy, check out her trashy early films, *Five Minutes to Love*, *The Rotten Apple*, and *Hollywood After Dark*, all available on DVD. It's only fitting that McClanahan's recipe is for cheesecake.

Rue McClanahan's Non-Dairy Cheesecake

2 cups graham cracker crumbs

⅛ cup of sugar

¼ cup margarine, softened

2 (8-ounce) containers non-dairy cream cheese

1 cup sugar

Juice of one lemon

1 teaspoon vanilla

Fresh raspberries

Combine graham cracker crumbs, sugar, and softened margarine and mix well. Press onto the sides and bottom of a 10-inch pie pan. Chill for 30 minutes. Preheat oven to 350°. Whip together non-dairy cream cheese, sugar, lemon juice, and vanilla. Pour into crust. Place the filled pie shell on a cookie sheet and bake for 30 minutes. Allow to cool. Chill for several hours before serving with fresh raspberries.

POST MORTEM

This lemony pie is so much tastier than you'd ever imagine. It's not a cheesecake by a long shot, but you'll want to sing, "Thank you for being a vegan!"

aFTer-Dinner Viewing

THe episode THaT Takes THe Cake

According to the Internet Movie Data Base, the women of *The Golden Girls* consumed more than 100 cheesecakes during the seven-year run of the show, and Bea Arthur hated cheesecake. Of all those cheesecake moments, perhaps the most adored occurs in the first season's final episode entitled "The Way We Met." The girls' hilarious banter moves from a squabble over how to best store raisin bran to a recounting of the "Great Herring War" to the revelation that Rose has an incredible sweet tooth. When the sweetheart of St. Olaf produces a chocolate cheesecake from her bag of groceries, Dorothy says, "I think this could be the beginning of a beautiful friendship." Was it ever!

InDEX

desserts

    Alice Ghostley's German Chocolate Cake, 287

    Dody Goodman's Zabaglione, 292

    Dom Deluise's Doodlewoppers, 271

    Donna Reed's Bisque Tortoni, 211

    Dusty Springfield's Banana Pudding, 55

    Eddie Albert's Flan, 197

    Ellen Corby's Apple Cake, 225

    Erich von Stroheim's Strudel, 253

    Fanny Brice's Super Chocolate Cake, 249

    Fernando Lamas's Empanadas, 327

    George Peppard's Louisiana Pecan Pie, 349

    George Reeves's Super Cookies, 308

    Gilda Radner's Dutch Apple Cake, 291

    Greer Garson's Capirotada, 77

    Humphrey Bogart's Coconut Spanish Cream, 305

    Janet Leigh's Gâteau Doré, 173

    John Denver's Flemish Apple Cake, 51

    John Ritter's Favorite Fudge, 269

    Karen Carpenter's Chewy Pie, 53

    Katharine Hepburn's Brownies, 77

    Klause Nomi's Lime Tart, 164–65

    Liberace's Sticky Buns, 57

    Lucille Ball's Apple John, 103

    Lucille Ball's Persimmon Cake, 104

    Mabel King's Banana Fritters, 211

    Madeline Kahn's Foot Cookies, 289

    Mae West's Fruit Compote, 245

    Michael Jackson's Sweet Potato Pie, 59

    Moira Shearer's Apricot Pudding, 237

    Richard Deacon's Bitter and Booze, 93

    Rock Hudson's Cannoli, 307

    Rue McClanahan's Non-Dairy Cheesecake, 359

    Telly Savalas's Butter Cookies, 349

    Virginia Graham's Coffee Toffee Pie, 21

    Vivien Leigh's Fruta Almina, 79

Doohan, James, 122–23

Douglas, Mike, 10–11

E

Ebsen, Buddy, 178–79

eggplant

    Dennis Weaver's Eggplant Parmigiana, 347

    James Coco's Stuffed Eggplant, 91

    Juliet Prowse's Moussaka, 235

eggs

    Alfred Hitchcock's Quiche Lorraine, 171

    Buddy Ebsen's Chiffon Eggs, 179

    Dody Goodman's Zabaglione, 292

    Eddie Albert's Flan, 197

    Gypsy Rose Lee's Linger Longer Omelet, 243

    John Wayne's Favorite Casserole, 303

    Leonard Frey's Scotch Eggs, 153

    Otto Preminger's Deviled Eggs, 27

    William Haines's Bachelor Omelet, 151

entrees. *See also* beef; fish; pasta; pork; poultry

    Bette Davis's Red Flannel Hash, 81

    Dennis Weaver's Eggplant Parmigiana, 347

    Dolores Del Rio's Enchiladas, 323

    Gene Roddenberry's Lima Beans and Ham, 125

    James Coco's Stuffed Eggplant, 91

    John Wayne's Favorite Casserole, 303

    Juliet Prowse's Moussaka, 235

    Lucille Ball's "Chinese-y Thing", 100

    Merv Griffin's Stuffed Squash, 19

F

Falk, Peter, 344–45

Fawcett, Farrah, 342–43

Fields, Totie, 277

fish

    Agnes Moorehead's Lobster Mousse, 183

    Anthony Perkins's Tuna Salad, 169

    Carolyn Jones's That Fish Thing, 205

aBOUT THE auTHOr

FRANK DECARO is best known for his six-and
-a-half-year stint as the flamboyant movie critic on
The Daily Show with Jon Stewart. A writer and performer, DeCaro is heard each weekday morning on
his own live national call-in program, "The Frank
DeCaro Show," on Sirius XM Satellite Radio, which
now boasts more than 20 million subscribers. His
guests have run the gamut from Ernest Borgnine to Tom Ford—on one three-
hour show!—and his following across North America is as loyal as it is diverse.

An accomplished home cook and an even better eater, DeCaro writes the
"Icons" column for CBS's *Watch!* magazine. Previously, he wrote the "Style
Over Substance" column for *The New York Times*. A graduate of Northwest-
ern University's Medill School of Journalism, he has written for myriad pub-
lications including *The New York Times Magazine, Martha Stewart Living,
Newsweek, Vogue* and *TV Guide*.

In addition, the award-winning DeCaro is the author of the groundbreaking
A Boy Named Phyllis: A Suburban Memoir, which *Vanity Fair* called "hilarious" and *The Advocate* credited as opening the door for David Sedaris and

"the gay American humorist as everyman." His follow-up work, a coffee-table biography called *Unmistakably Mackie: The Fashion and Fantasy of Bob Mackie*, earned a B+ in *Entertainment Weekly*. DeCaro's first major venture into new media resulted in the 2010 YouTube sensation "Betty White Lines," a rap video tribute to the *Golden Girls* star that was featured on the *Today* show, *Showbiz Tonight*, and dozens of blogs and got more than 100.000 hits in the first week online.

Please visit the author at FrankDeCaro.com and deadcelebritycookbook. com, "like" him on Facebook, and follow him on Twitter: @frankdecaroshow.